FabJo

Become a Hair Salon Owner

JULIE MORAN

FABJOB® GUIDE TO BECOME A HAIR SALON OWNER
by Julie Moran

ISBN: 978-1-897286-58-6

Library and Archives Canada Cataloguing in Publication

Moran, Julie L., 1963-
FabJob guide to become a hair salon owner / Julie Moran.

Includes CD-ROM.
ISBN 978-1-897286-58-6

1. Beauty shops. 2. Beauty shops--Management.
3. New business enterprises--Management. 4. Beauty
operators--Vocational guidance. I. FabJob II. Title.
III. Title: Hair salon owner.

TT965.M66 2010   646.7'2068   C2010-901407-3

Important Disclaimer: Although every effort has been made to ensure this guide is free from errors, this publication is sold with the understanding that the authors, editors, and publisher are not responsible for the results of any action taken on the basis of information in this work, nor for any errors or omissions. The publishers, and the authors and editors, expressly disclaim all and any liability to any person, whether a purchaser of this publication or not, in respect of anything and of the consequences of anything done or omitted to be done by any such person in reliance, whether whole or partial, upon the whole or any part of the contents of this publication. If expert advice is required, services of a competent professional person should be sought.

About the Websites Mentioned in this Guide: Although we aim to provide the information you need within the guide, we have also included a number of websites because readers have told us they appreciate knowing about sources of additional information. (**TIP:** Don't include a period at the end of a web address when you type it into your browser.) Due to the constant development of the Internet, websites can change. Any websites mentioned in this guide are included for the convenience of readers only. We are not responsible for the content of any sites except FabJob.com.

FabJob Inc.
19 Horizon View Court
Calgary, Alberta, Canada T3Z 3M5

FabJob Inc.
4616 25th Avenue NE, #224
Seattle, Washington, USA 98105

To order books in bulk, phone 403-949-2039
To arrange a media interview, phone 403-949-4980

www.FabJob.com

PRINTED IN CANADA

Contents

About the Author

 Julie Moran holds a Master of Professional Writing degree from the University of Southern California and a law degree from Fordham University. She has published four other books, including two FabJob guides, and written numerous articles for national consumer magazines.

Acknowledgements

Thank you to the following experts (listed alphabetically) for generously sharing hair salon industry insider information, and business and marketing advice in this FabJob guide. Opinions in this guide are those of the author or editors and not necessarily those of experts interviewed for this guide.

- *Dalgiza Barros*
  Owner, Creative Energy Hair Studio,
  Hanover, Massachusetts

- *Don Bewley*
  Co-founder, Eufora International
  www.eufora.net

- *Johnathan Breitung*
  Co-Owner, Johnathan Breitung Salon
  & Luxury Spa
  www.johnathanbreitungsalon.com

- *Federico Calce*
  Owner, Federico Salon,
  New York, New York
  www.federicosalon.com

- *Rita Ciotoli*
  Managing Director, Charm Salon &
  Spa and Way 2 B Spa,
  Ontario, Canada

- *Elizabeth Coy*
  Owner, Indigo Salon,
  San Carlos, California

- *Lisa DeStefano*
  Owner, DeStefano's Salon,
  Carlsbad, California

- *Derrick Diggs*
  Layers Hair Salon,
  Richmond, Virginia
  www.layershairsalon.com

- *Harley DiNardo*
  Owner, Shampoo Avenue B,
  New York, New York
  www.shampooavenueb.com

- *Suki Duggan*
  Owner, Donsuki Treehouse Salon,
  New York, New York
  www.donsukisalon.com

- *Larry Dunlap*
  Owner, Haircolor Xperts,
  Raleigh and Cary, North Carolina
  www.haircolorxpertsraleigh.com

- *Cindy Feldman and Ira Ludwick*
  Owners, Progressions Salon Spa
  Store, Rockville, Maryland
  www.progressions.com

- *Barry Fletcher*
  Owner, The Hair Palace,
  Mitchellville, Maryland, and
  founder/developer of Barry Fletcher
  Hair Products
  www.barryfletcher.com

- *Susie Galvez*
  Beauty industry expert, author, day
  spa founder and cosmetic formulator
  www.SusieGalvez.com

- *Michael Peter Hayes*
  Owner, Michael Peter Hayes Art
  Salon, Locust Valley (Long Island),
  New York
  www.mphsalon.com

- *Justin Hickox*
  Owner, Hickox Studio,
  Portland, Oregon
  www.hickoxstudio.com

- *DaRico Jackson*
  Owner and Celebrity Stylist, Amiri
  Salon, Beverly Hills, California
  www.myspace.com/daricojackson

- *Valery Joseph,*
  Owner, Valery Joseph Salons, New
  York City and East Hampton
  www.valeryjoseph.com

- *Debbi Kickham*
  Owner of PR firm
  Maxima Marketing,
  Westwood, Massachusetts
  www.marketingauthor.com

- *Billy Lowe*
  Celebrity hairstylist, owner of Billy
  Lowe Salon, Los Angeles, California
  www.billylowe.com

- *Joanna Meiseles*
  Founder and CEO of Snip-Its
  children's hair salon franchise
  www.snip-its.com

- *Bridget Miller*
  Physician's Asistant
  Baldwinsville, New York

- *Jill D. Miller*
  Business Development Consultant,
  Creative Solutions, Wichita, Kansas
  www.jilldmiller.com

- *Sean M. Moran, L.L.M., J.D., C.P.A.*
  Tax partner at the law firm of Dewey
  & LeBoeuf, LLP
  www.dl.com

- *Stephanie Nimmer*
  Manager, Godiva Salon,
  Atlanta, Georgia
  www.godivasalon.com

- *Michael O'Rourke*
  Founder, Carlton Hair Care Salons
  and Founder of Sexy Hair™
  products
  www.carltonhairinternational.com
  www.sexyhair.com

- *Ouidad*
  Owner, Ouidad Salons, New York,
  NY, and Santa Monica, California
  www.ouidad.com

- *Heaven Padgett*
  Owner, Hairem Salon,
  Houston, Texas
  www.thehairemsalon.com

- *Robert Patrizi*
  Owner, Halo [For Men] spa and
  salons, Chicago, Illinois
  www.halochicago.com

- *Philip Pelusi*
  Creator of P2 hair products and
  Owner of Tela Design Studio,
  New York, New York
  www.telanyc.com

- *Tony Promiscuo*
  Owner, Godiva Salon,
  Atlanta, Georgia
  www.godivasalon.com

- *Ronnie Pryor*
  Owner, Source Salon,
  Wilton Manors, Florida
  http://source-salon.com

- *Stacy Dabney Ramirez and
  Lindsey Dabney*
  Co-Owners, Bella Bethesda Salon,
  Bethesda, Maryland
  www.bellabethesda.com

- *Thee Viron Roe*
  deNovo Aesthetics Center,
  Dallas, Texas

- *Alex Safar*
  Owner and Top Stylist, Salon acote,
  with two Boston locations and one
  Miami location
  www.salonacote.com

- *Anne Marie Sheeley*
  President, Director of Education, and
  Master Stylist, Salon Diva,
  White Plains, New York

- *John Stevens, MS, RN, NP-C*
  Owner, deNovo Aesthetics Center,
  Dallas, Texas

- *Jeff Sturgis*
  Vice President of Franchise Sales,
  Fantastic Sam's Salons
  www.fantasticsams.com

- *Nancy Trent*
  Founder of PR firm Trent &
  Company, Inc., New York, New York
  www.trentandcompany.com

- *Al Urbanowski*
  Owner and Operator, Al's Barber
  Shop in Denver and Boulder, CO,
  American Crew International All-
  Star Educator

- *Marlene Weber*
  Owner, Marlene Weber Hair Salon,
  Poughkeepsie, New York
  www.marleneweber.com

- *Michele Wright*
  General Manager, Haircolor Xperts,
  Raleigh and Cary, North Carolina
  www.haircolorxpertsraleigh.com

Also thanks to editor Brenna Pearce, writer Mary Snyder, and editorial assistant Jenna Beach for their contributions to this guide.

1. Introduction

Congratulations on taking the first step on your journey to opening your own hair salon! This exciting, high-energy industry ranges from the small-town salon where you can get a basic hair cut and color to exclusive upscale salons that offer a variety of luxurious beauty treatments, to the glamorous world of cutting-edge hair styles and models parading on fashion runways.

Hair salons are bustling social centers where clients can relax and chat while being polished and pampered. The beauty industry is a feel-good industry, and the hair salon plays an essential part. When you open a salon, your aim is to offer your clients a pleasant experience, top-notch artistry, and to make sure each and every one of them leaves your shop looking and feeling wonderful.

Unlike many other businesses, there is less risk involved in opening a hair salon. The beauty industry is largely recession-proof, because no matter how well or poorly the economy is doing, people still need their hair cut or colored. And, unlike making restaurant-quality meals at home, for example, hair services are not something people can do for themselves — at least not very well. While people pare down personal luxuries when the economy slows, getting a great hair cut, perm, or other beauty service is something virtually everyone needs and can afford even when times are tight.

> *"I feel that a hair salon can be open at almost any time. This is one industry that is recession proof. Almost everyone needs a haircut. Even if they wait an extra week or two, eventually, they will get it cut."*
>
> — Rita Ciotoli, Managing Director,
> Charm Salon & Spa and Way 2 B Spa

Hair salon owners come from a variety of backgrounds. You may be an aspiring business owner who has come to recognize the solid, steady growth and relatively low-risk opportunity that owning a hair salon provides. Perhaps you're a hair stylist or esthetician yourself who has spent years working for others and is ready to strike out on your own. If you are a hair stylist, owning a hair salon is a great opportunity to explore your creativity while being in charge of your own destiny and reaping more of the financial rewards of your efforts.

If you've had business experience but you couldn't trim someone's bangs to save your life, you can still use your business savvy and skills to enter this dynamic and ever-growing field and achieve your dreams, and all without ever having to pick up a pair of shears.

1.1   Owning a Hair Salon

Hair salons come in an almost endless variety. The type of salon you choose is entirely up to you, and this guide will help you make that choice. For instance, you may choose to offer such basic services as shampooing, styling, and coloring, or you might offer additional services like hair extensions, straightening or weaves. A few innovative salon owners combine salons with another aesthetic or creative business, such as an art gallery, or combine social gathering places such as a pool hall with a men's barber shop or a wine bar in a salon setting.

According to census data collected in the U.S. in 2006 (the last year such statistics were available), the most common salons are those run by entrepreneurs with fewer than four employees. On the other end of the scale are high end salons offering a wide variety of services, including spa treatments, esthetics services, and so on, that employ dozens of people. Most salons offer an assortment of retail products as well, from hair and skin products and makeup to expanded retail offerings such as jewelry, gifts, or artwork. Here is a list of services that can be provided in a hair salon:

- *Hair cuts:* These can be anything from simple, routine cuts, such as those offered in men's barber shops, to the latest in celebrity style trends.

- *Hair styling:* Most services such as hair cuts, coloring and perms are finished with a blow-dry and styling. Styling can be complementary as part of the shampoo and cut process or an additional service such as creating fancy styles for proms or weddings.

- *Hair coloring services:* Most salons for women (and many catering exclusively to men) offer coloring services. These can include basic natural color matching services to the more exotic. Typical coloring services include highlights, streaks, lowlights, and foils to add variety, depth and dimension.

- *Hair straightening:* This involves straightening and taming curly and wavy hair and making it more manageable through the use of chemical agents and flat-irons.

- *Hair extensions:* Adding length to hair and making it look natural is an art as well as a real skill.

- *Wig choice and styling:* These are generally for people suffering from hair loss. Some salons specialize in working with individuals with hair loss while others offer these services in addition to other hair services.

- *Permanents:* Yes, people still get perms, although not as many as they once did. This is still considered a standard salon service, and perms can be either full or partial (to add height to a particular area, such as the crown).

- *Shaving/Men's grooming:* While there are still some traditional men's barber shops, the men's grooming specialty has evolved, with more men's-only salons cropping up. In addition to hair services, these salons offer hot shaves (some complete with hot towel treatments), as do some unisex salons seeking to cater to their male clients. Other men's specialty services some salons offer include hair trimming/removal (e.g., mustache/beard, ear and nose hair) and shoe shines.

- *Selling Specialty Salon Hair Care Products:* Offering a line or several lines of products for sale in the salon is a way to provide clients with hair, skin, makeup and other products they need and use at home, and can be an important additional income source for your business.

- *Other services:* Some hair salons also offer nail services such as manicures and pedicures, makeup application, and esthetic or day spa services such as facials, tanning, and massages.

1.2   A Growth Industry

There has never been a better time to get into the salon industry. According to Susie Galvez, beauty industry expert and author, hair care is a basic necessity for people irrespective of economic conditions. She contends that "during times of economic stress, making a great first impression visually is one of the easiest ways to weather the tough job market." While people might fall back on home use products for spa treatments and nail care Galvez argues, "taking care of hair, which is always totally visible, is one of those important things to leave to a professional."

According to the U.S. economic census of 2007 (the latest year for which complete industry statistics are available), annual revenues for all hair salons and barber shops in the U.S. were over $18 billion dollars. This is an increase of 25% over the previous five years. Salons owned by sole proprietors earned more than $14 billion across the U.S., an average 7.5% increase in revenues over the previous two years.

The situation is similar in Canada. Over just one year from 2006 to 2007, revenues in the personal care services sector (which includes salons and barber shops) increased from $3.9 billion to $4.2 billion. This represents an increase of almost 8% over the one year period. "That's the interesting thing about the beauty industry in general," says Jeff Sturgis, Vice President of Franchise Sales at Fantastic Sam's Salons, "it's a steady and stable growth industry...it grows every year and is more stable." Dalgiza Barros of Creative Energy Hair Studio agrees: "This is a business which will continue to thrive; and in fact, when times are tough people seek out products and services that will make them feel better."

Recent national statistics in the U.S. uphold our experts' opinions and point to continuous growth in the industry. According to a National Accrediting Commission of Cosmetology Arts and Sciences (NACCAS) report, as of January 2007, the total number of salons had increased by 18% since 2003. More than 1.6 million cosmetology professionals are employed in more than 370,000 beauty, skin care, nail and barber shops and salons throughout the country.

A typical salon, according to the report, provides full services from an average of five stations, employs three full-time and two part-time professionals, and serves an average of 127 customers per week. Retail sales in salons are also on the rise with retail product line revenues in excess of $12 million a year.

1.3   Benefits of Being a Hair Salon Owner

"I find one of the most rewarding aspects of owning a salon is the same thing that brought me into the industry. Making people feel amazing. When you're a stylist you get to spend 30 minutes with someone and completely change the way they feel about themselves. This can be a truly remarkable experience. When you own a salon, you get to do that on a much grander scale."

　　　　— Justin Hickox, Owner, Hickox Studio

Financial Rewards

Salon ownership can be very lucrative. While the size and complexity and even the number of salons owned by individuals varies greatly, there is potential for steady and solid earnings at every level of salon ownership.

While hard and fast salary statistics for salon owners are hard to come by, the salon owners we spoke with confirmed a 2003 Job Demand Survey conducted by the National Accrediting Commission of Cosmetology Arts and Sciences (NACCAS). This survey indicated that the average salary for salon owners was a little above $50,000 a year, but with a large potential upside in the six figures ($120,000-$250,000) for large, upscale salons or chains. Creating your own line of hair care products can bring in even more.

According to Business Development Consultant Jill D. Miller of Creative Solutions, "I would say an average salary range is $36,000 for salons bringing in around $500,000 a year up to $120,000 a year for salons that bring in over $1 million."

Our experts all agreed that to maximize your profits and achieve the higher end of the income spectrum, coupling salon services with retail sales is essential. This is because, even in a salon with several stylists and technicians working, there are a finite number of clients each stylist or technician can serve in a given day. Even in a fully booked salon this limitation caps the earning potential.

A Relaxing and Comfortable Workspace

Creating your own work space is another great benefit of salon ownership. Far too many work settings are boring or dreary, and having an attractive salon space where you and your clients feel comfortable and relaxed makes your workday an enjoyable one. There are a wide range of color schemes and types of ambience your salon can have. Choosing the right look and feel of your salon can be exciting and fun, and can serve as a creative outlet for you to express yourself.

Being in Charge of Your Own Destiny

Many aspiring salon owners, especially cosmetologists who have rented booth space from other salon owners, are tired of forking over a large percentage of their hard-earned cash to someone else. By receiving the profits from your work and income from the stylists who rent from or are employed by you, you can take charge of your future and maximize your earnings.

Setting Your Own Hours

An important corollary of being your own boss is getting to set your own hours and having a flexible work schedule. While your salon hours will be dictated in large part by the needs of the clients you serve, if you are the owner you can still set your hours and work the times that suit your temperament best.

You have even more flexibility if you are an owner who is not a cosmetologist (or a cosmetologist who has chosen to come out from "behind the chair" for good and simply manage the business aspects of the salon). In fact, some hair salon franchises emphasize that their owners can run the business partly from home and partly in the salon. While you will need to maintain steady contact with your employees and devote a good amount of regular time in your salon overseeing the business, you do not necessarily have to be there every day from open to close to run a successful hair salon.

Helping Others Feel Good About Themselves

This is one of the greatest and most often repeated benefit from the salon owners we spoke with. The beauty industry, and hair salons in particular, are all about making people feel good about themselves by helping them look their best. People go to hair salons to improve their appearance (and receive a little pampering in the process). Delivering on this service promise is a great way to help others feel good, and this in turn makes you feel good. As DaRico Jackson, celebrity stylist and owner of Amiri Salon explains:

> "Whether I am working on a celebrity or a non-celebrity, the gratification comes from seeing the self-esteem magnified when a women gets out of my chair. Sometimes women come to my salon down in the dumps, for whatever reason…but after an uplifting conversation, a glass of wine, an outstanding shampoo with a head massage, and a fabulous new look, their whole outlook changes. I love to see them walk out with their head lifted high, and that extra sway in the hips. When this happens, I know I've done my job."

Leadership Role and Respect

For all salon owners, and especially for salon owners who train and manage a team of employees, being a salon owner is a leadership position. If you like being in charge of a business and being in an environment where you can control and oversee how things are done, you will find satisfaction in this as a salon owner.

A natural outgrowth of this is the respect your leadership role as a salon owner garners from others. As Rita Ciotoli, Managing Director of two salons, Way 2 B Spa and Charm Salon & Spa, in Ontario, Canada, describes it, "the greatest reward for owning my own salon is that I am respected by many people. The accomplishment of running two successful salons is something that also makes me proud."

Artistic Freedom

Let's face it, hair design and styling is an art form. For many salon owners who are stylists/cosmetologists themselves, having your own salon is the ultimate way to follow your own artistic inclinations. Especially in salons where employees are a well-trained team under the direction of a salon owner, there is a deep personal satisfaction for the owner in achieving creative and artistic balance and consistency in their own work and that of their employees.

> *"As a kid, I wanted to brush people's hair and play with dolls. But as a boy growing up in Georgia, that was often frowned upon. Today, however, it doesn't even feel like I go to 'work.' It just seems like I am making up for lost time as a kid playing with dolls. It seems magical to me to be able to help people look and feel great, and to have them spin around in the chair and tell me, 'I feel great!'"*
>
> — Billy Lowe, celebrity hairstylist and owner,
> Billy Lowe Salon

Building Long-term Friendships

Salons by their very nature are social centers. Most everyone is familiar with the notion that people confide in their hairdressers, which underscores the deep friendships people often develop with those who help them care for themselves and look their best. Employee relationships are also a large part of a salon, as many employees and other personnel spend more time at work than they do at home. As a result, salon employees often become a 'family' of sorts.

Many salon owners find a deep satisfaction in forging deep, long-term friendships with both employees and clients. While a cosmetologist who works for others has little say in who else works at the salon, as a salon owner, you have total control over who will work at your salon, which gives you the ability to choose talented people with whom you enjoy working.

"One of the most rewarding aspects of my career as a salon owner has been watching my people have families and be able to buy cars and houses and later send their kids to college because they were successful working for me."

— Don Bewley, Co-founder of Eufora International

1.4 Inside This Guide

The FabJob Guide to Become a Hair Salon Owner is organized to help take you step-by-step through the basics you will need to open and operate your own salon. The chapters are organized as follows:

Chapter 2 (*"Hair Salon Basics"*) will help you decide what kind of salon you should open. This chapter discusses different types of salons and business niches within the industry, the range of services you can provide and products you can sell, and will explain what is involved in your role as owner and in the roles of your employees.

Chapter 3 (*"Getting Ready"*) explains how you can acquire the skills you will need as a hair salon owner. It covers ways of learning from experts and through observation. You will also discover how to get valuable experience and build a reputation through volunteer work or how to "earn while you learn" by getting a job in the salon industry. You'll also find resources in this section for learning more about the beauty industry.

Chapter 4 (*"Starting Your Hair Salon"*) will help you decide whether to buy an existing salon, operate a franchise, or open a new salon. It also explains what you need to get started, including your business plan, start-up financing, store name, and other important matters.

Chapter 5 (*"Setting Up Your Hair Salon"*) offers the information you need to actually set up your salon. It gives advice on how to choose a location, get merchandise to sell, and arrange displays. You will also discover what equipment and supplies you will need.

Chapter 6 (*"Running Your Business"*) takes you into the day-to-day challenge of running your salon once it's open. It explains how to develop a procedures manual, and covers inventory management, financial management and pricing, marketing your business, and working with staff and customers.

Chapter 7 (*"Getting and Keeping Clients"*) teaches you how to hit the ground running and grow your business by implementing an effective plan for promoting and marketing your business and by delivering memorable top-notch services and great customer service that will make your clients happy and keep them coming back.

By following the steps in this guide, you will be well on your way to living your dream — opening your own successful hair salon.

2. Hair Salon Basics

If you're going to run a hair salon, you may first want to know more about the variety of salon types and the products and services they offer. You'll want to learn as much as possible about how a salon operates and about new products and treatments. Techniques are constantly changing or being developed, which makes this industry an exciting and dynamic one.

While you certainly can't say that all salons are the same, in general they have basic elements that clients expect:

- Customer calls or comes in to schedule an appointment

- Customer arrives for his or her appointment; is often given a robe to protect their clothing, and their stylist or technician is alerted they have arrived

- Customer receives the selected hair or other beauty service(s)

- Customer "checks out" after receiving their beauty service(s), looking and feeling great

That's it! These things pretty much sum up about 95% of a normal day in the operation of the salon. Most salons have these same basic traits and routines in common, and salon clients share similar expectations about the services offered. However, despite the similarities, there is a wide variety of salon types.

2.1 Types of Salons

"Be known for something. Being a generalist is not the way to go. Instead niche it down. Be known as the one to go to for: perfect cuts, highlights and color, most stylish looks, healthy hair, etc. Of course you can do all of these things, but concentrate on being the best at one or two of them and the word will get out."

> — Susie Galvez, beauty industry expert

"There is definitely room for growth in niche markets. Given the current economy, people are careful how they spend their money. Many won't give up a good haircut to save a few bucks, but they want to know that they are getting the most for their money. Niche markets and specialized segments allow consumers to get exactly what they want without spending time and energy searching for the best option or taking a gamble on goods and services that end up being less than what they were looking for and hence a waste of money anyway."

> — Robert Patrizi, Owner,
> Halo [For Men] spa and salons

Salons come in a variety of sizes and settings. They can be small or large, specialize in one or two types of clients (e.g., children or men) or a limited number of services (e.g., a salon specializing in hair color services). Or they may offer a huge variety of services to a variety of clients. Salon services can be basic, lower priced and no-frills, mid-priced, or more expensive and upscale.

There are also some general industry trends to consider before deciding on your salon specialty. According to Philip Pelusi, creator of P2 hair products and owner of Tela Design Studio, there are challenges at all levels of the salon industry. "Chain salons that are mid-level are growing smaller," he notes. "There is still room in mid-level salons, but it is slowly becoming a smaller section of the industry. High-end salons are growing, but the high-end level is precarious and a tough industry that requires a high attention to detail." The more basic, lower priced salons are still successful, he told us, while cautioning the would-be salon owner that to be competitive, "the low-end level needs an overarching theme, strong brand message and competitive price point."

The type of salon you will open will be based on factors such as:

- personal preference

- your background and interests or expertise

- the start-up capital you have available

- the space you have available (if you have a location in mind)

- what your market research or gut instinct says is needed in your area

You don't need to decide on a type of salon right away, so take some time to learn a bit about your options early on. Below you'll find information on the many possibilities for your salon. Maybe something in this section will even spark an idea for how your salon can stand out with something new or unique.

2.1.1 Traditional Salons

This is the most common type of salon that is found in virtually every city and town in North America. They can be large, small, or in between. Traditional salons are most commonly unisex and many also do kids' hair cuts. Generally, they offer a full range of hair services, such as cuts, styling, perms, various coloring techniques, as well as sometimes offering nail and waxing services.

At one end of the spectrum are salons offering average prices or featuring less expensive (and usually quicker) cuts, and at the other end are upscale, more expensive salons that may even be associated with a celebrity hair stylist. Most traditional salons welcome walk-ins as a courtesy but encourage clients to make advance appointments. Some traditional salons, especially some well-known franchises, cater to the cost-conscious or to individuals who don't have the ability to set appointments ahead of time. Such clients may also be those who are simply short on time and just want quick and inexpensive hair services.

Marlene Weber of Marlene Weber Hair Salon cites the need to address client concerns about pricing. "I think given the current economy, people will be looking for low cost alternatives to their expensive salon services," she observes, "which leads me to believe one trend will be to have junior stylist prices available or alternative pricing during off times." She believes package pricing may also become important as salon clients seek other ways to economize on hair care services. According to Weber, this might include "offering clients an opportunity to prepay several services to get a discount and packaging services in a series even for cuts and colors will be a big gift card item. Another salon trend will be more services condensed into less time, i.e., multiple services at once."

You may be familiar with one or more of the nation-wide franchises offering these types of budget services. At one time, industry insiders believed that large, chain-store type salons would eventually dominate the industry, pushing out single salon owners. But, says Michael Peter Hayes, owner of Michael Peter Hayes Art Salon, "The theory presented in the 90s that in the future, 10% of all salons would do 90% of all salons' services and retail sales, has been drastically changed and debunked. Too many variables came into play." He cites "employee and client attrition, the high costs associated with keeping large inventories of stock, and other factors, which often resulted in a low or even negative rate of return on these large salons' investments," as the reasons the industry did not fully embrace the large scale salon business model.

According to Hayes, the traditional salon is alive and well, and will be so into the future. "I foresee instead a trend of smaller one to four chair salons, with more emphasis on services and comfort," he told us. "I feel it will become the norm, and the industry will see a surge of these smaller, smarter-styled salons."

There are other trends in the industry, such as catering to teens' needs. In general, teens are returning to more natural hairstyles that don't require a lot of extra care at home. "The emerging trend in the hair industry is a return to natural looking wavy, curly hair," says Michele Wright, general manager of Haircolorxperts. "The new group of teens has seen nothing but straight hair for the last few years and is moving towards wearing a more natural look instead of pressing and ironing it into submission."

Coloring Services

Hair color is an art unto itself, so it's not surprising that some salons specialize exclusively in color and color correction techniques. The menu of services offered in these salons can be relatively limited, due to their focus on coloring services. However, services often include perms and relaxing, haircutting or even waxing and nails, along with all types of color services. Generally, since expert color is their specialty, the colorists at these salons are among the best in their field.

An excellent example of this type of salon is Haircolorxperts (**www. haircolorxpertsraleigh.com**). According to operating partner Larry Dunlap, "Hair color has an almost unlimited potential for growth in the U.S. Due to the aging of our population and our obsession with youth, more and more people are using hair color to hide the effects of aging."

Curly Hair

Another traditional salon niche that deals with a specific type of hair are salons geared toward curly hair. According to Ouidad (pronounced "weedahd"), owner of Ouidad Salon in New York City and Santa Monica, California, a majority of people have some form of curl in their hair, but the rarity of salons geared toward this special hair type means that it is a largely underserved market niche.

She explains what makes her approach to curly hair so successful: "You must understand the different curl pattern on each head of hair and know how to puzzle it to perform together and not just go wild because it has no direction. My trademark Carving and Slicing technique [see sidebar on the next page] helps to achieve this precise cutting style."

> ## Specialized Training for Cutting and Caring for Curly Hair
>
> Ouidad Salon owner Ouidad and her specially trained associates teach classes on Carving and Slicing for curly hair. This demanding training course is based on her trademark techniques for cutting and shaping curly hair. The training takes place monthly at Ouidad's facility at 37 West 57th Street in Manhattan.
>
> Interested salons submit an initial application, and all stylists seeking to apply for training need to have a minimum of five years' experience. Ouidad also requires applicants to write a personal letter on their views and philosophy toward curly hair to demonstrate their passion and seriousness. For more information about these classes or to fill out an application, go to **www. ouidadPRO.com**.

2.1.2   Men's Salons and Barber shops

"Now is a great time to open a men's hair salon. An evolving trend in the industry is the increased desire for male-specific services beyond just a trim. More and more men are looking for a professional shave, style or treatment in addition to their cut."

> — Al Urbanowski, Owner and Operator,
> Al's Barber Shops

Barber shops were once a staple in American cities and towns, where men went for a hot shave and a haircut. These began to disappear a few decades ago, and with it, the male culture and camaraderie they once offered. More recently, would-be salon owners began to realize that traditional salons generally do not meet men's needs or wishes. Men are not only uncomfortable receiving services such as manicures, hair coloring or perms in "mixed company," but if they just want a basic haircut, they are often uncomfortable in the glitzier salon settings where women are getting their hair colored, cut, or permed.

Finding male-oriented services such as a barber-style hot shave or a beard and mustache trim in traditional salons can be difficult as well. While some salons offer separate private areas for male clients (and spas often provide separate locker room areas for men and women), there is a clear market niche for hair salons that cater to men (and/or boys) only. Everything from the décor to the menu of services in a male-oriented salon caters to their different grooming and psychological needs, delivering a more comfortable salon experience.

A good example of this type of salon is Bob Patrizi's Halo [For Men] spa and salons in Chicago. He designed his salons to appeal to men by using, he told us, "TVs, sports, rock music, a relaxing atmosphere, guy friendly décor such as exposed brick and ambient lighting — a generally un-fussy feel." If opening this type of salon appeals to you, keep in mind this caution from Patrizi: "One of the bigger mistakes that a lot of male salons make is to go overboard on a theme or try too hard to be 'manly'." He notes that "overdoing the sports theme or trying too hard to establish a 'gentlemen's club' where everything is covered in leather just feels contrite and uncomfortable. No one likes the guy who tries too hard. Just make them feel comfortable without drawing too much attention and making it seem overdone."

2.1.3 Children's Salons

Like men, young children have different hair cutting needs than women, and their needs are often unmet in the traditional salon setting. Going for a haircut can sometimes be a bad experience for kids, ranging from tedious to downright traumatic. Also, stylists whose clientele are comprised largely of adults are often unprepared to handle a fearful or squirming child (not to mention other clients at the salon who may be put off by noisy or misbehaving children).

Children's salons seek to make the inevitable need for regular haircuts a non-frightening, as well as an entertaining, experience. These salons provide haircuts and styling for kids and often provide children's entertainment ranging from toys and games to TVs and DVD players as well as snacks and drinks that appeal to kids.

This largely underserved niche is no trivial part of the industry. In the U.S. alone, children's haircuts make up more than $5 billion of the annual revenues in the entire hair care industry, according to Joanna Meiseles, founder and CEO of the Snip-its children's hair salon franchise. There has been a recent upward trend in the growth of new hair salons geared toward children. Within the last decade, as a result of this trend, several children's hair salon franchises have cropped up to meet this market need. We'll discuss several of these later in this guide, in section 4.2.2.

2.1.4 Ethnically Oriented Salons

Another type of niche salon is one that caters to the hair care and styling needs of men and women of various ethnic groups. For example, the hair products used and sold in salons catering to African Americans are engineered for their unique hair care needs. Similarly, hair services and cutting and styling techniques are also designed just for them. The principles involved apply to all ethnic groups with unique hair care requirements.

DaRico Jackson, celebrity hairstylist and owner of Amiri salon, who styles the tresses of celebrities that include Tasha Smith, Kelly Price, Johawrah Jones, and Tishina Arnold, emphasizes the importance of taking advanced classes to stay on top of the latest trends. Salon owners need to keep learning, because educating yourself on the science of hair and advanced techniques is key to styling success. It was during DaRico's early career as a regional designer for Sebastian that he changed his perspective on how he viewed black hair and how it should be. "It was then that I got out of my mind 'black hair won't do that!'," DaRico explains. "Hair does anything you want it to — you just have to understand the science of it, and you do this by educating yourself." Another important trait that sets him apart and keeps his African American clientele coming back again and again is the way he expertly creates beautiful haircuts that are also easy to maintain at home:

> "In today's world, African American women don't have enough time to sit in the salon [or] spend time maintaining their hair, so as a stylist, I have adapted to the idea of maintenance-free styling… By using the proper tools, you can create looks that will give a black woman a 'get up and go' hairstyle, just like their white counterparts. Instead of trying to change and fight with the texture of the hair with heat, try working with the texture they have, and recommend the usage of product to enhance it. This cuts down on time, and increases your retail profitability."

2.1.5   Other Specialties

Executives/Wealthy/Celebrity Clients

This is a variation on the traditional salon or salon and spa, the difference being the amount of elegance and privacy, as well as the level of exclusivity these types of salons provide. Salons that cater to high profile clients tend to be in more private locations not visible from the street, and they tend to be elegantly designed and furnished. They may also provide certain amenities their clients expect or need, such as Wi-Fi service and televisions delivering the latest business or stock market news, meal delivery service for clients on their lunch hour, or even on-site child care. The expenses of these salons are high, but then again, so are the prices.

Salon and Spa

Combining a hair salon with a spa is an increasingly common type of salon. These salons combine an area for hair services with other beauty services such as nails, waxing, tinting, and makeup with a separate spa area featuring spa treatments such as massages and facials. The focus in these salons is not only on looking good, but on pampering the client. Thus, even beauty services like manicures may involve additional touches such as a foot or calf massage. This type of salon requires separate areas for the salon and spa area, which needs space for lockers and dressing rooms in addition to private treatment rooms. If you are interested in providing spa services, you can find more detailed information in the *FabJob Guide to Become a Spa Owner*.

Hair Loss Specialists

Hair loss is another hair care niche that calls for special expertise. Many people suffer from permanent balding and hair loss from birth, from age-related illnesses, from taking certain medications, or from medical treatments such as chemotherapy. There are some traditional salons and even a few specialty salons that offer wig fitting and styling and other techniques for dealing with balding and hair loss.

Satellite Salon Locations

This is a variation of the traditional salon. Satellite salons are full service salons located on the premises of other established businesses such as high-end department stores or gyms. An excellent example is the Mario Diab Salon (**http://mezzaninespa.com/doctor_mario.html**), which is in the process of opening satellite salons within Equinox Health Clubs in New York City.

> *"Urban areas are great for specialty salons because you generally need a larger pool of clients. Urban areas in general tend to have a higher density of people and a greater range of personality types to accommodate a specialized market."*
>
> — Robert Patrizi, Owner,
> Halo [For Men] spa and salons

Environmentally Friendly Salons

Another variation of the traditional salon that is likely to represent a future growth trend in the industry is the environmentally friendly salon. The services at these salons are basically those of traditional salons, but the differences lie in carrying products composed of natural, sustainable ingredients packaged in post-consumer recycled materials. Other aspects of eco-friendly salons are using fluorescent lighting, which reduces CO_2 emissions due to their lower electricity consumption, actively developing ways to reduce waste, and recycling and reusing as much as possible. Some product lines, like Aveda for example, are manufactured using only wind power or other renewable energy sources.

An example of an environmentally friendly salon is Source Salon (**http://source-salon.com**) in Wilton Manors, Florida. Owner Ronnie Pryor advises that "Product lines and salons must become 'greener' to remain competitive. Salon owners should consider sustainability in every area of their space, from flooring and lighting to display units and décor."

Traditional Salon Combined with Another Retail Business

Combining a hair salon with another retail business is another newer (and still relatively rare) type of salon niche. The range of businesses that could work well with a traditional salon is likely limited only to your imagination. However, some real-life examples of successful salons that combine well with other businesses are:

- Rik Rak in Miami: offers traditional salon and spa services, but also features an extensive gift store that includes salon products, but also jewelry and other gifts.

- Harley DiNardo's Shampoo Avenue B Salon in lower Manhattan: a hair salon that doubles as a street art gallery, complete with art openings and live performances.

- Michael Peter Hayes Art Salon in New York: a two-chair hair salon that features a fine art gallery with exhibits that change every four-eight weeks, complete with wine and cheese receptions to announce new exhibits.

- Philip Pelusi's Tela Design Studio: located in New York's trendy meatpacking district; features a rotating art exhibit, weekly jazz performances, and café with an all-organic menu that includes wine and tea.

Medi-Spas

Medi-spas are a relatively new niche in the hair salon industry. These types of salons offer a full spectrum of beauty services, from traditional hair salon services to day spa services (e.g., facials, wraps, baths, massages). Other services might include medically supervised beauty services such as Botox and collagen injections and even facelifts, eyelifts, and other cosmetic surgery techniques. As an example, deNovo Aesthetics Center in Dallas, Texas, combines cosmetic surgery with a day spa and salon services. Owner John Stevens cautions that these salons should be considered medical offices (and thus properly licensed and staffed accordingly, whether or not required by the state where your Medi-spa is located).

> *"There's a lot of opportunity for medical and salon professionals to work together, including chiropractors and podiatrists. Work very carefully with legal counsel and your State Board of Healing Arts as you start this kind of business. Many new regulations are being passed by medical and cosmetology boards to safeguard customers from dangerous practices."*
>
> — Jill D. Miller, Business Development Consultant, Creative Solutions

2.2 Hair Salon Services

2.2.1 Hair Care and Styling

In this section we'll look at the variety of typical hair care and styling services that you can offer in your salon. In addition, we'll give you an overview of the techniques and equipment involved in performing each service.

Hair care services include techniques such as:

• Haircuts

• Blow-dry and style

• Styling (curling, up-dos)

• Hair conditioning rreatment

• Up-dos

• Permanent waves

• Spot perms

Haircut

Performed By:	Licensed Stylist
Time Required:	Approximately one-half hour (sometimes more, depending on length and complexity of cut required).
Equipment Used:	Shears, brush, comb, scissors, and sometimes a razor or shaver. Plastic drape for client. Often also requires shampoo and conditioner, and hair spray or other hair styling products.
Description:	A stylist discusses what a client wants done and makes suggestions, then cuts and shapes client's hair, often completing the service with a blow-dry and styling. Hair can be cut wet or dry, but usually hair is shampooed and conditioned beforehand and cut while still wet.

Approx. Retail Cost:	$15-$120, depending on location and type of salon and experience/reputation of stylist

Deep Conditioning Treatment

Performed By:	Licensed Stylist
Time Required:	One-half hour
Equipment Used:	Shampoo, specially formulated deep conditioner, blow-dryer, brush, comb, plastic drape and towels for customer.
Description:	A stylist inspects the hair and evaluates for condition and/or damage. Hair is shampooed and rinsed, then a special conditioner is applied. Plastic wrap is then placed over the conditioner, which is kept on while client sits under a dryer for approximately 20 minutes. The conditioner is then rinsed out, the hair is shampooed again, and the hair is styled.
Approx. Retail Cost:	$40 and up

Blow-Dry and Style

Performed By:	Licensed Stylist
Time Required:	Approx. 15 minutes to one-half hour, depending on length of hair and complexity of style.
Equipment Used:	Shampoo, conditioner, brush, comb, blow-dryer, curling iron, hair spray or other styling products. Plastic drape for client.
Description:	After a client's hair is shampooed and conditioned, a stylist blow-dries and styles client's hair.
Approx. Retail Cost:	$15-$100, depending on location and type of salon and experience/reputation of stylist

Hot Roller Set

Performed By:	Licensed Stylist
Time Required:	Approx. one-half hour to 45 minutes

Equipment Used:	Hot rollers, plastic cap. Brush, comb, hair spray. Plastic drape for customer.
Description:	A stylist rolls client's hair in hot rollers, clips them, then sprays them lightly with hair spray. Then the client sits under a dryer until the curls are dry and set. The curlers are then removed and the hair is styled, and usually more hair spray is applied to retain shape.
Approx. Retail Cost:	$25 and up

Up-Do (usually for special occasions)

Performed By:	Licensed Stylist, sometimes with an assistant
Time Required:	30 minutes to an hour, depending on length of hair and complexity of style.
Equipment Used:	Shampoo, conditioner, brush, comb, bobby pins, rubber bands, curling iron (sometimes a straightening iron, depending on hair type), hairclips, barrettes, hair spray and other styling products. Plastic drape for client.
Description:	A stylist washes and blow-dries, then styles client's hair in an elegant up-do. Up-do styles include variations on ponytails, braids, and buns, as well as French rolls/twists, demi-twists, etc. Up-dos can also incorporate flowers, lace, ribbons and jewelry, into the style, for a more formal, elegant look.
Approx. Retail Cost:	$35 and up; may offer discounts for groups, such as wedding parties

Permanent Wave

Performed By:	Licensed Stylist
Time Required:	About 1 3/4 -2 hours
Equipment Used:	Permanent chemical solution, neutralizer, squirt bottles, rods, papers, brush, comb, clips, plastic cap, cotton neck strip, protective skin cream. Blow-dryer, styling products. Plastic drape and towels for client.

Description:	After a client's hair is washed and conditioned, a stylist separates client's hair in small sections held with plastic clips. Working each section into small strips of hair using a comb tail, the stylist then rolls the client's hair in permanent rods. Cotton strips are wrapped around the edges of the head and a thin layer of skin cream applied to prevent perm solution from getting into clients' eyes or on their skin. Once the hair is entirely up in rods, a permanent solution is squirted evenly over the hair. A plastic cap is placed over the head and then the client sits under a dryer to process for approximately 20-30 minutes. Then a neutralizer solution is applied to the whole head and kept on for approximately 20 minutes. The perm rods are removed from the hair, which is shampooed and conditioned thoroughly and then blow-dried and styled.
Approx. Retail Cost:	$75-$120 (and up), without cut or $120 and up with cut

Spot Perm

Performed By:	Licensed Stylist
Time Required:	1 1/2 – 1 3/4 hours
Equipment Used:	Permanent chemical solution, neutralizer, squirt bottles, rods, papers, brush, comb, clips, plastic cap, cotton neck strip, protective skin cream. Blow-dryer, styling products. Plastic drape and towels for client.
Description:	The process for a spot perm is the same as for a regular perm except that only a particular part of the head is done (usually the crown or the front to add height to the area). The only difference (and why the process takes about 15 minutes less than a regular permanent) is that less time is required for the rods because fewer rods are being used.
Approx. Retail Cost:	$50 and up

Makeovers and Bridal Services

Makeover

Performed By:	Stylist, colorist, makeup artist, esthetician, nail technician
Time Required:	2 1/2-4 hours
Equipment Used:	Haircutting, coloring and styling equipment, makeup, manicure equipment.
Description:	First, a team evaluation is made by consulting with hair, color, makeup, nail and other beauty (e.g., waxing or facial) technicians.
Approx. Retail Cost:	Priced by consultation only depending on package of services to be performed. Some salons designed pre-packaged makeovers with a slight discount on the services put together.

Bridal Services

Performed By:	Stylist, colorist, makeup artist, nail technician
Time Required:	1-3 hours
Equipment Used:	Hair styling equipment, makeup, manicure equipment
Description:	Generally a team of cosmetologists get the bride (and sometimes also her bridal party) ready for the big day by styling her hair and doing her makeup and nails.
Approx. Retail Cost:	Priced by consultation only depending on services to be performed

2.2.2   Hair Coloring

There are a number of coloring services that you can offer to your clients. Most typical salons offer these services in addition to their regular styling and cutting services.

Highlights

Performed By:	Licensed Stylist/Colorist
Time Required:	Approx. 2 hrs.
Equipment Used:	Shampoo, conditioner, coloring chemicals, foils, application brushes, cap blow-dryer, brush, comb, styling products.
Description:	A colorist evaluates the color to be used and mixes it, then either takes strands of hair and pulls them through a cap or places them on foils and then brushes each strand with chemicals. This process is slow and can take up to an hour. The hair is then allowed to process for about 20-30 minutes. Then the cap or foils are removed and the hair is washed and conditioned, then blow-dried and styled.
Approx. Retail Cost:	$100-150 and up for highlights plus haircut; less for men ($40-60)

All Over One Color (Single Process)

Performed By:	Licensed Stylist/Colorist
Time Required:	1 hour
Equipment Used:	Bowl and brush, hair, comb, cap, shampoo, conditioner, coloring chemicals, blow-dryer, styling products. Drape and towels for client.
Description:	A colorist evaluates the color to be used, mixes it, then applies it to the hair. The hair is allowed to process for about 20-30 minutes. Then the coloring agent is rinsed out and the hair is shampooed and conditioned and then styled.
Approx. Retail Cost:	$100-150 and up for color and cut; less for men (e.g., grey touch up for men approx. $40-60)

2.2.3   Other Hair Services

Hair Straightening

Japanese Hair Straightening

Performed By: Licensed Stylist

Time Required: About 4-6 hours

Equipment Used: Straightening solution, shampoo, conditioner, heat lamps, flat iron, brush, comb, hair styling products, blow-dryer.

Description: The hair is shampooed and conditioned, then a straightening solution is applied to the hair, which is then heated under a hot lamp, then blown-dry, and then flat ironed piece by piece. The process is then repeated. A long and expensive process, Japanese straightening can last up to a year but may need a touchup after six months. This technique is also known as thermal reconditioning, straight perm, and Japanese straight perm.

Approx. Retail Cost: $350 and up, or about $80-100 per hour

Traditional Hair Straightening/Relaxing

Performed By: Licensed Stylist

Time Required: About 2- 2 1/2 hours

Equipment Used: Shampoo, conditioner, brush, chemical relaxer, cream, cap, comb, blow-dryer, flat iron, hair spray or other styling products. Plastic drape for client.

Description: After a client's hair is shampooed and conditioned, a chemical relaxer is added to the hair, which takes approximately one hour to apply. The hair is covered with a cap and allowed to process for about 20-30 minutes. Then a neutralizing agent is applied and allowed to process for about 20-30 minutes. Finally, the hair is blown-dry and styled and a flat iron is used to press it straight.

Approx. Retail Cost: $150-$250, depending on location and type of salon and experience/reputation of stylist

Hair Extensions and Wigs

- *Hair Extensions:* Done by a licensed hairstylist, this varies from 1-4 hours or more, depending on type and complexity of extensions desired; price varies greatly, but starts at approximately $200 - $750 and up. Techniques for applying hair extensions include weaving, gluing, heat fusing, and affixing the extensions with waxes or polymers. Hair extensions can be either human hair or synthetic hair.

- *Wig and Hairpiece application:* Done by a licensed hairstylist, this can involve a partial hair replacement blended in with client's own hair or a complete replacement if the client is bald. Price varies greatly with quality and size of hairpiece and the complexity involved, but run approximately $1000 up to several thousand dollars.

2.2.4   Men's Grooming Services

Men's grooming services, in addition to shampooing, cutting and styling, can include any or all of the following:

- Hot shave

- Beard and mustache design/trim

- Ear and nose hair trim

Hot Shave

Performed By: Licensed Barber

Time Required: About 30 minutes

Equipment Used: Hot shaving cream and brush, hot towel, straight-edge razor, aftershave lotion. A plastic drape and towels for client.

Description:	The face and/or neck area to be shaved is often wrapped in a hot towel to soften the whiskers. The towel is removed, then warm shaving cream is applied. A razor is skillfully used to provide a close shave. The face is then wiped clean and an aftershave lotion is applied.
Approx. Retail Cost:	$35-50

Beard and Mustache Trim

Performed By:	Licensed Barber
Time Required:	About 15-30 minutes
Equipment Used:	Comb, scissors, electric shaver, razors, towels, drape for client.
Description:	The barber carefully trims and shapes the beard and mustache.
Approx. Retail Cost:	$15-20

Ear and Nose Hair Trim

Performed By:	Licensed Barber
Time Required:	About 15-30 minutes
Equipment Used:	Comb, small scissors, electric shaver, electric nose/ear hair trimmer, tweezers, towels, drape for client.
Description:	The barber carefully trims and removes long or stray hairs in and on the nose and ears.
Approx. Retail Cost:	$15-20

2.2.5   Related Services

Complimentary Services

Many salons also offer their clients certain complimentary services, including serving them free light beverages and snacks (e.g., coffee, tea, bottled water, cookies, pastries, fruit) during their visits. Other free services include:

- Initial beauty consultation to make recommendations for cut, color, and other hair services

- Free bang trims between appointments for hairstyles with bangs

- Complimentary shampoo and conditioning with any hair service (although salons do charge extra for premium conditioning treatments and reparative treatments)

- Free blow-dry and styling with haircuts, perms, or color services

- Hot towels (usually in men's salons)

- Complimentary shoe shines (in some men's salons)

Don't just view these related services as merely a time-consuming or burdensome cost. Dalgiza Barros of Creative Energy Hair Studio explains that "one of the reasons the senior stylists—including me—have maintained our clientele for so long is because of our shampooing technique. We've spent time learning massage techniques that relax and revive. It's a double shampoo that generally lasts up to eight minutes and is very relaxing." Complimentary services like this can go a long way in building client loyalty.

Babysitting

Another great service worth mentioning, though not technically a free service, is babysitting. The Johnathan Breitung Salon & Luxury Spa in Chicago has a 300 square foot babysitting facility staffed by trained babysitters where clients can drop off their children. Parents are given a beeper in case they need to return to the babysitting room. The salon also provides cameras and obtains comprehensive insurance for the room.

A babysitting service allows clients to get services done without being disturbed, for a small fee. The charge for the service is $10 per hour with a $30 cap. "We have made the room so inviting," says co-owner Johnathan Breitung, "that it is easy for children to become preoccupied with all the toys in the room so that they leave their parents alone." This much-appreciated service, oddly enough, is hard to come by. In fact, according to Johnathan, they are the only salon in Chicago that currently offers this feature.

2.3 Salon Retail Products

As a hair salon business owner, you will also be selling retail products. There are a variety of product lines that you can consider for your salon, and these should tie in to the types of services you will be offering. As discussed previously, selling retail products is a crucial way to add to the profitability of your salon.

In many salons, employees and independent contractors receive a commission on the sales of retail products. This motivates them to help increase your sales. The drawback is that they might get overzealous in this regard and become pushy or aggressive salespeople, which can be a big turnoff for clients. If the products are positioned well, in a highly visible location near the register, they will often sell themselves.

Justin Hickox, owner of Hickox Studios, maintains that you and your stylists shouldn't be motivated by the bottom line or commissions, but by a need to educate clients about your products: "One mistake I feel salon owners make is to push their stylists to push products in order to pad the bottom line instead of focusing on product education for their clientele." When clients take home products from your salon, the aim is that they will be able to care for their hair and get similar results by using the same quality products you use in your salon. "Educating clients on how to style and care for their hair (or skin) at home is important in helping them achieve salon results at home. It's no compliment to me when someone says 'I'll never be able to do this at home,'" explains Billy Lowe, celebrity stylist and owner of the Billy Lowe Hair Studio in Los Angeles.

"My job as a salon professional," says Lowe, "is to educate my clients on the tools and products they need to achieve salon results and the hows behind it." He notes that these "educational moments" are important from your perspective as a salon owner because "you want your clients to have winning moments at home when they are styling their hair. You also want them to purchase the products and tools they need from your salon and not from your competitor. "

Hair Care and Styling Products

Some of the products you might consider for your salon are:

- Hair care and styling products, such as shampoos, conditioners
- UV ray protector for hair
- Hair sprays
- Gels
- Mousse
- Styling wax
- Brushes and combs
- Barrettes, and hair styling combs

Men's salons can sell hair products manufactured or scented for men. This category of products works particularly well, as men seeking salon services often need advice on how to care for their hair at home.

Salon products are generally more expensive than many products sold in other retail outlets, but are also selected by salon owners for their higher quality ingredients and superior results. Stylists can also demonstrate the use of a hair care or styling product in person, giving the client a chance to 'sample' the product before making a purchase.

Skin Care and Personal Care Products

These include skin care products such as skin lotions and hand creams, body washes and shower gels, soaps, massage oils, foot care products, magnetic products, vitamins, slimming or detoxifying or cleansing supplements or systems, and sunscreens. Men's salons can offer skin lotions and creams specially scented for men, shaving products, mustache wax, and colognes. Salons with spas also sometimes offer relaxing CD recordings for creating a peaceful ambience at home.

Jewelry, Accessories, and Gifts

Jewelry is another common retail item sold in salons, especially full-service salons whose clientele are primarily women. Jewelry and other stylish accessories like sunglasses or scarves do not take up much room and can be popular sales items, provided you select products that appeal to your client base.

Gifts such as perfumes, colognes, shaving kits, trinkets and other items may also be appropriate, depending on your clientele. Small items like these also make good 'impulse buys', so having them near the register where clients check out (along with a handy countertop mirror for them to see how they look) will help increase sales.

You can also go beyond smaller gift items and offer a more extensive line of products. Rik Rak Salon Boutique and Bar in Miami, for example, offers its clients a selection of fashion items and accessories like dresses, skirts, shoes, and hats, as well as handbags and jewelry. You can offer your clients almost any product that is related to improving their appearance.

Food

While many salons offer complimentary beverages such as coffee and tea and small snacks such as pastries and fruit, many salon experiences span enough time that a client may want something more. Some salons, especially those that cater to a lunchtime business professionals crowd, make arrangements with local restaurants to deliver meals to clients during their visits. If you will be offering services that are long in duration and expensive, you should consider contacting local restaurants to work out an arrangement such as this.

Art

As we mentioned in section 2.1, a small but distinctive niche in the salon industry is the salon space that incorporates an art gallery. This makes sense, as salons are a place where people are made to look and feel more beautiful or stylish, and art is all about appreciation of the chic and the beautiful. The Michael Peter Hays Art Salon in Locust Valley (Long Island), New York ("where art meets hair") combines these two successfully, as does Harley DiNardo's Shampoo Avenue B in lower Manhattan.

2.4   Hair Salon Personnel

2.4.1   Your Role as Salon Owner

You don't need to have worked in a hair salon business for 20 years or be a financial wizard to succeed as a hair salon business owner. The growth of the industry has created opportunities for experienced professionals as well as people stepping into the business for the very first time.

What you do need is enthusiasm, a desire to be on the job on a daily basis and a willingness to learn more about your business. A new business needs constant attention, and establishing and growing your business most likely will take several years. Remember, too, that you are about to take on a great deal of responsibility.

As a hair salon business owner, you will be responsible for all aspects of the business. However, there are certain tasks that you will perform that your staff will not, and there are tasks that you might need to be responsible for at first but can delegate later, once your staff is trained.

Some of these tasks include:

- Ensuring that the salon is clean and the equipment is in working order
- Supplying the stylists, technicians and estheticians with products they need to perform their jobs, such as client drapes and customer gowns, clean towels, styling and coloring equipment and products, etc.
- The day to day or weekly job of checking and re-ordering supplies and restocking inventory
- Providing and stocking beverages and snacks for clients and employees or independent contractors.
- Finding new ways to minimize costs and maximize revenues
- Pricing retail products (and salon services if stylists or technicians are employees)
- For retail items, searching online for new and unique items
- Changing retail and other displays
- Supervising staff members
- Assisting accountant with sorting out any financial issues
- Ensuring all certificates, licenses and accreditations required by the business and staff are current

- Being highly visible and addressing client concerns professionally

- Interviewing, hiring and training employees or contractors

- For owner stylists, coaching new talent through client consultations and services and product sales

- Scheduling staff appropriately

- Gathering bills and coordinating with bookkeeper, accountant, etc.

- Encouraging and allowing employees to take continuing education courses, making them aware of new educational opportunities

- Making sure client schedules run smoothly

- Making clients feel welcome and well taken care of

- "Keeping the peace" between employees

- Appraising performance, rewarding and disciplining (sometimes firing) employees

- Marketing the salon to new clients and coordinating with PR reps, graphic artists and other marketing and promotions professionals

A Day in the Life of a Salon Owner

Salon owners are generally expert multitaskers who can juggle many things at once for several hours at a time. They are also good peacekeepers and good leaders who can manage and motivate others and help resolve problems. One key difference between those who rent out chair spaces and those whose stylists and technicians are employees is that the owner has less oversight of contractors' client schedules and operations at their stations. However, many salon owners have similar duties and daily experiences, such as the following:

Many owners arrive before the salon opens. They make sure the salon is clean and tidy, that there are enough clean towels and that all salon and retail supplies are properly stocked (and either wash and dry towels or make sure the employee whose job it is does this). This often includes taking inventory of product stock and noting or placing new orders.

They either make coffee and put out snacks for employees and clients or make sure that this has been done by the appropriate employee. They may also check the appointment books and see what appointment times need to be filled and make the receptionist aware of this. Owners who take online orders for products must check for new orders and fill any open orders. They may on some days schedule employee meetings before clients arrive.

If the owner is also a stylist, they also take care of their own clients throughout the day. Regardless of whether or not an owner has clients, he or she must oversee the quality of the work of their employees (although this is not usually part of their duties if the other stylists or technicians in their salon are independent contractors). The owner must also see that everything from the front desk to the salon area are running smoothly throughout the day. They must solve client issues and problems to clients' satisfaction (again, less so if the stylists are renters and the client is an independent contractor's client) as well as settle any squabbles and keep the peace among the stylists, technicians, and other personnel.

Also throughout the day, they must continually make sure the phone is being answered, the retail area is neat and well-stocked, the coffee, tea and snacks are replenished, and that there are enough clean towels and other needed supplies. At the end of the day they must make sure the salon is clean and tidy, return any remaining calls, and check that the appointment schedule and personnel's work schedules are in order and the salon is ready for the next day.

"One key to successful salon ownership is being available and on top of everything 24 hours a day. A typical day as a salon owner is extremely hectic. From the minute you walk in until the minute you leave, your hands are full. I actually sleep with my Blackberry next to me just in case I need to be reached."

— Valery Joseph, Owner,
Valery Joseph Salons

2.4.2   Hiring Employee Stylists vs. Renting Chairs

"Make sure you hire a great staff. Every employee must embrace the salon's philosophy of outstanding artistry and customer service. The front desk person is truly a critical piece to the overall success of any salon. They should be a person or persons you trust completely and can give them authority and responsibility to make decisions."

> — Derrick Diggs, Owner,
> Layers Hair Salon

Salons vary considerably as to how many staff members are needed to help things run smoothly. Of course, this is usually determined by the size of the shop and the variety of services offered. The more you have of either of these, the more people that are required to run the salon.

Some very successful salons operate with as few as two people. Others are large and have many employees (literally dozens in some cases). Keep in mind that there may be several people working in a salon but, depending on the set-up, they may be employees or independent contractors or a combination of both. Choosing whether hiring employees or contractors will work best for you depends on a number of factors, including the type of business you envision for yourself, your startup budget, and who your clientele will be.

Hiring Employees

According to Ronnie Pryor, owner of Source Salon in Wilton Manors, Florida, "salons are moving away from booth rentals and back to employee team-building. This leads to a sense of ownership and pride, and allows an owner to maintain direction and artistic vision as a whole."

Federico Calce of the upscale Federico Salon in Manhattan explains why he would never rent chairs or booths to stylists, which reflects an important consideration for aspiring salon owners:

> "When you rent out a chair, you lose control. You lose artistic control and you lose control over how the stylist treats clients, yet you are still legally liable if that stylist and you are sued. Also, if a client is unhappy, she won't say she's unhappy with the stylist, she'll say she's unhappy with the salon. My advice would be to have commission people because they are actually employees, not independent contractors."

Employees versus Contractors

Legally, if you hire an employee, you will have to pay payroll taxes on that employee, and probably make unemployment and workers' compensation contributions to the appropriate government agency. On the other hand, you can train those employees the way you like, and you can require them to do their work at certain hours and at places you choose.

If you hire contractors, those people will have learned their job skills elsewhere. As celebrity hairstylist and Amiri salon owner DaRico Jackson points out: "There's something to be said about supervising children who listen versus grownups, who have their own ideas about how things should be, especially when they are renters, because they are actually running a business within yours."

Contractors can choose how and when to do the work. This means you have less control over stylists who rent chairs in your salon, including how they perform cuts and styles, and when they schedule their client appointments. However, part of the arrangement is that you and your stylist contractor will mutually agree on what services will be performed, as well as when they will be performed. But you cannot require them to be at your salon or anywhere else for a certain number of hours daily. It is often best to spell out what you expect and what the contractor is to do or deliver in an agreement.

Other differences between an employee and a contractor are:

- Employees work only for you. Contractors may have other clients as well as you, and can work for any and all of them.

- Employees are paid on a regular basis. Contractors are paid per appointment.

- Employees work for a certain number of hours. Contractors set their own hours, as long as they get the job done. That can be great for them if they are really fast, or not so great for them if they are really slow. As long as they are taking enough appointments and getting through them in a timely fashion, it's great for you. On the other hand, if an employee stylist is slow, this is bad for you.

- Employees can be fired or quit. Contractors can't be fired in the usual way while they are working under contract. You may decide to have them stop working in your salon, but you will be obliged to pay them according to your contractual agreement unless you are able to renegotiate the contract or successfully sue them if you are unhappy with their work. (Of course that would only be in extreme cases; it is best to avoid lawsuits altogether!)

Renting Chairs

Although the current trend leans toward hiring staff as commissioned employees, there are still a good number of salons where stylists rent chair spaces from the owner as independent contractors.

Some salon owners see significant advantages of renting booths or chairs. Dalgiza Barros of Creative Energy in Hanover, Massachusetts explains why she chose to rent chairs instead of hiring employees:

> "Renting chairs allows each individual an opportunity to own their own business and that entrepreneurial spirit is felt throughout the salon. The stylists that rent chairs appreciate the fact that they have a comfortable, functional space for their clients, but not at the cost of giving up a significant portion of their earnings. As a result, there is a greater camaraderie and salon politics are non-existent. And for me, it's a comfort knowing that each individual is responsible for herself."

Another benefit of this arrangement, as Michael Peter Hayes of the Michael Peter Hayes Art Salon in Locust Valley, New York points out, is that "a salon owner can have an easier outlook on the future (financial projections) with a rental income."

2.4.3 Salon Staff Roles

There are many people whose skills contribute to the success of a hair salon. Your salon may have some or all of the following types of staff members. You may also find that, at least in the beginning, you will take on some of these roles yourself.

Receptionist

Sometimes referred to as a front desk manager or salon coordinator, receptionists answer the phones, schedule client appointments, check clients in and notify stylists and others when their clients have arrived. Other tasks they perform are to check clients out when they are finished, and ring up retail purchases. If they do not perform any personal care services these individuals do not need a cosmetology license.

Receptionists are not paid well, usually minimum wage, but the position can sometimes offer an opportunity for aspiring stylists to 'learn the ropes' of how a salon runs. Often receptionists are hired immediately upon graduation from beauty school. While receptionists are a must for medium to large salons, some smaller salons do not need or have receptionists. Also, not all receptionists are beauty school graduates, so you may also be able to hire a high school graduate or mother or retiree seeking to re-enter the workforce, as long as they have good phone, interpersonal, and organizational skills.

Manager

This position may also be called by another name, such as salon coordinator. A salon manager can be someone with only a stylist background, but because the more important skills needed for this position are business management skills this individual generally should have a prior business management background or work experience. Managers who do not perform any personal care services do not need a cosmetology license.

Usually smaller salons are managed by the owner, but this is not usually the case in larger salons, where a separate manager is often a necessity. In any case, the owner oversees and sometimes overlaps duties with the manager.

The manager must be able to order and stock supplies, track and rotate stock, and deal with wholesalers and other suppliers (including vendor contracts, and placing and checking deliveries). They must be able to do inventory checks, and oversee the retail aspects of the salon. If the salon has employees, the manager usually must oversee employee health, retirement, and other benefits, as well as handle payroll and sometimes bookkeeping and accounting. They also might oversee the building and building repairs as well as salon equipment maintenance and repairs. They may handle customer relations for the salon.

One important consideration on whether you need a manager (besides how large or busy the salon is) is whether you have many clients of your own. Some salon owners are much more comfortable with hair related aspects of the salon than its business side.

As Valery Joseph, owner of the upscale Valery Joseph Salon in New York elaborates:

> "An artist should be an artist and a manager should be a manager. Do what you are best at. When you are styling hair, you can't be worried about what's happening at the front desk or you will lose your train of thought. You need to concentrate on your creation and spend your time with the client. A lot of people can do twenty things at once, but it will never be done right. Take the time to concentrate on one thing at a time, that way it will develop flawlessly."

Assistant Manager

The assistant manager does just that: assists the manager. They may even cover for the manager when he or she cannot be at the salon. Many of the assistant manager's tasks will be the same as the manager's tasks, although they will have less responsibility for more important aspects such as employee management and bookkeeping. If they do not perform any personal care services, these individuals do not need a cosmetology license.

Shampoo Assistants

Shampoo assistants, like receptionists, tend to be paid at or near minimum wage. They, too, are also often aspiring hair stylists, so this job is often ideal for beauty school students seeking to earn money and experience while they attend school. Their main function is to shampoo and condition clients' hair, escort them to and from the stylists' or colorists' chairs, occasionally assist stylists (e.g., handing them curlers, papers or foils), place clients under dryers and set timers, and sweep up hair and tidy the sink and styling areas and do laundry. Shampoo assistants do not need a cosmetology license.

Some salon owners we spoke with made a point of noting that they do not use assistant stylists or shampooers during the process of doing their clients' hair, but rather perform the entire process from beginning to end. They note that the process is more intimate and makes the client feel more special when the stylist is involved at every stage. They also say that this gives them artistic and quality control throughout the process, which greatly reduces any risk of mistakes or less than perfect results.

Stylists/Hairdressers

These are licensed cosmetologists (i.e., beauty school graduates) who specialize in hair. They shampoo, cut, color, style, straighten, and perm hair, apply and style wigs, hairpieces, and hair extensions, and give clients advice on caring for their hair at home. This position requires a cosmetology license.

Barbers (Men's Salons and Barber Shops)

Barbers shampoo, trim, shape, style and cut hair, usually working only with men and boys. They also shave men, as well as trim mustaches and beards, and ear and nose hair. Some also do men's nails or provide skin treatments, such as facials. A state license is required to be a barber. In some states, they are also licensed to color, highlight, bleach, or perm hair.

> "At cosmetology school stylists only receive about 10 hours of training in men's hair cutting, compared to approximately 1,000 hours spent training to cut women's hair. As owner of my own barber shop and with over 14 years experience as an American Crew International All-Star Educator, I've seen first-hand the impact knowledgeable, well-trained men's grooming specialists can have on a men's salon's success."
>
> — Al Urbanowski, owner of Al's Barber Shops and American Crew International All-Star Educator

Other Staff

Cleaning Staff

Usually in larger salons one or more people are hired to sweep floors, do laundry (clean dry towels are a constant need in salons), scrub out sinks, dust, clean bathrooms, etc. Otherwise, cleaning tasks are often shared by all the employees or independent contractors within the salon whenever they have time to help with this function throughout the day.

Estheticians

These are licensed cosmetologists (and thus beauty school graduates), but this term usually refers to cosmetologists who do not do hair. They may be trained in and specialize in other beauty treatments, such as facials, waxing, brow arching, lash and brow tinting, and makeup. These individuals may also have alternative titles, such as makeup artist or beautician. Keep in mind that anyone performing any of these functions with the exception of makeup artists must have a cosmetology license.

Manicurist or Nail Technician

A manicurist or nail technician is a cosmetologist with training in nail services. They perform manicures, pedicures and related treatments. Foot massages are often included in their services. These individuals must be properly licensed.

Business Manager

Some salon owners hire a separate person to handle business-related aspects of their business, such as marketing, managing the website, payroll, accounting and financial reporting, taxes, vendor contracts and other legal matters. Sometimes a salon manager may handle some of these matters (e.g., accounting and payroll, advertising, marketing, employee benefits) or these duties may be separated.

In section 6.7 you will find information about all aspects of hiring employees, including advice on recruiting, hiring, paying, and training new employees.

3. Getting Ready

This chapter will help to give you a realistic feel for the traits and skills you will need to succeed. In addition, you will find guidance and resources to help you acquire the experience or educational background (if any) you may need to acquire or develop further before opening your own salon.

The first part of this chapter discusses the personal traits, and interpersonal, business, and cosmetology skills that can come in handy. The information provided here will help you spot areas where you may need to improve or to acquire and develop new skills. The second part covers practical ways in which you can further develop the knowledge and skills you will need as a salon owner, including acquiring work experience, researching other salons, and educational resources, from courses to professional trade shows and organizations.

3.1 Skills and Knowledge You Will Need

Before continuing, it's important to note again that not all salon owners are beauty professionals. Owners we spoke with ranged from top hair designers and stylists to business executives who were tired of building someone else's business, to a professional nurse with a business vision but no hair styling knowledge whatsoever. Remember, too, that being a top hair designer does not necessarily mean one has the required business savvy to run a successful salon. Whatever your background, if you take the necessary steps to plan and prepare for opening your own business, you can make your dream of salon ownership a reality.

3.1.1 Personal Traits

The following are personal traits that many successful salon owners share. Some are shared by business owners in general, while others are more specific to this type of service business. If you lack some of these traits, don't panic: you can seek to develop them as you prepare to open your salon business. However, knowing beforehand what traits come in handy when overseeing and properly managing a salon business can help you avoid some nasty surprises later on. The many successful salon owners we spoke with listed the following as important personal traits:

- *Patient:* Any business that deals with the public, has many clients, and involves managing employees requires a great deal of patience.

- *Friendly:* Again, you are dealing with the public in a service business, so a friendly personality is a must.

- *Passionate about your salon and its purpose:* You will need a passion for your salon, and for the business you envision, to carry you through good times and bad and keep you striving to be the best at what you do, day in and day out.

- *Pride in your salon and your work:* This is key to success, as pride breeds careful work and great craftsmanship. The quality of the services you provide (either yourself as a stylist or through your employees) is the very lifeline of your business.

- *Healthy:* Because salon ownership is physically demanding and a hands-on business, it's important to be healthy enough to handle the daily tasks required.

- *Energetic:* Salons generally have long hours and salon owners often juggle several tasks at a time for many consecutive hours.

- *A good people manager:* You must be able to separate your business duties and your ability to make decisions that are good for your business from your personal relationships with your stylists and other employees. While many salon owners mentioned the importance of hiring a salon team that works well together, many also said they regretted allowing their friendships with their employees to prevent them from making the right decisions or being more authoritative with their employees.

- *Decisive:* You'll need to be able to make good decisions and problem solve on a daily basis, and often quickly. As mentioned above, you also need to have a strong personality and be strong willed when dealing with employees.

- *Willing to perform tasks great and small:* You may be a world-class hair designer, but to be a successful salon owner you must be willing to do anything from hair cutting to sweeping the floors and taking out the garbage (even if you have employees). Running a successful salon is a group effort, from the shampoo assistants all the way up to the owner.

- *Good communication skills:* This is a people business, so you need to be able to communicate effectively to your stylists/technicians, clients, and suppliers.

- *Reliable:* You can be the greatest artist when it comes to hair design, but you need to be able to make and keep appointments, as should all your stylists and technicians. A business and its employees must be reliable to succeed.

However, by far the most important trait, echoed by dozens of successful salon owners, was the ability to lead. You will need to be able to hire, manage, and fire employees, coach them on a daily basis, and set goals for them and for your business in order for it to thrive and grow. As DaRico Jackson, celebrity stylist and owner of Amiri Salon explains:

"As a salon owner, you have to not only be an expert in the field, but you have to possess some type of leadership skills, and an authoritative stature to gain the respect of your employees as well as your clients. I think that when someone comes to the salon they look for the person in charge to be the best at what they do and be a good problem solver."

On the flip side, you need not be stoical to the point of never seeking help from others. In virtually any business venture, you will occasionally need the assistance of others, so although you need to be a strong leader, you must also not be afraid to ask for help when you truly need it.

3.1.2 Interpersonal Skills

There are a number of interpersonal skills that can help you develop excellent relationships with your customers — and your employees, suppliers, landlord, banker, and everyone else you do business with. This section offers some tips on how to enhance those skills. The sections that follow have tips for specific situations.

Listening

> *"Listen. Listen. Listen. If you listen to your staff and your clients, you will hear about what's working and what's not. And your staff will likely have at least as much experience as you do, and can offer different perspectives and solutions you may never have thought of."*
>
> — Ronnie Pryor, Owner,
> Source Salon

While listening seems like an easy skill to master, most of us experience challenges in at least one of the following areas involved in listening: paying attention, understanding, and remembering. You can become a better listener by focusing fully on someone when they are speaking. Here are some ways to do that:

- Don't interrupt the other person. Hear them out.

- Keep listening to the other person, even if you think you know what they will say next. If you make assumptions, you may miss the point they're making.

- Ask questions in order to clarify what the other person has said. Take notes if necessary.

- Don't be distracted by outside interference. Loud noises, the other person mispronouncing a word, or even an uncomfortable room temperature can break your concentration and distract you from the conversation.

- Give feedback to the other person. Nod occasionally; say things like "I see," and smile, if appropriate. Let them know you're listening.

- Use paraphrasing. In other words, repeat back in your own words your understanding of what the other person has said. It can help alleviate misunderstandings later on.

Verbal Skills

Clear communication is essential because you will need to explain your salon's sales or return policy, and you will need to describe to customers your current inventory. When making sales, customers can become frustrated if they find it difficult to understand what you're saying. To improve your verbal communication skills, ask friends or a vocal coach for feedback on any areas that could be improved, such as: use of slang, proper grammar, or altering your tone of voice to eliminate any harshness. (You can find vocal coaches in the Yellow Pages.)

Reading Non-Verbal Messages

In addition to hearing what people say, a skilled business owner also notices non-verbal communication (tone of voice, facial expression, body language, etc.). These signals can give you valuable clues about what the other person is thinking.

For example, did a customer fold their arms when you made a particular suggestion? If so, they may be communicating that they disagree, even if they don't actually say so. Although body language can't tell you precisely what someone is thinking, it can give you clues so you can ask follow-up questions, even as basic as "How do you feel about that?" If you want to improve this skill, you can find some excellent advice in the book *Reading People*, by Jo-Ellan Dimitrius and Wendy Patrick Mazzarella.

3.1.3 Business Skills

"I have met with over 3,000 salon owners from all across North America and the most common issue is lack of leadership. You will need to be dedicated to continually improving your management and leadership skills if you are to build a team of dedicated employees who will support you in creating the type

of salon of your dreams. Salon owners are not bosses. They are coaches. Building a winning team requires an unwavering commitment to understanding your people and what motivates them. You not only need to set goals for yourself, but you will need to help your team to do the same."

— Don Bewley, co-founder,
Eufora International

"Personally, I think the right time to open a salon is when you feel you have outgrown the ability to work as an employee. But the years spent as an employee have hopefully prepared you well; it's vital you understand the management side of the business along with having learned how to deal with everyday challenges that come with dealing with the public. And, to stay in business, you need to know how to grow your business and market your salon."

— Dalgiza Barros, Owner,
Creative Energy Hair Studio

As Dalgiza Barros suggests in the quote above, if you are well prepared to be a business owner, the better the chances are that your salon will be a success. It's crucial to know at all times where your business stands financially. While you don't have to learn it all, staying on top of your accounting will help you avoid finding yourself in the awful position of being out of cash to pay your bills or replenish your inventory.

Keep in mind that even if you are an extremely talented hair stylist, this does not necessarily mean you are prepared to run a business. If you lack experience in managing a successful salon or lack the needed business background, this is an area where you first must develop the appropriate skills. Be aware that working as a stylist or other technician in a salon and running a salon are very different matters. Running a successful salon requires an in-depth knowledge of the industry and well-developed business skills that include marketing and promotion, business management, bookkeeping and accounting (unless you hire someone to do these for you), customer service, retail and inventory management, and related skills.

If you are a talented stylist with an established following who can draw clients in to a salon with your superior skills but you lack the right temperament or skills to run a business, you may want to consider having a business partner who has the appropriate business skills. For example, Stacy Dabney Ramirez who co-owns the successful bustling Bella Bethesda Salon in downtown Bethesda , Maryland, with her sister Lindsey Dabney, explains how this arrangement works for them:

> "Lindsey is the stylist and I run the business. It works really well. I am available to talk with clients, solve issues, network, and meet with stylists, while Lindsey can focus on one on one time with her clients."

Running a successful hair salon requires an overlap of a variety of business skills. Aside from knowledge and expertise about hair, hair care, and the retail products you sell (and training employees to be knowledgeable as well), you will need to know about:

- Business planning

- Financial management

- Merchandising

- Operations management

- Inventory management

- Hiring and supervising employees

- Marketing and sales

The more you can keep your expenses down while building a solid customer base to build sales volume, while at the same time turning over inventory frequently, the more successful your salon will be. For some of these tasks, you can hire employees or contractors to help you, such as a bookkeeper or someone who can handle the marketing and promotion for your business. Keep in mind, though, that the fewer people you need to hire to help you manage your business, the lower your overall costs of running the business. Developing business skills takes time, so be thorough, and don't be in such a rush that you neglect to fill in any gaps in your knowledge or skills.

Experience you have in other retail environments can be helpful, and there are a number of ways you can develop your skills and knowledge in all of these areas. In this chapter, you'll find specific ideas to help you increase your experience and knowledge of running a salon. You'll also find detailed advice throughout the remaining sections of this guide.

You will probably find reading the entire guide before you launch your business helpful, but you can quickly identify particular areas you may want to focus on by reviewing the table of contents. For example, section 6.6 provides advice on financial management, covering everything from budgeting to bookkeeping to building wealth, and section 4.5 gives you advice about start-up financial planning. Both these sections provide website links to online resources to help you find further help in these areas.

One tool for helping you to focus on what business skills are involved in being a business owner is business planning. Section 4.4 looks in detail at how to develop a business plan to get your business up and running by outlining and clarifying what products and services you will offer, deciding how you will finance your business, creating a market plan, etc. In addition to addressing these important business issues, a business plan will also help you to understand some of the other basic "hard" skills required of a business owner, such as marketing and accounting skills.

The Canada Business website at **www.canadabusiness.ca** has a great deal of helpful information for anyone thinking of starting their own business. They offer the following tips to new entrepreneurs for identifying and creating a unique service:

- Take advantage of a market switch
- Capitalize on a growth trend
- Take advantage of new fads
- Cover market gaps or shortages
- Imitate a successful product or idea
- Transfer a concept from one industry to another
- Invent a new product or service
- Create a market demand
- Serve unique customer groups
- Take advantage of circumstances
- Find people with under-used skills

Other Business Skills

In addition to the business skills listed above, you will need to deal with a fair amount of paperwork. This includes handling important business and legal issues pertaining to your business such as collecting and paying sales taxes, obtaining proper licenses to operate your business, and maintaining adequate insurance for your business. We'll discuss some of these issues in greater detail later on, but it's important to note that you will want to educate yourself on these issues and develop these skills if you do not already have them before you open your business.

Research Skills

Having good research skills is another important asset. You will need to use these skills from the moment you begin developing your business plan (including the population demographics of any areas you are considering), searching for the right location for your business, finding vendors and suppliers, learning about new trends and products, and other purposes.

Computer Skills

You will also need to know how to operate computers and software and use the Internet, as these are key for tracking sales data, inventory, and other important information. Computer skills can be learned, and many local school districts, community and other colleges offer continuing education or extension courses on how to operate a PC or Mac, as well as how to use several major software programs and making use of the Internet for research and marketing.

Resources for Developing Business Skills

The following resources can help you develop your business skills:

SBA

The Small Business Administration (SBA) is a leading U.S. government resource for information about licensing, taxes, and starting a small business. You can find a range of resources including information on financing your new business, business plans and much more at **www. sba.gov**.

SCORE

The Service Corps of Retired Executives (SCORE) is an organization of U.S. volunteers who donate their time and expertise to new business owners. You can find information on taxes, tips for starting your business, or even find a mentor who will coach you and help you maximize your chances of succeeding as a new business owner. Visit them at **www.score.org**.

Canada Business Services for Entrepreneurs

This Canadian government website offers information on legislation, taxes, incorporation, and other issues of interest to Canadian business owners or those who do business in Canada. For more information and a list of services they offer visit their website at **www.canadabusiness.ca**.

3.1.4   Cosmetology Skills or Knowledge

"Although I'm starting to see this changing, many stylists won't work for a salon owner who has not been a stylist. They believe that an owner that hasn't been behind the chair won't understand them and the business. Although I'm not sure I believe this is a valid concern, it isn't a bad idea for someone who is opening a salon to become a licensed salon professional of some kind."

> — Jill D. Miller, Business Development Consultant, Creative Solutions

Wikipedia, the online encyclopedia, defines cosmetology simply as "the study and application of beauty treatment". This simple definition hides a world of complexity. To start with, beauty treatments include hair styling, manicures and pedicures, cosmetics, skin care, etc. A cosmetologist is a person who is able to deliver one or more of these services. Most cosmetology courses focus on hair styling, but also teach students something about the other services, too. Whether you need to develop these skills depends largely on your reason for opening a salon, the kind of salon you plan to open, and the role you envision yourself playing in your business (see section 2.1 for more about different types of salons).

While cosmetology skills are not required to be a salon owner, understanding the craft can be very helpful. Naturally, many salon owners are accomplished stylists even before deciding to open their own businesses. If that describes you, and you plan to continue to work "behind the chair" after you open your salon, you likely already have well-honed, top-notch skills along with an established, loyal clientele.

As a salon owner with a cosmetology background, interviewing prospective employees thoroughly will be easier for you, too. Salon owners generally test prospective employees by having them cut, color and perm hair, either on people or on mannequins so they can see their level of skill, how quickly they work, and other important factors before hiring them to handle salon clients. Without a cosmetology background, you will need to find someone else who can help you properly evaluate the technical proficiency of prospective employees, as these are things a resume and references can show but not prove.

This is another area where franchise ownership can be a good choice for individuals who do not have a cosmetology background. In fact, Jeff Sturgis, Vice President of Franchise Sales for Fantastic Sam's Salons told us that "the majority of franchisees have no experience in this industry. Only about 20% of our franchisees actually are cosmetologists or come from the beauty industry."

Although most franchises will not actually locate or hire employees for you, they will provide extensive training for them as part of the franchise package. Of course, it's important for you to evaluate thoroughly any franchise opportunity you are considering in order to determine whether or not a particular franchise offers adequate training for your prospective employees. (To learn more about franchise options, see section 4.2.2.)

3.2 Learning by Doing

3.2.1 Work in a Hair Salon

"I would not own any business before working in that field at least a year prior to opening my own. That way you an see what works, what doesn't, and come up with your own ideas on how to make the business run smoothly... being a hairstylist does not prepare you to run a salon."

— Elizabeth Coy, owner,
Indigo Salon

"For someone who wants to own their own salon, I recommend first working in a salon. It's best to experience as much as possible about every aspect of the business — from the front desk to the shampoo station. It is critical to be educated in the craft as well as management. Being comfortable with the art of customer relations is a key element in leading a salon."

— Anne Marie Sheeley,
Salon Diva

Several of the business owners we spoke with said they had originally worked for another hair salon. This can be a valuable way to learn much-needed skills for running your own salon one day. Not only will you learn how to deal with customers, you will more than likely learn how to use the systems used by many salons (covered in Chapter 6 of this guide). You don't need to work as a hair stylist to work in a salon, so consider trying to find one of the other jobs that salons also offer (see section 2.4.3 to find information about the various salon employees).

Working in a hair salon (or in a day spa, or cosmetics shop/studio, or beauty products retail store), even if only on a part-time or volunteer basis, is probably the best way to prepare yourself for opening your own store. Working for a time in a hair salon will give you valuable insight into pricing merchandise, what sells (and, equally important, what doesn't), how to deal with customers, how to arrange merchandise to its best advantage so that it looks attractive to buyers, and exactly what it takes to keep a salon running smoothly on a day-to-day basis.

As Rita Ciotoli, managing director of the Way2 B Spa and the Charm Salon & Spa in Ontario, Canada, notes, it's not so much the experience with beauty services that counts as experience in the business aspects of running a salon. "I bought my first salon after three years of working as an esthetician in a hair salon," Ciotoli explains. "It didn't really matter that I had experience doing beauty services. It would've been better if I had business experience. I would suggest working with another business owner for a while and becoming manager at least three years before opening a salon of your own."

Visit the salon you'd like to work in as a customer whenever possible before applying for a job so you can get to know the owner (and the store) a little. Remember, it will help if the owner recognizes you because you have been there before. Never phone or write a letter; face to face works much better.

Here are some suggestions for introducing yourself and what you can do for a prospective employer:

- Explain that you are interested in learning retailing.

- Tell them if you've had any previous selling experience (whether it's shoes or ice cream).

- Think of some extra service you could offer, such as creating window displays.

- If no job is available and you really love the salon and want to work there, volunteer to work for free. It could pay in the long run.

Finally, when applying for a job in a hair salon ensure that your demeanor, personality and dress reflect the qualities that you would be looking for in an employee. These characteristics are outlined in more detail in section 6.7.2 ("Recruiting Staff").

3.2.2   Get Volunteer Experience

"Get involved with local charitable as well as professional organizations and see how you can get involved in special events."

— Nancy Trent, Founder of PR firm
Trent & Company, Inc.

Volunteering in your community can be a great way to get your name out there, build a sterling reputation, and gain some valuable experience along the way. Some suggestions for places to volunteer your salon-related services are:

- local theater groups

- fashion shows

- key public events

- government events

- local schools, and

- any other opportunity where you can get your name recognized in exchange for your services

As an example, you could volunteer to do hair or makeup for people who will be receiving awards or giving speeches. You can get your name mentioned in the program, which builds community recognition for you. Another valuable (though less glamorous) way to gain additional experience, especially when trying out new techniques, is to practice your haircutting and other skills free of charge on friends and family.

Johnathan Breitung, co-owner of the Johnathan Breitung Salon & Luxury Spa in Chicago, offers an example of a volunteer event his salon was involved in:

> "We were lucky enough to be able to participate in giving makeovers to a number of women from a battered women's shelter, which was very touching. These special women were so grateful and it made us feel fabulous."

You can find help in locating your community's non-profit groups through the Internet. GuideStar is a searchable database of more than 1.8 million IRS-recognized non-profit organizations in the United States. Visit **www2.guidestar.org** then click on "Advanced Search" to search by your city or state. You'll need to sign up to access the information. CharityVillage has a similar database of Canadian non-profit organizations at **www.charityvillage.com** (after you click on "Enter", click on "Links to NPO's" and choose "Volunteer Centres").

3.3   Be Your Own "Mystery Shopper"

You have probably heard of mystery shopping, where companies hire people to go into their various retail outlets and pose as shoppers. This is an excellent way for management to get feedback about what their retailers are doing wrong — and right. In order to take a first-hand look at how other people are running their own [retail business], you can become your own mystery shopper using these tips. You will find this information particularly helpful as you put together your business plan (see section 4.4) and marketing plans (section 7.1).

To begin, take a look in your local Yellow Pages under categories such as hair salons, beauty salons, and barber shops. Take time to visit several salons that interest you.

As you go to a number of stores and record your observations, a couple of things will begin to happen. First, you will begin to know what salons are in your area and which, if any, will be competition for you. Second, you will get a chance to see stores in action. There is no substitute for seeing first hand how hair salons really run and operate.

Take a small notebook and pen so you can discreetly take notes. After you have been to each salon, use a Salon Impressions Form like the one on the pages that follow to record your observations.

TIP: As you assess local salons, remember that what you see there should simply serve as ideas. There are no hard and fast rules about what your own store must carry.

In addition to observing anonymously, getting a hair salon owner's permission to let you observe them in action is also a wonderful way to learn. If you have a friend or a business contact that will let you spend a day seeing how they operate their business, it will be an excellent learning experience. In the next section you'll find advice on how to contact salon owners.

Salon Impressions Form

The Storefront

1. Is the salon easy to spot from the street?   ❏ Y ❏ N

2. Is it easy to park?   ❏ Y ❏ N

3. Is there plenty of free parking or street parking?   ❏ Y ❏ N

4. Is it an area with foot traffic?   ❏ Y ❏ N

5. How is the area?

6. What kinds of people do you see on the street?

Entering the Salon

1. What do you notice about the atmosphere?

2. What do you like about the way the salon looks?

3. What do you notice about the physical layout of the salon?

4. Does the salon seem inviting or uninviting? Why?

5. Is the salon clean?   ❑ Y ❑ N
6. How is the lighting?

7. How are the restrooms?

The Staff

1. Are you greeted?   ❑ Y ❑ N
2. Does the staff seem:

Approachable?	❑ Y ❑ N	Grumpy?	❑ Y ❑ N
Pleasant?	❑ Y ❑ N	Pushy?	❑ Y ❑ N
Bored?	❑ Y ❑ N		

3. When you ask a question, how do they respond?

4. Are they knowledgeable?   ❑ Y ❑ N

5. Are you able to get your questions answered to your satisfaction? ❏ Y ❏ N

6. Does the staff make you feel comfortable about asking a question? ❏ Y ❏ N

If You Get Any Services Done There

1. Do you like the service you receive? ❏ Y ❏ N

2. Do you like the way you look when you leave the salon? ❏ Y ❏ N

3. Does the staff instruct you on caring for nails, hair, etc., at home? ❏ Y ❏ N

4. Are they knowledgable? ❏ Y ❏ N

5. Do they try to push salon product purchases too much? ❏ Y ❏ N

6. Does the staff make you feel comfortable and pampered? ❏ Y ❏ N

7. Do you feel the service was well priced? ❏ Y ❏ N

Using the Retail Area of the Salon

1. Can you browse easily? ❏ Y ❏ N

2. Are you comfortable? ❏ Y ❏ N

3. How is the merchandise arranged?

4. What is the quality of the merchandise?

5. What are the floor displays?

6. Is the merchandise priced according to quality? ❏ Y ❏ N

Buying

1. Is the cash area organized?   ❑ Y   ❑ N
2. Is it easy to get served?   ❑ Y   ❑ N
3. Does the staff member speak pleasantly to you?   ❑ Y   ❑ N
4. Did you buy anything?   ❑ Y   ❑ N

   Why or why not?

Leaving

1. What are your impressions when you leave?

2. Does a staff member notice you are leaving?   ❑ Y   ❑ N
3. Does anyone thank you?   ❑ Y   ❑ N
4. Does anyone say goodbye to you?   ❑ Y   ❑ N
5. Do you feel positive about your experience?   ❑ Y   ❑ N

Overall Impressions of the Store

1. What did you like most about the salon?

2. What did you like the least?

3. What did you notice about the salon's logo, bags or other printed material?

4. Will you go back to the salon in the future?   ❑ Y   ❑ N
5. Will you recommend this salon to anyone?   ❑ Y   ❑ N

3.4 Learn From Other Business Owners

3.4.1 Talk to Hair Salon Owners

"My admiration of other successful business owners was a great source of inspiration. Over the years I have learned a lot by watching others."

— Dalgiza Barros, Owner,
Creative Energy Hair Studio

After speaking with dozens of salon owners, we recommend approaching salon owners via e-mail, through an organization of business owners, or by driving to a non-competing salon and asking their advice.

The hair salon owners we spoke with were eager to offer advice and point out many additional resources. A good resource for finding other salon owners is your local telephone directory, or, for an online directory with many salons and barber shops in the U.S., go to **www.hairdressersus.com**.

If you can get a salon owner to talk to you, you can learn an amazing amount of insider information from someone who could be doing just what you want to do. Keep in mind, however, that while some may be quite willing to talk, others may be too busy. But if you ask nicely for information many people are very glad to share it.

TIP: You will probably have a hard time if you approach a salon owner who could be considered your direct competition. There is a difference between sharing knowledge and giving away trade secrets. Make sure that the experts you try to contact are not your direct competition.

So, how do you contact salon owners? Try the following steps:

- Identify first what it is you are trying to accomplish
- Make a list of questions you want to ask
- Identify who you think you should talk to
- Make a list of contacts
- Take the steps to make contact (email, telephone, in person)

For example, let's assume you went to a great salon in a neighboring town. First (after you have made your list of questions), find out the phone number and the owner's name. Then call and ask to speak to the owner. Here is a sample phone script:

> "Hi, I am Stella Stylist. I was in your salon while I was on vacation and I was really impressed by it. Could you tell me who the owner is? *(After you are connected to the owner, Ima Infogiver, you proceed.)*

> "Hi, Ima Infogiver? My name is Stella Stylist and I am considering opening a salon in another part of the state. I was on vacation and had a chance to stop in your salon, and I loved it. *(Now, ask permission to ask — an old sales trick.)* I was wondering if you would be willing to let me ask you a couple questions about how you do things. I could use some expert advice."

> **TIP:** It never hurts to tell experts you think they are experts. Most people like being recognized for their accomplishments.

Make an appointment to call back the salon owner at their convenience. Then take some time and decide on a couple of questions you really want answers to. Ask only these questions. Also, offer to correspond with your contact using email if the expert prefers this. Always thank the expert for their time and make sure they know you appreciate the information. If you build this relationship slowly you can ask for more help and advice, and perhaps you can even find a mentor.

Remember to:

- Ask permission to ask questions

- Be sensitive to the expert's time

- Decide ahead of time what you will ask

- Don't overwhelm your expert with too many questions

- Build the relationship slowly and ask for more time at a later date

As you do research on the Internet, you will undoubtedly begin to see salon websites that interest you. All of these sites have contact information you can use to directly ask for help and advice.

Remember to adhere to the same advice in email that you would use on the phone. Be courteous, brief, and grateful. Don't worry if you have to send out a number of letters before you have a response; salon owners are busy people. If you are polite and persistent, some salon owners will be willing to talk to you.

Salon Consultants

"Take some business classes, or work with a consultant to put in systems to ensure that your business runs smoothly. While setting up a training model, employee manual, treatment protocols, office procedures, etc. take time in the beginning, not being prepared could cost you your business. Know what you are good at, and what you need to delegate to ensure that all areas of your business work properly. This is the biggest mistake that I have seen in my consulting of businesses – no working systems."

— Susie Galvez, beauty industry expert and author

As Susie Galvez points out in the quote above, one road to early success is to ensure that you're knowledgeable in all the working business systems in your salon. If you're unfamiliar with setting these up, you may want to consider hiring a salon consultant.

The following advice on hiring a salon consultant has been adapted from the *FabJob Guide to Become a Spa Owner*:

Salon consultants will advise you on whether your unique concept is viable (something this guide obviously cannot do), if it fits with the demographics in your area, and if the space you've chosen and designed is going to make you money, or is set up in a way to fritter cash away. If experienced, the consultant will have other salons to compare your project to and can help you come up with realistic numbers of what you can make, and what it might cost you. A salon consultant will cost you anywhere from $500 to $5,000 a day, depending on the project and the consultant's experience.

When you are interviewing consultants (and you should interview several before you choose one), remember that you can afford to be picky. You have to ask yourself, "if this person knows so much about running a hair salon, why aren't they doing that now?" Or if you are up for it, ask the consultant for their answer. A good consultant will have one ready.

Go into any consulting agreement with a reasonable amount of skepticism and let them prove why using their services will be worth their fee. Remember that you can also look for mentors, such as those offered at Vocation Vacations (see below), as opposed to hiring a consultant. Another option is to contact the Service Corps of Retired Executives (SCORE), which has chapters throughout the U.S. SCORE members are trained to serve as counselors, advisors, and mentors to aspiring entrepreneurs and new business owners.

To find a salon consultant, try an Internet search using "salon consultants" and the name of your city or state (include the quotation marks in your search). You can also look in the Yellow Pages under "Consulting". For a wider search, use the online version at **www.yellowpages.com** (or **www.yellowpages.ca** in Canada).

Vocation Vacations

Vocation Vacations are in-depth mentorships designed to help give you a taste of what it's really like to be a stylist or salon owner. Your mentor will give you lots of practical advice for getting started, and you'll have the chance to learn more about a high end salon in action.

Vocation Vacations currently offers a two day mentorship (subject to availability) at Billy Lowe salon in Los Angeles. At present, the cost is $1,249 per person (not including air fare or accommodations). This includes two full days with Billy Lowe, a Myers-Briggs Type Indicator test, an opportunity to participate in one hour of pre- and post-VocationVacations career coaching, a special journal for documenting your journey of turning your dream job into a reality, and lunches with Billy. Visit **http://vocationvacations.com/DreamJobHolidays/billy-lowe.php** to learn more.

3.4.2   Join an Association

To learn more about the hair salon industry, consider joining a cosmetology association. These organizations are usually non-profit groups that charge a membership fee in exchange for various member benefits. These benefits might include conferences where you can meet other salon owners, suppliers and manufacturers' representatives, and attend workshops to learn more about the business.

Salon Industry Associations

The National Cosmetology Association

Website: **www.ncacares.org**

The National Cosmetology Association (NCA), whose membership includes hair stylists, manicurists, estheticians, and other professionals associated with the industry. Membership includes free admission to several major annual trade shows, and they offer other savings programs such as discounts on insurance, supplies, and educational programs. They also promote salons to the public and publish a free magazine for members called American Salon. Membership fees are $115 for professionals and $75 for students.

Professional Beauty Association

Website: **www.probeauty.org**

The Professional Beauty Association (PBA) is another organization for salon industry professionals. Benefits include advocacy, education, networking, and business tools (such as a front desk manual or a bridal services contract form you can use), and promotion discounts and tools for industry professionals from salon owners to product manufacturers. Dues are based on annual sales, and begin at $175 for sales under $500,000 annually to $250 for sales between $500,000 and $1 million annually on up to $7,500 for sales of $100 million or more.

Other Associations

Intercoiffure

Website: **www.intercoiffure.us**

Intercoiffure is an international organization for beauty industry professionals. It is the most prestigious beauty organization in the world, and thus only the top salons in a given area are selected for membership. Applicants must be both a salon owner and a licensed cosmetologist. To join, go to their website to view the list of requirements (which includes sponsorship by two Intercoiffure "A" members, photos of recent work, promotional pieces, a price list and services offered, photos of your salon, and more).

Salon and Spa Association

Website: **www.salonspaassociation.com**

The Salon and Spa Association offers discount comprehensive insurance benefits, business tools, savings on products, articles and other educational resources, free management software, and more.

American Association for Esthetics

Website: **www.americasbeautyshow.com**

American Association for Esthetics is a good choice for skin care specialists and practitioners seeking networking and educational opportunities. They sponsor the Americas Beauty Show, and membership provides free admission to this and other major skin, face and body shows per year. They publish a magazine for members called Skin, Inc. The annual membership fee is $115 for practicing aestheticians and $35 for students.

If you are planning to open a salon and spa, some additional organizations you may wish to join are:

- *The Spa Association*
  (Provides education and other resources for spas, including medi-spas)
  www.thespaassociation.com

- *The Day Spa Association*
  (Provides educational and networking opportunities)
  www.dayspaassociation.com

- *The International Spa Association*
  (Offers tools for marketing and promotion, international industry conferences, networking opportunities, and an industry publication, Pulse)
  www.experienceispa.com

Once you're an established salon owner, it's a good idea to join a national or state association because membership gives customers confidence to see the Association's logo displayed in your place of business. Another benefit is the networking that takes place.

3.4.3   Business Organizations

You can also join a number of excellent organizations designed for business owners to learn and network in an organized setting. One excellent resource is your local Chamber of Commerce. Chambers usually have an annual fee and are set up to aid the local businessperson with a variety of business-related issues. Members attend local meetings and can also take part in events designed to help them be more successful.

To find out how to contact your local chamber, visit the national websites. For the U.S. Chamber of Commerce visit **www.uschamber.com/chambers/directory/default.htm**. For the Canadian Chamber of Commerce Directory visit **www.chamber.ca/index.php/en/links/C57**.

3.4.4   Online Communities

Another good source of acquiring information from experts is through online message boards like the online forum at **www.behindthechair.com** (see below). Here you can meet with salon owners and ask questions of your own or read through the posts. You can also get insight into customers and what they are looking for. Yahoo! Groups also offers a Hair Stylists discussion group for all hair professionals, including salon owners.

- *Yahoo! Groups: Hairstylists (requires Yahoo! membership)*
  http://health.groups.yahoo.com/group/HairStylists

- Behindthechair.com is a very trusted online resource for hair salon owners. This site has a message board/online forum for members, current industry news and other information, and has many informative articles geared toward salon owners and other industry professionals (**www.behindthechair.com**).

- Salon Today is a website for beauty professionals created by the publishers of *Salon Today Magazine* (an excellent publication specifically geared toward salon owners). The site has a message board for members to exchange information and ideas. Just go to either website and click on the message board tab: **www. salontoday.com** (also available at **www.modernsalon.com**).

- Your Beauty Network (**www.ybn.com**) is a fee-based website for salon professionals and aspiring professionals. It has several online business management tools (including an online calculator to help you decide what prices you should charge), as well as informative articles, a members forum, and more. Membership fees apply; for a salon owner, the fees are $299.85/quarter or $1000 per year.

- Beauty 101 is an online forum on About.com where people can exchange ideas, tips and opinions on all aspects of beauty treatments. Although it is not limited to beauty professionals, there is some good information here for new and aspiring salon owners. Visit it at **http://forums.about.com/n/pfx/forum.aspx?nav= messages&webtag=ab-beauty**.

3.5 Educational Programs

NOTE: Information about courses and other educational programs is provided for the convenience of readers and does not represent an endorsement. Only you can decide which educational program, if any, is right for you.

A good working knowledge of hair care and styling will help you to hire competent employees and keep your salon abreast of the latest beauty treatments, techniques and products. Keep in mind that all hair stylists and technicians working in a salon must be properly trained and licensed by the state (for more information, see section 4.6.2, "Business Licenses"). Therefore, it can be helpful if a salon owner has at least some formal knowledge of hair cutting, styling, color, etc.

3.5.1 Beauty Industry (Cosmetology) Courses

The decision of whether or not to go to beauty or barber school largely depends on your background and your dreams. If you dream of being a stylist and working in your own salon, you can't get there without beauty school training and licensing. Proper training will also give you the ability to find and hire excellent stylists and other beauty professionals for your salon (or be able to select talented independent contractors). The skills of the people you hire will have a great impact on your salon's reputation.

Even for those who do not wish to "get behind the chair", having an in-depth understanding of the industry can be a big plus in the field. As mentioned above, many successful salon owners are not cosmetologists. However, they do have solid business skills and hire great beauty professionals, managing them and their retail businesses well.

A standard full-time barber or cosmetology program takes about nine months to complete. The requirements for becoming a licensed barber or stylist vary from state to state, and in many states, a high school diploma or GED is required to obtain a cosmetology license in addition to completion of a state licensed beauty or barber school program. Completing a cosmetology or barber school program will allow you to perform a broad range of beauty services, from hair cutting to coloring and perming, in addition to makeup and nails.

Finding Courses

If you're considering taking a beauty school or barber school course, the resources in this section will help you find a suitable program. Factors you'll want to keep in mind are location, cost, the types of licenses you will qualify for, the quality of the program, and how much time it takes to complete the program. Also, try to find a program accredited by the National Accrediting Commission of Cosmetology Arts & Sciences (**www.naccas.org**). You can find a searchable directory of NACCAS-certified schools and programs across the country at **www.naccas. org/Pages/ShowSchools.aspx**.

A good place to start your search is **www.beautyschool.com**. They have a clickable map that lets you find detailed beauty school listings for each state. The Careers in Beauty website , sponsored by the American Association of Cosmetology Schools, at **www.beautyschools.org/associations/7485/careersinbeauty.cfm?page=3**, has a directory of beauty schools searchable by city and state. (To find more results, in the drop-down menu leave "Select a City…" and choose your state). The Careers in Beauty Schools Directory website, **www.beautyschoolsdirectory.com**, lists schools in the U.S. and in Canada.

In addition to vocational schools, many salon product manufacturers have high quality educational institutes that teach advanced cutting and coloring and other techniques. Many salon owners we spoke with began in such programs (e.g., Aveda, Sebastian, Vidal Sassoon). These can be expensive programs but many people we spoke with who have attended them feel they are worth the time and cost of attending. Also, once you are a salon owner, you and your employees might want to take part in continuing education classes offered by such schools.

Go to the manufacturer's site for more information on seminars, locations and costs. Here are a few of the best known schools to help you get started:

- *Aveda*
  (Expect to pay about $16,000 in tuition; financial assistance is available)
  www.avedainstitutes.com

- *Paul Mitchell The School*
  (Tuition is in the $10,000 to $15,000 range; financial assistance is available)
  www.paulmitchelltheschool.com/pmsp/locations/index.cfm

- *Redken The Salon Professional Academy*
  (Approximately $8,000-$15,000 depending on your location for the cosmetology course; financial assistance is available)
  www.thesalonprofessionalacademy.com

- *Wella Schools*
  (Located in Columbia, South Carolina; contact school for more information.)
  www.wellaschools.com

Many community colleges offer courses in cosmetology as well. You can find listings of colleges in your area at **www.petersons.com** or, in Canada, **www.schoolfinder.com**. Many of the courses offered at local colleges are available on a part-time basis, too. Search on keywords such as "hair styling", "hair stylist", "cosmetology", and "beauty".

In addition to the school resources listed above, some high schools offer cosmetology courses as part of their curriculum, as do many community colleges. Both of these options are reasonably priced. Some offer inexpensive continuing adult courses for adults that may include cosmetology courses. For more information, contact your local public school district.

Several top hair stylists and salon owners recommended that those who want to serve the most discerning, upscale clients should study hair design in Europe, if at all possible. Michael Peter Hayes, owner of the Michael Peter Hayes Art Salon studied with the top schools, designers and stylists in Europe. This alone can set you apart from your competition because, as he discovered, not many hairdressers in the U.S. have studied abroad. "This was my initial reason to go," Hayes says, "and it has paid for itself over and over with an upscale clientele that is more educated and well traveled and with a lot more exposure to current trends and designs."

Hayes recommends Sassoon in London, Toni and Guy in London or Milan, and the Jacques Dessange academies in Paris. Revlon corporation also offers salon training in Spain (**www.revlonprofessional.com/english/beautyschools.html**). Offering these more exclusive hair services can result in a higher income in a shorter time, but keep in mind that studying abroad will cost you considerably more than studying in North America.

As mentioned above, we cannot say whether any of the programs listed in this guide will be right for you. You are the only one who can make that decision. Program costs and other details can change, so make sure you confirm information about any program before registering.

3.5.2 Business Courses

"I personally believe that in any business you should have a strong understanding of the industry. Business education courses would be a good idea no

matter what business you are in. Courses in customer service are particularly valuable."

> — Justin Hickox, owner,
> Hickox Studio

Earning a degree, diploma, or certificate in business can be helpful in running your own business. You can find more information and links to colleges and universities at Peterson's Planner at **www.petersons.com**, or in Canada, you can visit the Schoolfinder website at **www.schoolfinder. com**.

A formal business education is not necessary to run a salon. There are many successful business owners who are self-taught and have never studied business. Others have taken a course here and there but do not possess a degree. However, the skills you learn in business classes can come in handy.

Heaven Padgett, owner of the Hairem Salon in Houston, Texas notes that she did get a degree in business, which helped her a little, because "to be a good business owner you MUST have some business sense, be a natural leader and be willing to keep track of details and be disciplined." The danger of not having business knowledge, she says, is that "many businesses fail because they did not properly keep records or pay taxes properly, which gives a false sense of profit."

However, while business courses can be helpful in this regard, she also cautions that "most business courses are not directed towards the challenges of salon ownership, and being a leader to artists," which she likens to "herding cats."

Depending on which of your skills you would like to develop, consider taking courses on topics such as:

- Advertising

- Basic Accounting

- Business Communications

- Business Management

- Entrepreneurship

- Merchandising

- Retailing

Your local college or university may offer these and other business courses. Through the continuing education department you may be able to take a single course on a Saturday or over several evenings. If you can't find a listing for the continuing education department in your local phone book, call the college's main switchboard and ask for the continuing education department. They will be able to tell you about upcoming courses.

Also, many cities have small business development centers (affiliated with the Small Business Administration) that offer classes for aspiring business owners, either for free or a small fee.

If you are not interested in attending courses at a school, or you don't have the time, another option that can easily fit into your schedule is distance learning. Traditionally these were called correspondence courses and the lessons were mailed back and forth between student and instructor. Today, with the help of the Internet, there are many on-line courses available. Again, check your local community college, university, or business school to see if they offer online courses.

Your local Chamber of Commerce may also offer training courses and seminars for new business owners. Many also offer consultations with retired executives and business owners who are well-qualified to offer advice. Visit **www.chamberfind.com** to find a Chamber near you.

3.6 Resources for Self-Study

3.6.1 Books

Amazon.com lists thousands of books on the subject of small business ownership or small business management, but of course you do not have the time to read them all! So here is a selection of excellent books you may want to start with. Look for them at your local library, browse through them at a local bookstore, or order them online.

The hair salon owners we asked to recommend books, interestingly enough, did not generally mention books on hair design or color, etc.

They emphasize beauty schools and specific hair designers and simply getting experience for perfecting technique. The titles listed below were all recommended by successful salon owners, and a couple of them were recommended by more than one source.

- *The E-Myth Revisited,*
  by Michael Gerber
  (A great book on entrepreneurship that is very relevant to salon owners)

- *Secret Service: Hidden Systems That Deliver*
  Unforgettable Customer Service,
  by John R. DiJulius III
  (A great book on customer service)

- *First, Break All the Rules: What the World's*
  Greatest Managers Do Differently,
  by Marcus Buckingham and Curt Coffman
  (A great book on entrepreneurship that is very relevant to salon owners)

- *The Very Best of Robert Service,*
  by Robert Service

3.6.2   Trade Shows

"I always recommend private classes for fine-tuning cutting and color skills. But for inspiration attend trade shows. They will get your staff jazzed about their trade and let them do it as a group, which is very important!"

> — Ronnie Pryor, owner,
> Source Salon

"Try to attend shows that will provide you with the skills that set you aside from the competition. You always want to be a leader in your industry and staying on top of education is very important."

> — Dalgiza Barros, owner,
> Creative Energy Hair Studio

The largest and most prestigious in the United States is the International Beauty Show (**www.ibsnewyork.com**) held annually in March at the Jacob Javits Convention Center in New York City. There is also the International Beauty Show Las Vegas, **www.ibslasvegas.com**, which is held annually at the Las Vegas Convention Center in April. Both shows offer the opportunity to discover new and exciting products, to attend seminars and educational programs run by some of the top industry professionals, and network with other salon owners as well as product suppliers and manufacturers.

Other major trade shows include:

- *America's Beauty Show*
  Sponsored by the American Esthetics Association, held in early spring in Chicago
  www.americasbeautyshow.com

- *International Salon and Spa Expo*
  Held in Long Beach, California, in February
  www.probeauty.org/isse

- *Beauty Expo USA*
  Las Vegas, in January
  www.beautyexpousa.com

In Canada, major trade shows include the eight trade shows sponsored by the Allied Beauty Association held from March to October in Montreal, Toronto, Winnipeg, Vancouver, Edmonton, Regina, Calgary, and Moncton (**www.abacanada.com**) and the ABA trade show held in Toronto in February and sponsored by Cosmoprof (**www.cosmoprofbeauty. com/canada/shows.aspx**).

3.6.3   Trade Magazines

There are several excellent trade magazines to help you keep up with the latest news and trends in the salon industry. Here are some recommended publications:

The monthly *American Salon*, **www.americansalonmag.com**, published by the National Cosmetology Association, is considered one of the most comprehensive and best magazines for news and information about the salon industry. They also offer a sister publication for spa professionals called *American Spa* (**www.americanspamag.com**).

Another great publication geared toward industry professionals and geared toward hair, nail and other beauty professionals is *Modern Salon*, **www.modernsalon.com**. An excellent glossy monthly magazine geared specifically for salon owners and how to help them grow their businesses is *Salon Today* (**www.salontoday.com**). In Canada, the monthly *Salon Magazine* is the leading source for salon and beauty industry news and trends. Visit their website at **www.salon52.ca**.

For salon/spa owners, in addition to *American Spa Magazine* mentioned above, other excellent publications include *DAYSPA Magazine*, which is a monthly magazine geared specifically toward owners of day spas (**www.dayspamagazine.com**). Other related publications include *Massage Magazine* (**www.massagemag.com**) which is geared toward massage therapists, and *Spa Finder Magazine* (which, although published for consumers, contains detailed profiles of spas and other good information). Visit them at **www.spafinder.com**.

4. Starting Your Hair Salon

Now that we've looked at ways to develop your business skills, it's time to look at how to go about actually starting your own salon. This chapter of the guide will walk you step-by-step through the process.

Use the checklist below as a guideline to help you complete the steps necessary to get your business going. In fact, you may want to print the checklist and keep it nearby as you go through the rest of this guide so you can add items as you learn more about them.

Getting Started Basics Checklist

- ❏ Choose your niche.
- ❏ Prepare your business plan.
- ❏ Obtain a business license.

❏ Locate several potential locations and weigh pros and cons of each.

❏ Secure financing.

❏ Lease or purchase store space.

❏ Obtain any necessary permits or certificates.

❏ Purchase salon fixtures.

❏ Purchase software your salon will use for inventory.

❏ Decide what merchandise you will offer for sale, locate suppliers and purchase inventory.

❏ Start advertising your grand opening.

❏ Decide if you need help. Interview and hire additional employees, if necessary.

❏ If you are planning to hire employees, obtain an Employee Identification Number (contact details later in this guide).

❏ Complete your salon operations manual and finalize any salon policies.

❏ Make a plan for your grand opening.

❏ Set up systems for record keeping.

❏ Set up window displays.

❏ Open your business.

4.1 Choosing Your Niche

The first thing to consider for your salon is what types of products and services you will offer. This is your "niche" or specialty. Chapter 2 provides detailed information about the types of salon businesses and various services and products you can choose from.

Initially, as you consider what niche to fill with your own salon, remember that the simplest approach is to focus on something you are familiar with. Look at areas of your life and experience to help you decide. Stick with what is familiar at first, but don't make your salon's niche too narrow in your first year. Starting with a wider range of products and services will help you adapt to the needs of your clientele. Over time you will likely find some products and services are more profitable for you, and you can change your offerings as you learn more about what your customers want.

To help you choose your niche you'll need to do some market research to give you an idea of trends in the industry you are entering. You'll need to determine:

- Is there a need in your community for the services you plan to sell?

- Can you effectively compete?

The best place to start is by studying other successful salons similar to the one you are planning to open. Don't be afraid to ask other retail salon owners for their advice. You may hear that sales of certain types of services are booming, while some services may be losing popularity.

Also find out if any salons similar to yours have opened or closed in the area recently. If you're new to the area, you may have to speak to other business owners and locals to get this information. While your marketing and customer service might be better than the salons that closed, the fact that a similar salon has been unsuccessful might indicate that a particular type of retail outlet doesn't do well in your area. If at all possible, try to track down the previous salon owner through the local phone book and ask a few questions.

You'll find some additional resources for doing market research in section 4.4 on business planning to help you focus in on your market.

4.2 Options for Starting a Hair Salon

Once you have decided on your niche, you'll need to decide whether to buy an existing salon, buy a franchise, or open a new salon. Deciding which route is right for you is an important decision.

An established salon will cost more than starting from scratch, but it also comes with customers, inventory, and reputation, which means it's likely to continue with its pre-established success. A new salon typically costs less to start up, and you can tailor it specifically to your own vision. Unlike buying an established salon, though, you will need to spend more on advertising, gaining clientele, and making a reputation for your business — and new businesses have a higher risk of failure. Franchises might be another option to consider. We'll explain more about how these work in section 4.2.2.

4.2.1   Buying an Established Salon

One way to start is to buy an existing business and make it your own. Buying an existing salon can show you a profit on the very first day you're open. You'll still need a business plan, financing, a lawyer and an accountant, but many of the other decisions – like what to call it and where to locate it — will already be made. In addition, you will acquire all or most of the equipment, furniture, supplies, and inventory you will need to get started. You also get clientele and the established business name.

However, you should also look very carefully at whatever else you might be acquiring. The business may have outstanding debts and you may have to assume any liabilities that come with the salon, such as bills it owes to its suppliers, or repairs or maintenance expenditures that haven't been paid.

If this option for starting your business appeals to you, begin by looking for salons for sale in your area. Do not be afraid to approach local salon owners and inquire if they are interested in selling their business, or if they know any salon owners considering retirement. And, don't forget to look in your local newspaper, local business publications, and contact the Chamber of Commerce for information on shops that may possibly be for sale.

What to Look for Before You Buy

Purchasing an existing business can be a good way to get into the retail trade immediately, but there are a few cautions. You could be purchasing a failed business with a poor financial history, bad reputation, or even some hidden liabilities as mentioned earlier. You need to perform a due diligence investigation, meaning you need to look at the operations of the business, including revenues, cash flow, assets and liabilities, licensing, and so on, before purchasing.

To protect yourself, before making a deal for any business hire an accountant to go over the company's books. This will help you to determine if the seller is representing the business accurately and honestly. Then, before signing an Agreement of Purchase and Sale, you should enlist the services of a lawyer to review the written agreement.

Following are a few things to look for as you start your search for an existing business to buy.

Why the Business is For Sale

Here are a few of the most common reasons why business owners offer their businesses for sale:

- The owner is retiring or has health problems

- The owner is moving on to another salon or another business altogether

- The business has failed and the owner wants to get out as quickly as possible

- The owner is afraid of increasing competition

- One key element of their business strategy is faulty, such as the type of inventory offered

- The business is part of a chain and is not doing as well as other salons owned by the same company

- A partnership has fallen apart and the partners are liquidating all or a part of the company's assets

Before purchasing an existing retail business answer the following important questions (with assistance from the seller whenever possible).

- Why is the vendor selling the business?

- What is the sales history of the salon?

- What is the average cost to maintain the salon?

- What assets or liabilities will come with the purchase?

- Are there any tax, legal or property issues you will have to contend with?

The previous owner may help you with many of these issues or you may have to do your own research, perhaps by consulting local government, realtors or other merchants. Whatever the situation, you should never buy an existing business without knowing all of the details.

You should have complete access to the previous owner's salon records, including financial statements. With these you will have information about the customer base and noticeable patterns in the salon's business practices. Unwillingness by the previous owner to provide financial statements for your complete inspection might be a tip-off that something isn't right with the business.

Potential buyers often work in the salon for a short time before purchasing it. Owners are often willing to train the buyer. If the business owner you are thinking about buying from is unwilling to do this, you should find out why.

Hidden Costs

When you purchase an established business it seems like you're purchasing a turnkey operation with license, location, traffic and inventory all in place and you just have to open the doors. However, there may be hidden expenses that you will have to pay for, such as back taxes, needed repairs or building code violations, so be sure to watch for these. You don't want an angry supplier showing up at your door demanding money for inventory purchased by the previous owner but never paid for. (You've already purchased the inventory from the owner and now you'll have to pay for it a second time.)

In addition to paying for the business, and any miscellaneous expenses, you will also need money to pay for equipment and supplies, and additional inventory. You may also want to start a marketing campaign in order to make people aware of the fact that you're the new owner and let the community know that you're open for business. This is particularly important if you've bought a business that might have been on the decline for whatever reasons.

Finally, if you plan to remodel a salon after buying it, perhaps to give it a fresh new image, then that could easily become another significant expense depending on the size of the job and the contractor you hire. Keep all these additional potential costs in mind as you consider buying the existing business.

Creating a Spec Sheet

A spec sheet is a summary of the business and includes the book value (total assets minus total liabilities and goodwill), market value (the book value figure adjusted to reflect the current market value of assets), and the liquidation value (how much the owner could raise if the business was liquidated). Earnings potential should also be considered.

If the value you arrive at is significantly different from what the owner is asking for the business, ask the seller how he or she arrived at the price. You can then make your offer based on your estimate of worth and the owner's asking price. You don't need to accept that the business is actually worth what the owner thinks it is.

The real worth of a business is in its continuing profitability, so examine the financial records closely (especially the profit and loss statements and cash flow statements) to get a good idea of what your revenue would be, as well as your expenses and net income. Try to buy a business for its annual profit. Don't be distracted by the listed price.

One helpful resource is the Due Diligence Checklist at FindLaw.com. The full website address is **http://smallbusiness.findlaw.com/starting-business** (click on "More Topics", then on "Buying an Existing Business" then on "Due Diligence Checklist" under Tools & Resources). This checklist shows you everything that you should check out about any business you're thinking of purchasing in areas like the business's organization and good standing, financial statements, physical assets, real estate, and much more. Be sure to consult this checklist or one like it as you perform your due diligence investigation.

The Canada Business Services for Entrepreneurs website has an excellent page at **www.canadabusiness.ca/eng/125/140** that details what you need to consider when purchasing an existing business. Canada Business also provides links to articles with helpful information on how to determine asset and earnings value and how to valuate a business.

Purchase Price

Purchase prices are determined by a number of factors. These include region and neighborhood location, profit and local economy, potential growth, and the owner's own sense of what the company is worth based on reputation or goodwill. BusinessesforSale.com, Business Nation, BizQuest and others offer listings of many types of businesses that, for whatever reason, are being offered for sale. These sites list each business's asking price, and usually state its turnover and profit.

Expect to pay anywhere from $20,000-$50,000 to upwards of $250,000-$350,000 for an existing hair salon or hair salon and spa. This usually will include all contents of the shop and often means taking over an existing lease or rental agreement for the location. Starting your own salon requires a lot of energy and devotion — whether you build from scratch or buy an existing salon. You should plan on waiting two to five years to earn back your purchase price.

Recent listings of hair salon businesses for sale on these websites included:

- A full service hair salon in Ashland, Massachusetts, in business for 23 years asking $75,000. The price included $40,000 in furnishings and equipment and $4,000 in stock and inventory. The rent was $1,000 per month with a five year lease. The salon featured 5 hair stations, 1 nail station and a tanning room. Annual gross sales listed were $175,000, with net annual profit of $51,000. The seller listed her age as a reason for wanting to sell but was willing to stay on as a stylist. The salon had three, long-term employees.

- A hair, skin and nail salon in Los Angeles near Sony Pictures Studio with a large salon retail business in business for 20+ years. The sale price of $80,000 included twelve stations and private rooms for nail and skin care, fixtures, and inventory. Gross annual sales were $85,000, with annual net profits of $40,000.

- A 3,200 square foot contemporary full-service salon and spa in a leased location in Largo, Florida. The business included 6 hair stations, 10 nail stations, and facilities for skin care, massage and tanning. The asking price of $350,000 for this 7-year old business included the salon fixtures and equipment.

- *BusinessesforSale.com*
  (Includes business for sale in the U.S., Canada, U.K. and other countries)
  www.businessesforsale.com

- *Business Nation*
  www.businessnation.com/Businesses_for_Sale/

- *BizQuest*
  www.bizquest.com/buy

- *BizBen (California only)*
  www.bizben.com

Try entering the keywords salon, spa, day spa, hair and beauty salons, hair salons, and barber shops into each website's search engine or search by industry.

TIP: Beware of websites that require a fee or ask for personal information to view their listings. Real Estate agents make their money on sales and not on people browsing.

Financing

Some owners will allow you to finance an existing business if you can come up with a good down payment but are unable to purchase it outright. Many of the owners of the businesses for sale at the websites above are willing to negotiate financing with potential buyers. Be sure you understand the terms of any financing you set up with the seller. See a lawyer before agreeing to anything.

If you are considering borrowing from a lending institution such as a bank then financing an existing, profitable business is much less of a risk than starting a new one. A lending institution will want to see your detailed business plan before agreeing to lend you any money. (See section 4.4 for more on how to write a business plan, and section 4.5 for more about financing your new business venture.)

Making an Offer

When you have done your research, figured out what the business is worth and decided you want to buy the business you may then decide to make an offer, possibly less than the asking price based on your own valuation of the business. Usually the owner then will make a counter-offer. Keep in mind that you may have less leeway to negotiate a better purchase price if the owner will be financing the purchase for you.

You will usually be asked to pay a non-refundable deposit. This is standard and ensures the owner that you are a serious buyer. Be sure to get a deposit receipt and get any purchase agreement in writing after you've arrived at a mutually agreeable price. Also be sure that every important detail about the purchase is mentioned in the contract. Because so much money is at risk, a lawyer should draw up or at least review the contract before either party signs.

Buying an Existing Building

A second option rather than buying an entire business is to buy an existing building in which to set up shop and then move your business into it. The obvious advantage here is that buying an existing building often is less expensive than buying an established business along with the building housing it. Another aspect to consider is that, as already mentioned, if you buy an existing business you inherit both advantages and disadvantages from the previous owner.

One advantage of buying a building is that it most likely has already passed fire and building codes, unlike a new project that will require inspections and approval by municipal authorities before you can occupy it. Be sure to check first with zoning laws to be sure you're safe to operate your business there.

There are disadvantages as well. The building may require heavy infrastructure repairs (such as utilities or plumbing) or you might have to completely remodel the interior. Repair and remodeling costs can be expensive, even into thousands of dollars, so be sure to inspect the building carefully for any structural problems before you buy it.

Do a thorough investigation of the building's interior and exterior. Check the electrical systems, cooling and ventilation systems, bathrooms, walls and ceilings. If possible, interview the previous owner and ask about any potential problems that might create extra costs for you.

You should consider hiring a building inspector to conduct a thorough, professional evaluation of the property. Hiring a professional building inspector, though an added cost to buying a building, could save you from a disastrous purchase (and thousands of dollars in repairs) so consider finding one to look at any property you're thinking about purchasing. To find building inspectors in your area, check the Yellow Pages under "Building Inspection Service."

4.2.2   Franchising

If you are eager to start your own salon, but are concerned about the many facets involved in getting everything set up, you may want to consider franchising.

Franchising is a business model which allows someone (you) to run a local business using an established regional or national company or corporation name, logo, products, services, marketing and business systems. The original company is known as the "franchisor" and the company that is granted the right to run its business the same way as the franchisor is known as the "franchisee."

You have probably bought products and services from many franchises. Burger King, Wendy's and many other fast-food outlets are franchises, as are many others. Recent figures from industry analysts estimate that franchising companies and their franchisees accounted for more than $2 trillion in annual U.S. retail sales from 900,000 franchised small businesses. So, clearly, franchises can be very successful business models to start with.

Pros and Cons of Franchising

Often, people who choose to franchise do so because they want to minimize their risk. By working with an established system, franchisees hope to avoid costly mistakes and make a profit more quickly, especially since the business probably already has name recognition, products and marketing concepts that are popular among the public.

Franchising offers some unique advantages. Buying a ready-made business means you do not have to agonize over the minute details of a business plan, you do not have to create a logo and letterhead, and the organization of your salon is already done. Plus, there is less risk with a ready-made business with a proven track record.

Franchises are good for people who want support running their businesses. The franchisee may receive assistance with everything from obtaining supplies to setting up record keeping systems. Many franchisors are continuously working to develop better systems and products and you can take advantage of those developments.

Franchisors typically provide a complete business plan for managing and operating the establishment. The plan provides step-by-step procedures for major aspects of the business and provides a complete matrix for the management decisions confronted by its franchisees.

If you choose to franchise, remember that although you own the salon you do not own any of the trademarks or business systems. A franchisee must run their business according to the terms of their agreement with the franchisor. In exchange for the security, training, and marketing power of the franchise trademark, you must be willing to give up some of your independence. If you are a person who likes to make most decisions on your own or to chart the course of your business alone, a franchise may not be right for you.

Since someone else is ultimately "in charge," you may be wondering how having a franchise is different than being an employee. In fact, there are significant differences. You have more freedom than an employee; for example, you might choose your own working hours. And you could ultimately earn a lot more money than an employee.

On the other hand, franchisees must pay thousands of dollars up front for the opportunity to work with the business. In addition, you will be required to cover your own operating costs (including the cost of staffing your salon to the levels required by the franchisor), pay a franchise fee and a percentage of total sales.

Costs

Entrepreneur Magazine describes a franchise fee as a one-time charge paid to the franchisor "for the privilege of using the business concept, attending their training program, and learning the entire business." Other start-up costs may include the products and services you will actually need to run the business, such as supplies, salon fixtures, computer equipment, advertising, etc.

The fees for operation will vary from franchise to franchise, and may rely heavily on location, but expect the franchise fee to be somewhere between $15,000-$25,000, with additional start-up costs.

There are a variety of factors involved in determining the initial investment. For example, if you are interested in operating a Fantastic Sam's franchise, the average investment will cost anywhere between $118,000-$230,100 depending on the geographic location and the size of the salon. Most franchise owners obtain financing for their business by providing approximately 35% of the total capital, and then arrange a business loan from a local bank for the balance of the total investment required. (See section 4.5 for more information on start-up funding.)

In addition to your initial investment, you can expect to pay the franchisor ongoing royalties, generally on a monthly basis. These royalties are usually calculated as a percentage of your gross monthly sales, and typically range from 2 percent to as much as 10 percent; the exact amount will depend on the company you franchise with. This is the corporation's cut for providing you with their business model and good name.

Choosing a Hair Salon Franchise

It is important to do your homework on the company you are interested in franchising with — gather all the information you need to make an informed decision. Speak with other people who have invested in the company you are investigating and have an attorney examine the franchisor's contract.

Get some professional opinions on any franchise opportunity you're interested in. Work with an attorney who understands the laws associated with franchising. Also, you may want to work with an accountant to examine your anticipated expenses, your financing needs, and your prospects for achieving your desired level of profitability before you sign any agreement.

Key points to research:

- The type of experience required in the franchised business

- Hours and personal commitment necessary to run the business

- Background of the franchisor or corporation

- Success rate of other franchisees in the same system

- Franchising fees to open the franchise

- Initial total investment required to open the franchise

- Cost of operation to continue the right to operate the business as a franchisee

- Any additional fees, products or services, such as advertising, that you must buy from the franchisor and how they are supplied

For excellent advice on franchising, visit the following websites:

- *Canadian Franchise Association*
  www.cfa.ca

- *Entrepreneur's Franchise Zone*
  www.entrepreneur.com/franchises

- *Small Business Administration: Buy a Franchise*
  www.sba.gov/smallbusinessplanner/start/buyafranchise/

There are a large number of companies offering franchise opportunities in the hair salon market. Their specialties are varied so no matter what type of retail franchise you're interested in, you'll probably find one that fits your needs and interests.

Here are a few well known franchises for you to consider. Please note that this list does not represent our endorsement of any of these businesses. They are provided for informational purposes only. Only you know which franchise, if any, is right for you.

Full Service Salons

Fantastic Sam's

This company is one of the largest and most well-recognized hair franchises, with over 1,350 locations currently, including 12 locations in Canada (and in 2007, they were ranked #39 in Entrepreneur's Franchise 500). Fantastic Sam's are full service, unisex, all-ages salons. All stylists and other technicians are employees of the franchise owner (as opposed to independent contractors). Fantastic Sam's offers comprehensive business training for its franchisees as well as no-cost advanced training for the stylists in their employ. Some 80% of Fantastic Sam's franchisees are not licensed cosmetologists.

Address:	50 Dunham Road 3rd Floor Beverly, Massachusetts 01915
Phone:	(877) 383-3831 (franchise sales)
Contact:	(877) 383-3831 or fill out online form
Website:	**www.fantasticsams.com/FantasticSams/Franchise**
Franchise Fee:	$30,000, variable royalty fee
Initial Investment:	$118,000-$230,850 (including the franchise fee)
Min. Net Worth:	$250,000 net worth, $60,000 liquid assets

Great Clips, Inc

Great Clips, Inc. was founded in 1982 and began franchising in 1983. Today, the company has over 2,700 franchise locations throughout the United States and more than 50 in Canada. Most locations are in strip malls, all locations welcome walk-ins, and they offer extended hours that include weeknight and weekend hours. Currently seeking franchises in both the United States and Canada.

Address:	7700 France Ave S #425 Minneapolis, MN 55435
Phone:	(800) 999-5959
Website:	**www.greatclipsfranchise.com**
Franchise Fee:	$20,000, royalty fee of 6% on gross sales

| Initial Investment: | $109,400 to $202,500 (including the franchise fee) |
| Min Net Worth: | $300,000 ($50,000 liquid) |

Hair Cuttery

Hair Cuttery has been in business since 1974, but only began to franchise in 2004. However, the brand is well tested, with over 800 locations in the U.S.

Address:	1577 Spring Hill Road #500 Vienna, VA 22182
Phone:	(877) 876-7400
Website:	**www.haircuttery.com**
Franchise Fee:	$15,000-$25,000; royalty fee of 4.5-5% on gross sales, renewal fee of 25% of franchise fee
Initial Investment:	$120,500-$283,000 (including the franchise fee)
Min Net Worth:	$500,000 ($250,000 liquid)

Hcx/Haircolorxperts

Haircolorxperts specializes in hair color only. Their color treatments start at $20 and target the consumer who would otherwise do their own hair color at home. They have 43 franchise locations in 13 states. Franchise opportunities are available throughout the U.S.

Address:	4850 West Prospect Road Fort Lauderdale, FL 33309
Phone:	(954) 315-4900
Website:	**www.hcx.com**
Franchise Fee:	$20,000, royalty fee of 6% on gross sales
Initial Investment:	$273,800-$421,200 (including the franchise fee)

Regis Corporation

Regis Corporation is one of the largest franchisors in the hair salon industry with more than 2,000 locations across North America. Their stable of franchise opportunities includes City Looks (U.S.), Cost Cutters (U.S.), First Choice (Canada only), Magicuts (Canada only), Pro-

Cuts (U.S.), and Supercuts (U.S. and Canada). Franchise costs and fees vary considerably depending on the franchise you choose. They also have more than 2,000 locations in Europe, including salons Jean Louis David, Saint Algue, Intermède, Coiff & Co. and City Looks.

Address:	7201 Metro Boulevard Minneapolis, MN 55439
Phone:	(888) 888-7008
Website:	**www.regisfranchise.com**
Franchise Fee:	$12,500-22,500, royalty fee of 2-7% on gross sales
Initial Investment:	$94,100-$373,000 (including the franchise fee)
Min. Net Worth:	$300,000-$500,000 ($100,000-$150,000 liquid)

Men's Hair Salons

American Male

American Male salons offer an upscale grooming experience for men in a relaxing atmosphere that includes TVs and complimentary beverages. They currently have 14 franchise locations in the U.S. in California, Illinois, Nevada, New Jersey and Pennsylvania. They are seeking to expand their franchises throughout the United States.

Address:	345 Morgantown Road Reading, PA 19611
Phone:	(866) 925-9760 (877) MEN-HAIR
Contact:	**info@americanmale.com**
Website:	**www.americanmale.com**
Franchise Fee:	$28,000, royalty fee of 5% on gross sales, renewal fee of $500
Initial Investment:	$170,000-$312,000 (including the franchise fee)

Knockouts

These salons feature attractive female stylists in skimpy outfits. All services are boxing themed and haircut packages include vigorous shampoos and scalp massages. With many current new and soon to open franchise locations in 13 states, they are expanding rapidly and have sold more than 450 franchises.

Address:	6341 Campus Circle Drive East Suite 110 Irving, TX 75063
Phone:	(972) 714-9300
Website:	**www.knockouts.net/fran/fran_step.php**
Franchise Fee:	$22,500, royalty fee of 6% on gross sales, renewal fee of $500
Initial Investment:	$94,100-$190,550 (including the franchise fee)

Sport Clips

These sports themed salons specializing in non-fussy male grooming are aimed at men and boys. The company began franchising in 1995, and now have well over 400 franchise locations in the United States, where they are currently seeking additional franchises.

Address:	P.O. Box 3000-266 Georgetown, TX 78627-3000
Phone:	(800) 872-4247
Website:	**www.sportsclips.com/ best-franchise-opportunity.aspx**
Franchise Fee:	$49,500, royalty fee of 6% on gross sales, renewal fee of $6,500
Initial Investment:	$153,200-$276,900 (including the franchise fee)
Min. Net Worth:	$300,000 ($100,000 liquid)

Too Hotties

These are salons that feature attractive stylists in revealing outfits who cater to men. Services include a free shave and before and after shampoos. In addition to haircuts, shaves and other grooming services for men, these salons feature pool, video games, Wi-Fi, TV, and complimentary peanut butter sandwiches. They currently have 10 locations in the U.S. in Nevada, Arizona, Colorado, Florida, Missouri, Texas and South Carolina and are seeking to expand their franchises nationwide.

Address:	4560 South Campbell Avenue Suite C Springfield, MO 65810
Phone:	(417) 889-1909
Contact:	**franchiseinfo@toohotties.com**
Website:	**www.toohotties.com**
Franchise Fee:	$25,000
Initial Investment:	$198,000-$372,000 (including the franchise fee)

Family and Children's Hair Salons

Pigtails & Crewcuts

The company was founded in 2002 and began franchising in 2004. There are currently 14 locations in the U.S. They are seeking franchises nationally within the U.S.

Address:	1100 Old Ellis Road #1200 Roswell, GA 30076
Phone:	(877) 752-6800
Website:	**www.pigtailsandcrewcuts.com/franchise.aspx**
Franchise Fee:	$25,000, royalty fee of 5% on gross sales
Initial Investment:	$93,750-$168,250 (including the franchise fee)
Min Net Worth:	$150,000 ($75,000 liquid)

Sharkey's Cuts for Kids

This company was founded in 2001 and began franchising in 2004. They specialize in children's haircuts and birthday parties. There are currently 28 locations in the U.S. and Canada and they are seeking franchises nationally as well as worldwide.

Address:	37 Highland Road Westport, CT 06880
Phone:	(203) 637-8911
Website:	**www.sharkeyscutsforkids.com**

Franchise Fee:	$64,995-$119,000, royalty fee of 1,000/month, renewal fee of $500
Initial Investment:	$68,920-$175,500 (including the franchise fee)
Min Net Worth:	$150,000 ($50,000 liquid)

Snip-Its

Snip-its salons, which are aimed at children from newborn-9 years, not only provide quality haircuts for kids, they keep them enthralled with games, unique costumed cartoon characters (such as Snips, Maranga Mirror and Flyer Joe Dryer), videos, and even a machine that grants a prize to kids for the cost of a snip of hair at the end of their visit. Snip-its salons also host children's birthday parties. They are currently seeking franchises in several states throughout the U.S.

Address:	1085 Worcester Road Natick, MA 01760
Phone:	(877) SNIP-ITS
Website:	**www.snip-its.com/franchising**
Franchise Fee:	$25,000, initial royalty fee of 5% on gross sales, 6% annually thereafter.
Initial Investment:	$164,700-$273,200 (including the franchise fee)
Min. Net Worth:	$250,000 net worth/$50,000 liquid assets

The Lemon Tree

The Lemon Tree features family salon services available daily from early morning until late at night. The company began franchising in 1976, and have 60 franchises located in Florida, New York, Pennsylvania, New Jersey, and Connecticut, where they are currently seeking additional franchises. Salon experience is not necessary but they suggest some general business background.

Address:	6800 Jericho Turnpike, #120W Syosset, NY 11791
Phone:	(516) 393-5860
Website:	**www.lemontree.com**

Franchise Fee:	$20,000, royalty fee of 6% on gross sales
Initial Investment:	$68,600-$115,100 (including the franchise fee)
Min Net Worth:	$100,000-$200,000 ($50,000-75,000 liquid)

Salon/Spa-Related Franchises

Glamour Secrets

Glamour Secrets has been in business over 15 years and has more than 70 locations in Canada, 9 in the U.S., and even a location in Kuwait. These salons offer a variety of services from a full menu of hair salon services to spa services, makeup, nails and ear piercing. They currently are seeking franchises in both the U.S. and Canada.

Address:	101 Jevlan Drive Woodbridge, Ontario L4L 8C2
Phone:	(905) 264-2799
Contact:	**franchising@glamoursecrets.com**
Website:	**www.glamoursecrets.com/franchising.html**
Initial Investment:	$165,000-$220,000 (royalty 6% of sales with up to 3.5% returned to owner)
Min. Net Worth:	$300,000

4.2.3   Opening a New Hair Salon

Of course, you can always start from scratch and open a brand new salon. That way, you can have complete control over every step of the process and make sure that your shop is everything you want it to be. The information in the rest of this chapter will show you how to do just that.

Throughout this guide you will find numerous websites that can assist you in various aspects of starting and running a hair salon business. In this section, we focus on several key resources that can help you quickly increase your business knowledge. Each of these websites is a wealth of information that you can refer to throughout the process of starting your business.

Starting a Business Websites

For general information about starting a business, visit the websites listed below.

SBA

The Small Business Administration (SBA) is a leading U.S. government resource for information about licensing, taxes, and starting a small business. You can find a range of resources including information on financing your new business, business plans and much more at **www.sbaonline.sba.gov**.

SCORE

The Service Corps of Retired Executives (SCORE) is an organization of U.S. volunteers who donate their time and expertise to new business owners. You can find information on taxes, tips for starting your business, or even find a mentor who will coach you and help you maximize your chances of succeeding as a new business owner. Visit them at **www.score.org**.

Canada Business Services for Entrepreneurs

This Canadian government website offers information on legislation, taxes, incorporation, and other issues of interest to Canadian business owners or those who do business in Canada. For more information and a list of services they offer visit their website at **www.canadabusiness.ca**.

4.3 Choosing a Salon Name

If you decide to start up your own salon from square one, choosing a name may be one of the most important decisions you make for your new business. You want something catchy that will draw people into the salon while clearly indicating it is a hair salon.

If you have the financial resources, you could hire a naming professional to help you choose the right name for your company. Known as name consultants or naming firms, these organizations are experts at creating names, and can help you with trademark laws.

TIP: Business names don't have to be trademarked, but having them trademarked prevents anyone else from using the same name. Trademark laws are complicated, so if you think you want your company name trademarked it's a good idea to consult a lawyer with expertise in that area.

Most people starting up a new salon, however, don't have the money necessary to hire professional name consultants. The cost of these services can start at a few thousand dollars. Instead, to come up with a name yourself, consider your niche and what types of customers you are trying to reach. You might even hold a brainstorming session and enlist family and friends for suggestions. If somebody comes up with a really good one, you'll probably know it right away.

Here are name samples from the salon owners we surveyed:

- Godiva Salon

- Hairem Salon

- Charm Salon & Spa

- deNovo Aesthetics Center

- Halo [For Men]

In most jurisdictions, once you have chosen your business name you will also have to file a "Doing Business As" (DBA) application, to register the fictitious name under which you will conduct your business operations. The DBA allows you to operate under a name other than your own legal name.

Filing a DBA usually takes place at the county level, although some states require that you file at the state level, publish your intent to operate under an assumed business name, and sign an affidavit stating that you have done so. However, in most cases it's usually just a short form to fill out and a small filing fee that you pay to your state or provincial government. You can find a link to DBA filing requirements by state at **www.business.gov/register/business-name/dba.html**.

Trademarked Business Names

A trademark database lists all registered and trademarked business names. In the U.S., the essential place to start is with the U.S. Patent and Trademark Office. You can hire a company that specializes in this type of service to do a name search for you, if you choose. However, you can do an online search of the federal trademark database yourself to determine whether a name has already been registered.

You can also do this at the county level or at the state level when you file for a DBA using the fictitious names database of the agency you're filing with. The fictitious names database is where non-trademarked business names are listed.

You can check trademarks at the United States Patent and Trademark Office (**www.uspto.gov/main/trademarks.htm**). In Canada, the default database for name searches is the Newly Upgraded Automated Name Search (NUANS). You can search the NUANS database at **www.nuans. com**. There is a $20 charge for each NUANS search.

If you would like to learn more about this subject, you can read an in-depth article about naming your business entitled "How to Name Your Business" at the Entrepreneur.com website. This article includes tips on how to brainstorm ideas for naming your business, as well as establishing trademarks and how to file a DBA. A related article, "8 Mistakes to Avoid When Naming Your Business" offers tips on avoiding some typical business naming mistakes. You can find both of these articles at **www.entrepreneur.com/startingabusiness/startupbasics/index144024. html** (click on "Naming Your Business" in the "Browse by Topic" section).

4.4 Your Business Plan

"Have a dream. Write it down. Tweak it 'til it tells you you're ready, then go forward with determination, a strong business plan, and 30% more money and time than you planned to spend."

> — Marlene Weber,
> Marlene Weber Salon

Many business owners fail not because their business ideas weren't great but rather because of their lack of planning. A business plan is a detailed breakdown of every aspect of your business, including its location, sources of start-up funding, aspects of financial planning and an in-depth description of your proposed business. A good business plan serves two purposes. It's your guide (one that can be used and modified as necessary on an ongoing basis) for how you want your company to progress and grow.

Your business plan also serves as a sales tool should you decide to seek outside funding for your business. A business plan is essential in meeting with your bank manager or other lending institution. They need to know you are a good risk before they loan you money. A business plan tells them that you are prepared and know where you're going.

Additionally, a well-thought out plan will help you to identify any factors that will affect your profits and your competitive advantages. A business plan will allow you to step back from your excitement about starting a business, and take an objective look at your plans.

A good plan will help you over the rough spots by identifying where you might have slow cash flow during certain seasons (e.g., during the summer when many people are away vacationing). A well-prepared plan will help you learn who your customers and competition are, to understand the strengths and weaknesses of your business, and to recognize factors that could affect the growth of your company.

You shouldn't treat your business plan as if its contents are written in stone, however. There are many reasons why you'll want to keep up-to-date with your business plan. As your business changes and grows, your business plan probably will need some tweaking to reflect new goals and changing customer purchasing patterns, for example. (You might find that certain products sell better than others as you move forward.) Your business plan description will need to change if you branch out into a different product niche in your salon.

In the next section, we'll guide you through the various elements of your business plan and how they fit into the overall conception of your new enterprise.

4.4.1 What To Include In a Business Plan

"Writing a business plan is not just for the banker. A good business plan is a feasibility study, a roadmap for success, and a way for investors to take you more seriously. Don't rush through the planning. You won't take time to do it after you're open. Once the business is open, refer to your plan often to help you remember the ideas you worked hard to develop."

> — Jill D. Miller, Business Development Consultant, Creative Solutions

A business plan can be a simple description of your business concept or a detailed report, including graphs and charts of potential growth. A typical business plan should include the following items. You will learn more about a number of the important items, such as marketing and salon operations, later in this guide.

Cover Page

The cover page should list your name, home address, phone number and any other contact information you wish to provide. This is an often-overlooked, yet essential, piece of the business plan. If you are presenting your plan to investors or the bank, they must know how to contact you.

Executive Summary

This should be an upbeat explanation of your overall concept. Think of the paragraphs on the backs of book covers. An executive summary encapsulates the major contents of your business plan just as the paragraphs summarize the plot of a book. You want to sell your idea, so you need to keep it positive.

You should write the Executive Summary after the rest of the sections are completed (except, of course, the Table of Contents). The Executive Summary is the synopsis of your business vision. It should be concise and explain the major contents of your business plan.

Be sure to include the following important points:

- Business start date and location

- Financial objectives for the year
- Commitment to resources (inventory, facilities, staff)
- Products and services
- A strong closing statement

Table of Contents

Make it easy for your investors by including a Table of Contents so they can easily turn to specific items such as your profit projections.

A Table of Contents, although it's the first thing to appear in the plan, should be the last thing you write. That way you already have all the content and page numbers in place.

Description

The description of your business should cover the products and services you plan to offer and be as specific as possible. You can also include industry information about other salons in your niche market. In this section of your business plan, you will include the following:

- *Products and Services:* What type of merchandise and services you will be offering to customers and any additional product lines or services you hope to add.
- *Customers:* This is the section to give an overview of who you think your typical customers will be.
- *Goals:* What would you like to achieve by opening your salon? To establish yourself as a specialist in a certain sector of the industry? Expand your salon to a larger operation in five years? Describe your business goals in this section.
- *Salon Appearance:* Describe how your salon will look from the front window display, the flooring, to the sign outside. Include merchandise display features, how traffic will flow through the salon, as well as the total square footage of your retail space.
- *Unique Features:* What will separate your shop from others? What strengths will your business have over other similar businesses

in your community? What previously unfilled product or service area of the industry are you filling? This will also be a part of your marketing section.

- *Management:* In this section describe the salon's ownership and explain its legal structure, whether or not you intend to hire employees, and what training you will offer to them.

- *Start-Up Costs:* Lenders are particularly interested in how much you need to get your business running. Provide an overview of your financing requirements, including your own investment contribution, and any additional sources of working capital; explain your business registration, licenses, and insurance. This will be only a summary description. More in-depth descriptions and details about finances will follow in your financial section.

While you should include some details about all of the items above, remember that the business description section provides only an overview. This is to give readers of your business plan a quick summary of how the salon will be set up, your starting financial position, and an overview of the management and operation of your salon. Some parts will obviously overlap with the more detailed information provided in the other sections.

Legal Structure

The next section to include is how your salon will be set up from a legal standpoint. Here you will describe the legal structure of your business, such as sole proprietorship, partnership or corporation. This section may be included with the description of your business, or you can include it under a separate heading. Like other parts of your business plan, you can rearrange the sections or group them together. (You'll learn more about business legal structures in section 4.6.1 a little later in this chapter.)

Location

If you have not already chosen a location, then explain the type of space you wish to lease or purchase, and why you think it is a prime location for your salon. If you need help finding a location, contact a local realtor to find out what is available for lease. If you have already chosen a location, then describe it and detail the positive points about where it is situated and why the site will be a good one for your business.

Your Market

Who are your potential customers and why? Use census information (see box below) to show you have done your homework. Include any information on upcoming construction or stores that may be planning to build in the neighborhood. You can get this information from your local zoning board, as new businesses will have to obtain permits from them.

For example, let's say that a complementary business or other facility, one that might bring additional customers into your salon, is scheduled to open the week before your salon opens. A new daycare facility opening nearby might bring in extra customers for a salon offering children's products, or a new movie theatre in the neighborhood might attract an evening clientele for a restaurant; these are examples of complementary businesses. The opening of such a complementary business could potentially bring you a lot of extra customers, just as a new school, new housing development, and many other establishments could provide new customers.

How to Find Information on Your Market

Before opening your salon in a particular area, find out if the market is right. For example, if the business you want to open requires a certain demographic (particular population characteristics) and that demographic is under-represented or lacking entirely, or if there are already several salons similar to your own in the neighborhood, then you will need to decide if it's worthwhile starting your business in that area.

It is important to research this topic thoroughly. It could be vital to the success of your business. Census reports will help you with general information such as the average age of a city's residents or the number of children in the area. You can locate your area's latest census data at the U.S. Census Bureau website (**www.census.gov**) or Statistics Canada's census pages at **www12. statcan.ca/English/census**.

A visit to your local realty office can also prove worthwhile. Many realty companies keep statistics on the types of families moving into the area. It is also a good idea to talk to your local government (the zoning board is a good place to start) and find out if any permits have been granted for housing or business development. New housing additions often attract young families, whereas condominiums and apartments may be more likely to attract singles to the area.

Another good place to look is on the website of your local municipality. These websites often have employment statistics about local industries, level of education of the populace, and other important economic data. The local Chamber of Commerce can also provide similar information. Another website you can check out is **www.city-data.com**, where you can click on your state then your locality to find basic population and other related data.

Competition

List your competition. While it may not be a good idea to list every single competitor, it is a good idea to list a couple of the toughest ones. This will show the bank or investors you have realistic expectations about your business and are aware of what you need to do to survive. You can find where these salons are located by asking area residents or checking your local Yellow Pages.

Inventory and Pricing

Here, you will explain how you plan to acquire goods. List any suppliers you plan to work with, and what items you will need for the daily operation of your salon.

You may have to estimate prices, so your homework on other salons and what they offer and the prices they charge will be invaluable. A good rule of thumb for estimating what you should sell an item for is to price it at double the price of your cost for the item. For example, if you have a product that you purchased for $10.00, then you would sell it for $20.00 (100% markup on purchase, or 50% on selling). You can obtain the latest prices for items from websites and current catalogs.

You should also include what your potential profit on these items will be. Your profit will vary depending on local market demand for your products, sales volumes for a particular product, and wholesale costs. See section 6.4 for more about how to determine retail prices and track profitability for your merchandise.

Marketing

How will you determine your target market and then get the word out about your new business? Be detailed here. List specific marketing campaigns you plan to use; for example, local newspaper ads, flyers, and special signs. (To learn more about marketing see Chapter 7.)

Management and Staff

This section should highlight your background and business experience. This is also a good place to explain your passion for what you will be selling. You are selling yourself in this section. List any type of business background, from working in retail to relevant classes you have taken.

This section also includes information about staffing. It is unlikely you can do all the work yourself. Even if you do not plan to hire others right away, you should have a contingency plan in case you are ill, or some other catastrophe strikes. At the very least, you should make it clear you have several family members or friends willing to step in and help in case of an emergency. If you do plan to hire staff, then state that here, and mention your projected labor costs.

Financial Statements

This is the bottom line that most banks and investors will want to see. This will include start-up budgets, an estimation of revenue and expenses and a projection of when profitability will occur. See section 6.6 for more information on creating financial statements and details about financial planning for your business.

4.4.2 Start-Up Financial Planning

In the next section, you'll find a sample business plan for a new salon. It includes samples of financial statements, including cash flow and income statements and a balance sheet. Before you look at those, let's examine the basics of financial planning and how it affects the success of your business when you're starting out.

Financial management is crucial to running a successful business. One of the first important questions you should find an answer for is how you will finance your monthly expenses until you turn a profit. These ongoing monthly costs will include things like mortgage, renting or leasing costs, employee wages, utilities, salon supplies and so on. In addition, you'll need to decide how much you will pay yourself and your staff, how much you want to save for unexpected expenses, and how much you will put back into the business to finance growth.

When writing your business plan, be realistic. It is better to overestimate costs and underestimate profit. If you make more than expected in your first few months to a year, then so much the better. You will be in great shape!

Budgeting Basics

"Always have 50% more of what you thought it was going to cost you. Things always run late, so plan accordingly."

> — Valery Joseph,
> Valery Joseph Salons

If you have ever sat down and calculated how much money you'll need for something like the family vacation by figuring out what your income and expenses are, you already know how to budget. The most difficult part of budgeting for a business is that unlike when you work for a steady paycheck, it's more difficult to project your expected income after you pay all your expenses out of your revenues.

To clarify the situation in your business plan you will need to determine, as best you can, both your start-up costs and your operating costs. The start-up budget will include all the costs necessary to get your business up and running. Your operating costs will be all of the ongoing expenses once the business is in operation. In your planning, be clear about where the money is going and why, and explain how you came to your conclusions.

For starters, having a buffer of at least six months' finances available to cover your basic expenses is a good idea, just in case the business does not create a profit immediately. Many businesses will take up to a year to see a profit. Your salon may show a profit sooner, but it's best to be prepared.

In the cash flow projections in the sample business plan coming up in the next section, you will see that the company starts out with $35,000 cash on hand. This comes partly from the owner's cash savings and partly from an expected loan. The $35,000 helps to carry the business through at least the first six months as the company finishes this period with an ending cash number of nearly $12,000. Without the cash on hand at the beginning, the company may not have made it through to the end of the first six months. Its total expenses for the period were more than $60,000 including start-up costs. As you can see, that initial boost covered most of the business's monthly expenses for the first half of the year.

Here are some things you should consider when completing your revenue forecast and financial projections:

- Market trends and cycles

- Any seasonality of the business

- Varied sources of revenue

- Holidays (note that in the sample plan, revenues for December were projected as being higher than the months before and after)

- Unexpected events (such as equipment breakdowns, personal illness, etc.)

- How will you monitor your cash flow?

The financial section of your business plan will include your financial projections, break-even analysis, a projected profit and loss statement (also called an income statement), and information about your personal finances.

Remember to include the following items in your budgets. Notice that some expenses overlap on the start-up and operating budgets.

- *Start-up budget:* Legal and professional fees, licenses and permits, equipment, insurance, supplies, marketing costs, accounting expenses, utilities, payroll expenses.

- *Operating budget:* Make a month to month budget for at least your first year of operations, including expenses such as: staff (even if it's only your salary), insurance, rent, loan payments, advertising and promotions, legal and accounting fees, supplies, utilities, dues and subscriptions, fees, taxes and maintenance.

You can get a good idea for the cost of many of these budget items by browsing business supply websites, talking with realtors for rental costs, and basing your wages at minimum hourly wage to start. You may want to pay higher than minimum wage to your staff in order to get more qualified employees. At times, you may have to make an educated guess based upon your research and your chats with other business owners.

List expected profits and/or losses for at least the first year, but preferably for three years. You will want to break this down on a month-to-month basis. Show where the money is going and how much you expect will come in. If the business plan is for a loan, explain how much you need to borrow, why you need that much (exact uses of money), and where you plan to obtain it.

Estimating Your Revenues

Depending on your geographic location, your revenues can be in the tens to the hundreds of thousands. Of course, this amount also varies greatly depending upon the demand for your products, what you pay to your suppliers, and how much you market your business.

Speak with other salon owners in your general region of the country who are not competition for you. If you live in Indiana, consult with salon owners in Ohio, Illinois and Kentucky. If you live in California, consult with salon owners up the coast, in Oregon or Washington for example. If you live in New York, consult with salon owners in New Jersey.

Sample Start-up Budget Amounts

ESTIMATED INITIAL INVESTMENT FOR A NEW SALON

Type of Expenditure	Amount (Low-High)	Method Of Payment	When Due	To Whom Payment Is To Be Made
Initial License Fee[1]	$30,000	Lump Sum	When you sign the Salon License	Salons Corp
New Owner/SFC Training Fee[2]	$-0- to $2,100	Lump Sum	Before your Training	Salons Corp or FSFC
Travel and Living Expenses For You and Your Employees During Training[3]	$1,500 to $3,000	As Incurred	During Training	Airlines, Hotels & Restaurants
Leasehold Improvements[4] *(including architectural fees)*	$20,000 to $75,000	As Incurred	Before you open your Salon	Landlord, Suppliers & Contractors
Rent and Utility Deposit[4]	$3,000 to $8,750	Lump Sum	Before you open your Salon	Landlord & Suppliers
Initial Haircare Product Inventory (60 day supply)[5]	$8,000 to $12,000	As Incurred	Before you open your Salon	Salons Corp or Other Distributor
Salon Equipment[6]	$20,000 to $30,000	Lump Sum	Before you open your Salon	Suppliers
Other Equipment, Fixtures, and Furnishings[7]	$3,000 to $7,000	Lump Sum	Before you open your Salon	Suppliers
Salon Supplies - Non Technical (60 day supply)	$2,500 to $3,500	As Incurred	Before you open your Salon	Suppliers
Salon Identity and Graphics Kit	$1,500 to $2,500	Lump Sum	Before you open your Salon	Salons Corp or Other Distributors
Advertising (first 90 days)[8]	$7,500 to $15,000	As Incurred	As Arranged	Suppliers
Insurance [8]	$1,000 to $2,000	Non-refundable as required	As Incurred	Insurance Company
Additional Funds - 3 Months[9]	$20,000 to $40,000	As Incurred	As Arranged	Employees, Suppliers & Utilities
TOTAL[10][11]	$118,000 to $230,850			

Reprinted with the permission of Fantastic Sam's hair salon franchise.

One way to figure out how much you will need to sell to make a profit is to figure out the average cost of your items. (We'll look at how to figure out a break-even point based on your estimated expenses, including inventory, a little later in this section.) Depending on the suppliers you will deal with, you might be able to get a copy of a wholesale catalogue or get access to wholesale prices on the supplier's website. You may have to open a merchant account with them first, though. Once you have done a little research on who your suppliers will be, you can go ahead and contact them to get more information about your initial inventory costs.

Sales Projections

Before you can start your budget, you must arrive at some reasonable monthly sales projections. Many business decisions will be based on the level of sales that you forecast, so if you're too optimistic, you might find your business in trouble. As mentioned earlier, it's always best to be conservative in your estimates.

Alternatively, if you underestimate the amount of sales, you might make decisions that hold back the growth of your business, such as deciding on a less-than-perfect salon location because the rent or building purchase price is cheaper. A certain amount of "guesstimating" is required, but you can learn as much as possible about your market beforehand in order to make the estimates more accurate.

There are two types of revenue forecasting methods: Top Down Method and Bottom Up Method.

Top Down

The Top Down Method is what retail operations most frequently use because you can fairly accurately estimate your total market size and from that the amount of money you can reasonably expect to earn from sales.

To use the Top Down Method you must first estimate what the total sales potential would be. This type of information often can be gathered through the Chamber of Commerce, government census data, or from local, state, or national retailers' organizations. Then, by estimating what share of that market you can reasonably expect, you arrive at your possible sales for the year.

Calculation for Top Down Forecasting

Step 1:   Total market size x average annual spending (by customers in businesses like yours) per family or per person = total market potential

Step 2:   Total market potential (from Step 1) x number of competitors = average market share

Step 3:   Average market share (from Step 2) x your estimated percentage of market share = potential annual sales

Bottom Up

The Bottom Up Method is most often used when forecasting revenues from delivering a service. Depending on your business, you might need to use both Top Down and Bottom Up.

The Bottom Up Method is what you will use to calculate revenues from offering services only. Service revenues are limited by the number of hours you can reasonably work. You must first calculate your rate per hour (if you have several services you're offering, use an average price per hour and average production time to make the calculations easier).

Calculation for Bottom Up Forecasting

Step 1:   Hourly rate x number of hours available to work in a day = average daily sales

Step 2:   Average daily sales (from Step 1) x number of days you can work per year = possible annual sales

Step 3:   Possible annual sales (from Step 2) x expected rate of efficiency = projected annual sales.

NOTE: Rate of efficiency is usually about 50% in the first year. Any guaranteed contracts would have a 100% efficiency rate.

Operating Budgets

The first step in creating an operating budget is to determine what your monthly costs are. Take any bills, such as insurance and taxes, that occur either quarterly or yearly, and divide them by 4 (quarterly) or 12 (yearly) to find out how much you pay for those expenses each month.

Sample Budget Analysis for a Salon

Step 1: Data collected for the year projections

Description	Expenses	Revenues
Yearly projected revenue		$175,000
Lease	12,000	
Wages	73,000	
Loan repayments	13,000	
General expenses	5,000	
Utilities	6,000	
Cost of Goods Sold*	10,000	
Taxes	20,000	
Equipment & maintenance	12,500	
Advertising	6000	
Totals	$157,500	$175,000
	Yearly Net Profit = $17,500 (10%)	

Step 2: Monthly Budget Analysis

Description	Expenses	Revenues
Monthly projected revenue		$14,583.33
Lease	1,000	
Wages	6,083.33	

Loan repayments	1083.33	
Office/Salon Expenses	416.67	
Utilities	500	
Cost of Goods Sold*	833.33	
Taxes	1,666.67	
Equipment & maintenance	1041.67	
Advertising	500	
Totals	$13,125	$14,583.33
Monthly Net Profit = $1,458.33 (10%)		

NOTE: The accounting definition of Cost of Goods Sold (COGS) is: opening inventory + cost of purchases – closing inventory. If you use inventory tracking software, you can get a good idea of your COGS on an ongoing basis, although this is not as accurate as doing regular physical inventory counts.

With these annual and average monthly figures projected, the retail owner can now take a look at where the money is being spent and make some informed decisions about how to cut back on some of the expenditures in order to grow profits. Coming up, we'll show you how to calculate a break-even point for your retail business based on the projections you have already made for your operating expenses.

If you'd like more information about budgeting for your business, check out the article, "Budgeting for the Small Business," on the U.S. Small Business Administration website. The web page address is **www.sba. gov/idc/groups/public/documents/sba_homepage/pub_fm8.pdf**.

TIP: Every month, take a look at your expenditures and your sales, and update your budget and financial statements. A large setback, say purchasing an item that won't sell, or a repair to your vehicle, will mean you must redo your projections and budgets.

Calculating Your Break-even Point

Break-even analysis is a good way to find out how much you must sell in order to cover your costs. (You can compare the result with your projected revenues to see how they match up.) This is without profit or loss; profit comes after the break-even point. Figuring out your break-even point involves a fairly straightforward calculation. You must, however, have all the figures ready in advance before you can get an accurate number. In addition, in order to calculate the break-even point, you'll first need to break out fixed (non-controllable) costs like rent from variable costs like supplies.

You should also be aware that this number does not represent the amount of sales you need to make in order to "break even" for the year. This number is for you to determine at what point during the year, given a certain amount of sales, your earnings will begin to outstrip your expenses. If it comes early in the year, you will be in great shape. If it comes late in the year, you may need to make some changes in order to show a profit for the year. This formula can also be applied to monthly sales and expenses to show you where you reach the break-even point during the month.

Sample Break-Even Point

The formula is:

$$\text{Break-even point} = \text{Total fixed costs} \div (1 - \text{total variable costs} \div \text{revenues})$$

Using the numbers from the sample budget analysis we did earlier, let's say your salon has fixed expenses of $22,200 for lease payments and $8,000 for loan costs (totaling $30,200) during the first year. The rest of the budget expenses are variable costs, totaling $63,325. Based on revenues, variable costs are 56% (or in other words, for every dollar in sales, 56 cents is variable costs).

Here's how to calculate your break-even point.

$$\text{Break-even point} = \text{Fixed costs } [\$30,200] \text{ divided by } (1 \text{ minus variable costs } [\$63,325] \text{ divided by revenues } [\$112,500])$$

$$30,200 \div (1 - 63,325 \div 112,500)$$

$$30,200 \div (1 - 0.56)$$

$$30,200 \div 0.44$$

$$\text{Break-even point} = \$69,000 \text{ (rounded)}$$

The salon will have to earn gross revenues of about $69,000 each year in order to break even. This company is operating at 112500/69000 or 163 % of break-even, meaning it is profitable. With these figures determined, you can now look at ways of reducing your variable costs as well as increasing your revenues to try to widen the gap between gross revenues and your break-even point. It's also a good way to see if your projected revenues are realistic when balanced against known expenses.

When Can You Expect to Turn a Profit?

"Opening a salon can be an amazing adventure. It's a business that is rewarding, fulfilling, and can be very lucrative. If you make sure to hold it to the same standards that you hold yourself to, you can do very well. Just make sure you are ready to put some time in before you start pulling in the profit. Just like growing a clientele as a stylist, growing a strong salon that functions in the black can take a year or more."

— Justin Hickox, owner, Hickox Studio

This varies widely from region to region, salon to salon, and owner to owner. Most salons break even sometime during the first year. You can reasonably expect to start making profits after that time period.

A lot will also depend on your overhead costs. If you are running an Internet store with low overhead costs, you may turn a profit very quickly. Or if you are running the business out of your home and have no rent, then you may turn a profit more quickly than someone leasing space in a strip mall.

One idea might be to start small with an Internet or home-based store and then move to a larger space as your business grows. This way, you'll see a profit much quicker without the risk involved in investing your own or someone else's money.

4.4.3 A Sample Business Plan

Keep in mind that this is a somewhat simplified business plan. You will need to provide more detailed information in some areas, particularly in the financial section (including financial statements) of your plan.

Sample Business Plan: Enchanté Salon Stella

Cover Page

Include the title, your name and contact information.

Executive Summary

Enchanté Salon Stella is an exciting new concept in the hair salon industry. While many salons exist, few service our immediate community, and none offer the kind of upscale services and atmosphere or unique amenities that Enchanté does. Later in this document you will be able to read about these innovative customer service concepts.

Our products and services include a menu of special services that will appeal to women and men seeking a relaxing and pampering experience when they need personal grooming. Using these products and services as a starting point, the salon will continue to add other products and services as driven by the demands of our clientele, and will consider specifically whether to add a menu of spa services in the future.

Start-up date for the store has been set for October 1st of this year. We will be located at 19 Newman Street in downtown Rancho Largo, which has a total population of 150,000. Of this 150,000, approximately one-fifth, or 30,000 people, fall within our upscale target demographic and live or work within a five-mile radius of our location. The salon's location is also excellent due to its high traffic volume and ample free parking, onsite and on nearby lots. In addition, no other upscale salon is located in this area, despite its high concentration of offices and retail businesses, upscale apartment buildings, two luxury hotels, and high draw for shoppers.

The store will be managed by owner Stella Stylist. Ms. Stylist has 15 years' experience as a stylist, having worked for six years with celebrity stylist Norman Frey at his salon in Los Angeles and another nine years as top stylist and president of the busy, upscale Rainier Salon in the resort community of Pearl Springs. She received her cosmetology license from the Parker-Fesson School of Beauty in Los Angeles and further studied advanced classes with Aveda, Sebastian, and at the prestigious Ecole de Beaute in Paris. In addition, she has completed a number of continuing education courses, including courses in business management, marketing, customer service, and accounting. Because she plans to maintain her busy styling practice, Ms. Stylist will hire an assistant manager and business partner, Barbara Goldwell, who has been in retail sales and small business management for more than 10 years, to provide additional management experience.

The salon will hire three additional full-time stylists with impeccable skills and established reputations on a salary and commission basis, as well as bring in one full-time manicurist and one part-time makeup artist, both as highly skilled independent contractors on a flat rental basis. As it is highly computerized, inventory tracking and the creation of a client tracking database using salon software will be simple and effective.

With only ten other upscale salons located in the city, and only one within a three-mile radius of our planned local area (which caters to an entirely different target market), we expect to turn a profit within the first year of operations. We estimate that, with the high volume of shoppers, residents, and business executives, and the lack of immediate competition coupled with our solid business concept, we will capture a minimum of 9-10% of the upscale salon market share (or approx. 2,840 loyal base clients who come in an average of four times per year) within the first year. If these clients spend an average of $88 per visit, including retail sales, this translates to an eventual $1,000,000 in retail and service sales, with an estimated gross profit of $100,000.

Both the location and the timing are perfect for starting this type of business in our community. We have identified a lucrative market niche that has gone unfilled before now. No other salon in the immediate area offers the kind of services that we do. With the extensive experience and savvy business acumen of its management, Enchanté Salon Stella will be one of the most profitable retail ventures in the area.

Table of Contents

To be completed last.

Description of the Business

Enchanté Salon Stella will be an upscale, full-service hair salon offering top quality salon services for both men and women in a soothing and elegant atmosphere. In addition to our menu of services, we will offer high-end quality hair and skincare products as well as casual jewelry pieces by well-known local artist Amy Kleinhardt and daytime and evening purses created by local artist Judith Couch. Aside from these accessories, our retail products will come from major wholesale beauty supply companies and manufacturers.

Our goals by the end of the year are to be profitable and to be the leading luxury salon in the community.

The salon will be open seven days a week, starting on October 1st this year. Hours of operation will be Mondays through Fridays, 9:00 a.m. to 9:00 p.m., Saturdays 10:00 a.m. to 6:00 p.m. and Sundays 12:00 p.m. to 5:00 p.m. Enchanté will offer the following unique services for our clients, services not offered by any of our competitors:

- *Quality:* The quality of the services we plan to offer are unsurpassed by any other local salons, as our stylists, manicurists and makeup artists will all be highly skilled professionals chosen for their superior artistry.

- *Elegance:* The surroundings and furnishings will create a soothing oasis of elegance, luxury, and comfort. The interior design of the salon will be overseen by Raymond Shafer, known for his superb designs, such as the Asian Gardens Sushi Restaurant in Rancho Largo and the University Club's elegant tea salon rooms.

- *Privacy and Convenience:* Unlike many salons located on street level with large picture windows, our clients will enjoy the privacy yet convenience of our second floor location within the prestigious Rancho Largo Business Plaza building in downtown, where many of our potential clients work. It is also within easy walking distance of two upscale hotels and several other retail businesses, office buildings and apartment buildings in the area.

- *Client Education:* At Enchanté Salon, no client will leave the salon without a discussion and thorough understanding of his or her individual daily and weekly grooming routine for hair, skin, and nails. Unlike clients at other salons who often leave with the feeling they will never be able to recreate their fabulous new look at home, our clients will have the confidence and ability to style and maintain their look so that they will look and feel as good every day as they do when they leave our salon.

- *A staff trained in the highest standards of customer service:* Clients will be pampered throughout their stay at our salon, as their comfort and care will be overseen by a highly attentive and friendly professional staff. Our clients will never experience the frustration of waiting for their services or being left forgotten under a dryer, and everyone will be provided with fresh coffee, tea, refreshments, magazines, and other comforts throughout their stay.

- *Free refreshments, Wi-Fi, newspapers, flat screen televisions, and other amenities:* Although many salons provide a few well-worn magazines and maybe a cup of coffee or bottle of water to their customers, our salon will provide them with every comfort throughout their stay. We will provide free Wi-Fi service throughout the salon for executives and other business people who need to stay in touch with work, as well as several flat screen TVs with satellite service to entertain them throughout their stay. In addition, our clients will enjoy complimentary refreshments such as fresh fruit, cappuccino, cookies, and pastries during their stay at the salon, and our client service areas, chairs, and lounge will be elegant, comfortable, and inviting. We will also provide luxurious touches such as hot towels for face and hands and a lunch delivery service from local cafes (delivery will be free and clients pay the same price as they would to dine in the restaurants). And of course, we will provide a wide variety of current magazines in addition to daily news and financial papers such as the New York Times and the Wall Street Journal.

The salon will be approximately 1,400 square feet in area. Approximately 1,000 square feet of floor space will be dedicated to the four stylists' stations, one manicurist station and one makeup vanity and a three-sink shampoo area. The retail area will be located near the reception desk so that customers will be drawn through the merchandise areas when checking in and checking out of the salon. This reception and retail area will occupy approximately 100 square feet. This area will include an elegant reception desk, a POS system, computer/cash register system, and elegant lighted glass cases to display merchandise. A private area at the rear of the store will include a small storage space, staff washroom, a dispensary and mixing area, a washer and dryer, and owner's office.

Description of the Industry

The salon industry is a steady growth industry. During both robust and slower economies, this industry grows at a stable, upward rate. Within the past decade alone, the industry has enjoyed an almost constant average growth of 4% per year. According to the National Beauty Association*, the average man, woman and child gets a haircut every six to eight weeks; further, more than fifty percent of women in the United States currently color their hair, 20% of these women get their hair colored in salons, as do a growing percentage of men over the age of 35. A recent article in the Hair Salon News stated that, while in times of economic slowdown, people may delay getting a haircut or color by one to two weeks, they do not eliminate haircuts or other personal grooming services from their budget. They also do not tend to downscale the cost or quality of the services they are accustomed to, and will cut other aspects of their budget rather than skimp on services such as haircuts, color, and manicures that affect their personal appearance.

> (* The National Beauty Association and Hair Salon News are a fictional organization and publication for this example. A real business plan needs real data sources, which you can find online or through industry magazines and organizational reports. Each industry has its own organization.)

Business Legal Structure

Limited Liability Corporation (LLC). We have chosen the LLC business legal structure because it allows the freedom of running the business as a sole proprietorship and simplifies tax returns while still protecting personal assets.

> (* Note to reader: This may not be the best choice for you. Please read section 4.6.1 on legal structure and consult with a lawyer or other professional, if you are still uncertain.)

Business Location

A 1,400 square foot retail space located on the second level at the Rancho Largo Business Plaza on Newman Street in downtown Rancho Largo is currently available for lease. The location has plenty of parking spaces and is visible from MacArthur Boulevard, a busy thoroughfare that cuts through the downtown area and is a direct exit off of Interstate 60. In addition, the location, a former cosmetic medical services office, is already equipped with spaces for client care, reception, a private office, sinks, and washer and dryer hookups. Large front windows will allow for plenty of light, yet the second floor location will assure the quiet and privacy our clients seek. Some further interior redecorating will be required, such as setting up dividing walls between the retail/reception area and the stylists' station areas, and removing two walls from patient treatment rooms. A new wood laminate floor will also be installed throughout the service and retail areas of the salon.

Target Market

The products and services will be marketed to affluent local individuals. There are more than 150,000 people living in the area. Of these, some 30,000 fall within our target demographic and work and live within a five-mile radius of our location. Because there are relatively few local salons competing for this demographic, and studies have shown that most salon clients come from within a five-mile radius of the salon location, we should be able to capture a significant portion (9-10%) of this target demographic within the first year. A local telephone survey conducted on our behalf by Hapsburg Marketing, Inc., indicates a strong interest in this demographic for an upscale salon service conveniently located in the downtown Rancho Largo area. Most of our target clientele are either unhappy with the quality of what is available or must travel outside their area to obtain the quality of services they seek. In addition, projected local growth appears to be a steady upward trend of approximately 6% per year, primarily of professionals due to the location there of several large financial and tech companies and its proximity to a prestigious private university.

We can capture at least 9-10% of this market with targeted advertising and word-of-mouth business especially, due to our central location. That would equal approximately 2,840 clients per year at an average of four visits to the salon per year with average client spending of $88, including projected retail sales of hair and skin products. (Because of the uncertainty of potential sales, no sales of jewelry or purses were included in these figures). This suggests an annual gross revenue stream in excess of $1,000,000, with an estimated annual net profit of $100,000.

Inventory and Pricing

Starting inventory of hair and skin care products will be obtained through discount wholesale beauty suppliers. Our initial stock will be equal to two months of projected sales. Once the store opens, most additional inventory will be purchased as needed by our assistant manager from our wholesalers. We will carry only salon-quality brands and all of our stylists and makeup artist will be well educated on the benefits and use of these products. In addition, all stylists will be encouraged to sell (without being pushy) the retail products to contribute steadily to our gross revenue. As an incentive, stylists will receive 10% of sales, provided they meet a monthly quota.

Hair and skin care products will be marked up by 100%, and cosmetics will be marked up 200%. Jewelry and purses will be offered initially on a consignment basis with the salon receiving 20% of the retail price of each item sold.

Promotion

We will bring brochures to the concierge of the two local luxury hotels as well as bring them to every office in our building and the surrounding office buildings. We will also run some limited advertising in the local newspapers, but will have a large direct mail campaign to both office addresses and residential addresses of our target demographic throughout a six-mile radius of the salon. We will also develop a website and an email newsletter as cost effective methods of keeping in touch with customers. Database software will help us keep track of customers so we can send them promotional offers and news. In addition, we will hold events like makeup demonstrations and sales, bridal days, beauty author appearances, etc., to draw new customers into the salon.

Competition

There are three other higher-priced salons within the city of Rancho Largo, only one of which is within the three-mile radius of our proposed location. Our only competition within the key three-mile radius for the salon market is Quikcuts, which caters to time-strapped individuals who are unable to make or keep regular appointments. It is a mid-priced salon, and not in a comparable high-end market. Quickcuts opened approximately six years ago and currently has a 65% market share; however, a sizeable percentage of this share is made up of children (who are not the likely clientele of Enchanté), families on a budget, and cash and time-strapped university students — again, not our likely clientele.

Because our demographic is different, we will not be competing for a large portion of their loyal customers; rather, we will be drawing away only those customers of Quikcuts who are already dissatisfied with the lack of upscale salon services in the area as well as drawing in those individuals who currently make the trip outside the area to get their hair and nails done. Since many of these individuals live or work within five miles of Enchanté, we are likely to capture a good percentage of this market within the first year of operations.

A second medium-priced salon located a bit further from our location is Glamour Hair & Nails. However, while they have a 12% market share, they are not in direct competition, as they cater primarily to African American women. While we may lure some of their clients to our salon, neither business, due to the distance between our locations and the differences in specialty niches is likely to pose significant direct competition to the other.

The other high-priced salon in Rancho Largo, Flying Colors, is located ten miles from our location. This full-service unisex salon also caters to a mid-priced market, but is a booth rental salon whose stylists in recent years have been mostly recent beauty school graduates, and the salon has a fairly high attrition rate of stylists (which likely also drives away clients), reportedly due to the difficult personality of the owner.

Thus, these other salons either cater to a very different demographic, or are far enough away or do not offer the same quality of services, and cannot truly be considered direct competition. The only arguably direct competition is the Jean-Claude Salon in neighboring Whitman, located five miles from the center of Rancho Largo in a high-end strip mall. Due to often heavy traffic on the beltway that connects the two areas, this can be a long and aggravating trip that clients will likely forego if there is a more conveniently located alternative in Rancho Largo. In addition to a more convenient location where clients can find top-notch services to which they are accustomed, our salon design will be more luxurious, and our surroundings and amenities will provide them with a more pampered and soothing salon experience.

Management and Staff

The owner and manager of Enchanté Salon will be Stella Stylist. Stella Stylist has worked in high-end salons as both a top stylist and manager of operations for many years and has attended many beauty trade shows and advanced coloring and cutting classes. Her thorough knowledge of the world of hair and beauty coupled with her business experience and knowledge in how the salon industry works will create success. In addition to her extensive work experience, she has completed several business courses through her local community college. As a result of this professional development strategy, she is aware of the most effective marketing techniques for salons and possesses accounting, inventory, customer service, business management, and other necessary skills for running a profitable salon business.

Barbara Goldwell, with more than 10 years' experience in a variety of retail settings, will act as assistant manager at a starting wage of $12 per hour. She will work approximately 50 hours per week, coming in at approximately noon each day to allow Stella to continue to service her many established hair clients and take on new ones during the afternoon and evening hours.

All stylists and the manicurist and makeup artist will be thoroughly screened and then tested as to their artistic abilities as well as their personalities and ability to deliver the finest customer service available. Stella will personally evaluate each potential employee and will oversee their work and provide for additional training from time to time as necessary to keep up with current hair and other beauty trends.

Financial Information

Risks

As with any business venture, there are risks associated with opening this salon. One possibility is that our main competitor, Quikcuts, might

Table 1: Competitor Analysis

Factor		Strength	Weakness	Competitor:	Importance to Customer
	Enchanté			*Jean-Claude*	
Products	Higher quality	X		High quality	Very High
Price	Same	X		Same	Low
Quality	High	X		High	High
Selection	Same	X		Same	Medium
Customer Service	Excellent	X		Excellent	High
Reliability	High	X		High	High
Stability	Low - if we do not do well, we will eventually close up	X		Very stable	Medium and established. This is a real strength of theirs
Expertise	Very High		X	Very High	Very High
Company Reputation	N/A			High	
Location	Prime location convenient for target clientele	X		Prime location but far from target clientele	High
Appearance	Elegant with many luxurious amenities.	X		Not as elegant but nice, with some amenities	High
Sales Method	Targeted advertising	X		Targeted advertising	Medium
Credit Policies	Accept cards, cash or check.	X		Same	High
Advertising	Planning a lot of		X	Does some	Medium
Image	Upscale		X	Upscale Luxurious	Very High

Table 1: Competitor Analysis (continued)

Factor		Strength	Weakness	Competitor:	Importance to Customer
	Enchanté			*Quickcuts*	
Products	Higher quality	X		Emphasis on average quality and price	Very High
Price	Charges more			Charges less	Low
Quality	Very High	X		Slightly less	Very High
Selection	Same	X		Same	Medium
Customer Service	Excellent	X		Service okay	High
Reliability	High	X		High	High
Stability	Low - if we do not do well, we will eventually close up		X	Very stable and established. This is a real strength of theirs	Medium
Expertise	Very high	X		Medium	Very High
Company Reputation	N/A			High	
Location	Prime location with lots of traffic	X		Good location. Little less traffic	Low
Appearance	Elegant With many luxurious amenities.	X		Low Budget Décor, Few Amenities	High
Sales Method	Targeted advertising	X		Targeted advertising	Medium
Credit Policies	Accept cards, cash or check	X		Same	High
Advertising	Planning a lot of	X		Does some	Medium
Image	Upscale Luxurious	X		Mid-price range Efficiency Services	Very High

decide to add more luxury services or a spa or add several amenities for the same price to try to effectively compete with our clientele. However, we see this as a remote possibility since its owner is the top stylist with six additional stylists, all of whom are busy and who service a sizeable and steady portion of the hair salon market — the mid-priced and budget-conscious market — in the community. Because they would not only leave this market with few convenient and budget options, and would have to reinvent their salon and image from the ground up, including changing their name, décor, image, and services, an expensive and unnecessary undertaking that would only position them in a different market and in more direct competition with Enchanté , this is highly unlikely.

Another risk might be that we fail to effectively lure the established clientele from Rancho Largo who travel to Jean-Claude Salon. However, since established market patterns reveal that most salon clients come from a three-mile radius and our telephone market survey conducted by a professional marketing firm indicates our salon is viewed by our target market as a needed service, offering these individuals a much more convenient alternative that is every bit as luxurious as their current salon and is located in their own hometown is almost certain to lure them to our salon.

We believe that our sales targets are realistic based on our market research, but there is always the possibility that our target sales will not be achieved for the year. We will closely monitor revenues on a daily, weekly and monthly basis to ensure that our retail and service sales targets are being reached, and if they are not, we will make every effort to discover why not and correct any issues we discover. Start-up capital will carry the salon's expenses through the first six months of operations.

Cash Flow

Excluding the spike in cash flow for holiday sales increases, we project positive cash flow beginning in April of next year.

Following are our cash flow projections for the first two quarterly periods of operations (note that these figures include sales projections for the first month of operations starting the first of October through October 31):

Enchanté Salon Stella Cash Flow Projections:
1st Six Months of Operations

	Oct	Nov	Dec	Jan	Feb	March
Cash on Hand	$45,000	$22,473	$19,490	$26,687	$15,904	$1,661
Sales Revenues	$44,000	$48,400	$58,080	$39,600	$35,640	$50,820
Total Cash and Sales	**$89,000**	**$70,873**	**$77,570**	**$66,287**	**$51,544**	**$52,481**
START-UP EXPENSES						
Construction	10,000					
Equipment/Supplies	15,000					
Inventory	16,700					
Licenses	1,000					
Insurance	2,000					
Total Start-up Costs	**$44,700**					
ONGOING EXPENSES						
Rent	$2,500	$2,500	$2,500	$2,500	$2,500	$2,500
Advertising	2,000	1,000	1,000	500	500	500
Utilities	2,100	2,100	2,100	2,100	2,100	2,100
Wages	9,000	37,556	37,556	37,556	37,556	37,556
Taxes	3,333	3,333	3,333	3,333	3,333	3,333
Office supplies	835	835	835	835	835	835
Inventory purchases		2,000	1,500	1,500	1,000	1,000
Loan repayment	2,059	2,059	2,059	2,059	2,059	2,059
Total Ongoing Expenses	**$21,827**	**$51,383**	**$50,883**	**$50,383**	**$49,883**	**$49,883**
Total Expenses	**$66,527**	**$51,383**	**$50,883**	**$50,383**	**$49,883**	**$49,883**
Cash Ending	**$22,473**	**$19,490**	**$26,687**	**$15,904**	**$1,661**	**$2,598**

[You should create a month by month cash flow projection sheet for the entire year to include in your business plan, rather than the six months in our example.]

Statement of Net Assets

Following is the balance sheet representing the personal assets and liabilities of Stella Stylist.

Personal Assets & Liabilities of Stella Stylist	
ASSETS	
Current Assets	
Cash	$10,000
Investments (401K)	80,000
Total Current Assets	**90,000**
Long-term Assets	
Automobile	12,500
Home Equity	125,000
Total Long-term Assets	**137,500**
Total Assets	**$227,500**
LIABILITIES	
Current Liabilities	
Car Loan Payment	$400
Mortgage Payment	650
Utilities and Other Expenses	750
Property Taxes	1,500
Total Current Liabilities	**$3,300**
Long-term Liabilities	
Car Loan	9,000
Mortgage	150,000
Total Long-term Liabilities	**$159,000**
Total Liabilities	**$162,300**
Net Assets	**$65,200**

[For a start-up company, one without business assets and liabilities, you should create a balance sheet like this to represent the owner(s) total personal assets and liabilities.]

Other Items

In addition to the items listed above, your business plan might include things such as a statement of personal finances (this can include a print-out of your credit history and tax returns), a resume, reference letters, and other items. It is up to you if you want to include these things. Always err on the side of giving more information, especially if you are unsure if you can secure a loan based on the information you're providing to lenders.

Another item you might want to add is a loan proposal or request for funding. In the example financial statements above, the owner will need an additional $25,000 in start-up funding to add to the owner's $10,000 cash in the balance sheet to carry the business through the first six months of operations. A lender or investor will want to see a loan proposal or request for funding detailing how much money you want to borrow, what you plan to spend the money on, and how you plan to pay it back. Under this heading, state the amount of money you are asking for, whether it is a debt or equity funding request (i.e. if you are borrowing money, that is debt funding; if you are asking someone to invest in your business as a shareholder or minority partner, that is equity funding), how you plan to repay a loan, or what an investor gets out of investing in your company. Your loan proposal should include:

- How much money you want

- How long it will take you to pay it back

- Details of how you plan to spend the money

- How you will get the money to pay back the loan

- A description of your own personal assets and other collateral that you can use to secure the loan

If your business will need start-up financing the next section will tell you how to go about finding it.

4.4.4   Business Plan Resources

You can find a free sample business for a salon business at **www.bplans. com/hair_and_beauty_salon_business_plan**.

Here are some additional resources that you might find useful in helping you to write your business plan:

- *SBA: Write a Business Plan*
  www.sba.gov/smallbusinessplanner/plan/writeabusinessplan/

- *SCORE: Business Plan Templates*
  www.score.org/template_gallery.html

- *Canada Business: Developing Your Business Plan*
  www.canadabusiness.ca/eng/125/138

- *Canada Business: Business Plans Templates and Samples*
  www.canadabusiness.ca/eng/guide/2089

- *BDC (Canada) Business Plan Template*
  www.bdc.ca/en/business_tools/business_plan/default.htm

TIP: When writing your business plan, pay close attention to spelling and grammar, and try to write clearly and concisely. You don't want to make reading the plan a chore.

4.5   Start-Up Financing

This section covers sources of start-up financing, and what you'll need to present to lenders in order to apply for funding. Additional advice on all aspects of financing your business can be found at the SBA's Small Business Planner website at **www.sba.gov** (under "Start Your Business", click on "Finance Start-Up" then choose "Financing Basics"). In Canada, visit **www.canadabusiness.ca/eng/125/142**.

4.5.1   Getting Prepared

"Keep a to-do list with you at all times, even next to your bed stand. The stress is sure to wake you in the middle of the night, so just write yourself a note and go back to sleep if you can."

> — Michael O'Rourke, Founder,
> Carlton Hair Care Salons

When looking for funding, you must first be well prepared before approaching any potential loan or investment sources. You will need the following things:

- *A Business Plan:* As you learned in the previous section, a business plan is the document that lenders will review to decide whether or not to give you a loan. This document is absolutely necessary for banks or other lenders, and even if you are getting the start-up money you need from a rich aunt, you should prepare your business plan and present it so the person lending you money can see that you have a clear and organized plan. (If you haven't read it already, see section 4.4 for advice on creating a business plan.)

Your financial statements are a particularly important part of your business plan.

- *A Personal Financial Statement:* This should be prepared as part of your business plan. It is important because you need to have a clear picture of your own financial state to know exactly where you are financially before you begin. This financial statement will tell you:

  - How much money you need every month to pay your bills

  - What kind of resources or assets you have

  - What kind of debt you carry. How will you repay this debt while you are putting your total effort into opening your salon?

- *A Start-Up Survival Nest Egg:* Many financial consultants think that having a nest egg to live on while you are starting up your salon is one of the most important things you can have. Some suggest at least six months' of living expense money — that is, all the money you will need monthly to pay all your personal living expenses, bills, and debts, so you can focus on your new retail business without stress. This is apart from any reserve start-up capital you might need for the business itself.

Asking for Money

Keep these tips in mind when you ask someone for funding:

- Get an introduction or referral. If you can get someone who is respected in the community to introduce you to a potential lender, it gives you credibility and that's a big advantage.

- Have an extra copy of your business plan available for the potential lender's inspection, and be able to speak clearly and concisely about your plans. Be able to discuss all aspects of your business plan, your long-range goals and your prospective market.

- Be professional. Shake hands, speak with confidence and look the person you're talking to in the eye.

- Dress to impress. You're going to be a business owner. Be sure you look the part.

- Be receptive. Even if you don't end up getting any money from a prospective lender or investor, you may be able to get ideas and suggestions from them. Perhaps they'll have some pointers regarding your business plan, or some suggestions about steering your business in a particular direction. Don't be afraid to ask questions, either.

Remember that if someone agrees to loan you money or invest in your business, they're doing so because they believe in you and what you can do. When you ask someone for money, you need to sell yourself and your ideas. Make sure you have a great sales pitch.

There are a number of online resources to help you find out more about financing options for your business. The SBA link noted above is a good place to start in the United States. In the "Start Your Business" section of the Small Business Planner, open the "Finance Start-Up" link and scroll down to find Loan and Funding information. In Canada, you can try Canada Business' "Grants and Finances" page at **www.canadabusiness. ca/eng/82**.

Now that you know the basics, you are ready to determine who you will approach for your funding.

4.5.2   Equity vs. Debt Financing

In business, there are two basic kinds of financing: equity financing and debt financing. Essentially, equity financing is when you agree to give someone a share in your business in exchange for an agreed amount of investment capital from that person. Debt financing is, as you probably already know, borrowing money at interest that you pay back in install-ments over time or in a lump sum at a specified future date. (Or repay-ment could be a combination of these; the point is, you'll pay interest). The decision to choose debt or equity financing usually will be based on your personal financial position and how much additional money you need in order to get your business started.

One form of equity financing is investment capital provided by ven-ture capitalists. You'll want to look for an individual or investment firm that is familiar with your industry. You'll have less explaining of your business concept to do and they might be more open to investing in a company such as yours whose premise they already understand.

While a venture capital investor won't expect you to pay interest and regular monthly installments, they will expect some kind of return on their investment. This could include dividends paid out of your net income, the right to interfere with operations if they think they could do better, or the right to resell their interest to someone else for a higher price than they originally paid for their share of your company. Make sure that you are comfortable with the terms of any investment capi-tal agreement, and that it clearly specifies what your obligations are. Check with a lawyer if you're not sure.

Another form of equity investment comes from your circle of friends and your family. You might be able to get a no-interest loan from a fam-ily member or a close friend, with the promise to pay them back at a time in the future when your business is self-sustaining. This is an ideal situation for you so long as the lender has no expectation of "helping" you run your business if you're not comfortable with that. You may also decide to bring in a friend, business acquaintance, or family member as a partner if they have some capital to invest to help cover start-up costs.

Debt financing is any form of borrowing, including a loan, lease, line of credit or other debt instrument on which you must pay interest in order to finance the original principal amount. Sources for this kind of financing include banks, credit unions, credit card companies, sup-pliers, and so on. If you buy a computer system for your company and pay for it in monthly installments over a couple of years, that is a form of debt financing since you will pay interest on the amount you finance. In the following sections we'll look at some of the sources of each type of financing and the advantages and disadvantages to each.

4.5.3   Borrowing Money

You can choose to utilize any mixture of the financing suggestions that follow. Many new business owners choose a mix of some of their own savings, a family loan, and a small business loan. Only you can decide which financing sources will be the best ones for your business and your personal situation. The most important thing is to make sure you agree to loan repayment terms that you can live with and that are realistic for you.

Commercial Loans

Commercial loans are loans that you can get from a financial institution like a bank or a credit union. You can go to your neighborhood bank around the corner to set up all your small business banking needs, or you can shop around for a bank that will offer you the best loan terms possible.

The terms of your loan will depend upon several things:

- Your credit score

- Your collateral

- Your ability to pay back a loan

There are a number of different loan types you can enter into with these financial institutions. They offer both long-term and short-term loans. For example, you might choose an operating term loan with a repayment period of one year. This will help you finance your start-up costs such as buying equipment and inventory or pay for any renovations you might need to do.

Line of Credit

"Rather than getting a traditional loan for the working capital, I suggest entrepreneurs talk to their bankers about establishing a line of credit for this

> *fund. That way the money is available if you really need it, but you don't have to borrow it and accrue interest if you don't need to."*

> — Jill D. Miller, Business Development Consultant, Creative Solutions

You might also choose a business line of credit if your situation warrants such an arrangement. In this setup, the bank will grant you what is in essence a revolving loan in a specified amount, and will honor any checks you write to pay for your ongoing business expenses. You will pay interest on any amounts outstanding under the line of credit.

Remember that lines of credit are to be used to pay for operating expenses as needed. Don't abuse the privilege by going out and buying thousands of dollars worth of office equipment or a new car for the business. If you do, then you won't be able to meet the projections you gave the lender when you presented the business plan to them. Those projections are why you got the line of credit in the first place.

Operating term loans and lines of credit, particularly if they are unsecured by assets (or other collateral), will have higher rates of interest attached. In some cases, the lender may require that you offer some sort of security for the loan, such as having a co-signer or putting up your personal assets against it. Some lenders may accept inventory (usually at 50% of your cost to purchase it) as a portion of collateral. Another consideration is that your interest rate will change as the bank's interest rates fluctuate.

Long-term Loans

You might choose a long-term loan, rather than short-term financing, if you need to do major renovations or building, or take out a mortgage if you intend to purchase a building as your retail location.

One advantage to this type of financing is that the interest rates are usually lower. This is because the loan is paid back over a longer period of time than an operating term loan or line of credit, and you pay interest at a fixed, instead of a variable, rate. Another reason interest is lower is that the loan is backed by the value of the asset you're purchasing. This makes repayment of the loan more likely. (The lender can always sell an asset like a building if you default on the loan.)

TIP: If you're looking for a long-term loan of less than $50,000 the bank will probably consider it a personal loan. As a result, they will be more interested in your personal credit history, and they may require you to put up personal assets such as real estate as security.

One major disadvantage to a long-term loan is that you will have a debt burden that you will need to carry for a number of years. This can affect your company's growth because you might not have the liquidity you need to pay for expansion or to pursue new lines of merchandise. You might also have to pay a financial penalty if you decide to pay back the loan earlier. Consider all your options carefully before you enter into any kind of long-term debt arrangement. Speak with an accountant and a lawyer first.

Personal Loans

One of the greatest resources for your start-up money will always be the people you know who believe in you and your ideas—your family and friends. Very often they will help you with money when all other resources fail you. They usually will agree to payback terms that aren't as strict as commercial lenders, and they are usually pulling for you, too. As with any other kind of loan, it is important to make sure that you and the other parties completely understand and agree to the terms of the loan. Also, make sure to put everything in writing.

Another possibility is to ask a family member to co-sign a commercial loan for you. Co-signing means that this person agrees to take on the financial responsibility of the loan if you should fail. Family members are often willing to help you out this way. Make sure, before friends or family members help you out by co-signing a loan, that they are really comfortable doing so.

4.5.4   Finding Investors

Venture Capital and Investment Capital Investors

Depending on the type and size of your business, you might consider finding investors to help you with your start-up capital. You may find that some investors are just not willing to invest venture capital in a small, single-location retail store, however, many small retailers have gone on to grow their companies into regional or national chains. So this type of investment may well be something you'll want to look into for the future. As you'll see later in this section, there are ways to find investors willing to put money into small businesses.

Remember that investors are looking to make money by investing their capital in your business. They may or may not be people you know, but they will want you to show them how they will make a profit by helping you. You have to assure them that they will get something out of it, because for them investing in your salon isn't personal (like it might be when a family member invests in your business), it is business. Investors work one of two ways:

- They want to see their initial money returned with a profit

- They want to own part of your business

While investment capital might seem like a great idea, be aware that many entrepreneurs have been burned when venture capital vanished when the start-up money was needed. As mentioned earlier, the investment agreement could contain unsavory terms that give too great a portion of control to the investor instead of leaving it in the hands of the company owner.

However, on the plus side, private investors can be more flexible to deal with than lending institutions like banks. They may not want to get too deeply involved with the day-to-day management of the company. They might also be more willing to accept a higher level of risk than a bank, trusting in your skills and knowledge of the industry and leave your assets unencumbered.

To find venture capital investors beyond your immediate circle of family and friends, you can investigate some of the resources found at the websites listed below.

- *VFinance*
  www.vfinance.com

- *Angel Capital Association Member Directory*
  www.angelcapitalassociation.org/directory

- *Canadian Venture Capital Association*
  http://cvca.ca

You can also find investment capital through the Small Business Administration's Small Business Investment Company (SBIC) program. While the SBA does not act as an intermediary on behalf of entrepreneurs, they do have a wealth of information about the process of finding investors on their website at the "SBA Entrepreneurs Seeking Financing" link below. You can use their services to help you put together a business plan and a request for funding package (see more about this in section 4.5.5), which you can then submit to SBICs that might be interested in providing you with investment capital. You can search for SBICs to match your needs at **www.sba.gov/aboutsba/sbaprograms/inv/esf/INV_DIRECTORY_SBIC.html**.

- *SBA Entrepreneurs Seeking Financing*
  www.sba.gov/aboutsba/sbaprograms/inv/esf/

- *PrivateEquity.com*
  (Click on "Private Equity Firms".)
  http://privateequity.com

- *The National Association of Small Business Investment Companies*
  www.nasbic.org/?page=SBIC_financing

You have to decide what you want. Do you feel you will be able to meet the investor's terms? Do you want to share ownership of your business with another person? For some new business owners, the perfect solution is to find a person who wants to partner with them, share the responsibility of their new store, and bring some money to invest.

Partners

One of the simplest forms of equity financing is taking on a partner. Having a partner in your business brings additional skill sets, business contacts and resources to the venture. Most importantly, a partner can bring money to help pay for start-up costs and assist with ongoing operations. You'll need to decide whether your partner will be active in the running of the company or just a silent partner who invests the money, receives income from the business, but has no say in how things are run. (You can read more about Partnerships as a form of business legal structure in section 4.6.1.)

You as an Investor

Never forget that you might be your own best source of funding. One nice thing about using your own money is that you aren't obligated to anyone else or any other organization—it is yours to invest. This can be an excellent solution for individuals with some credit problems.

To raise your own capital, you can:

- Cash out stocks, bonds, life insurance, an IRA, RRSP, or other re-tirement account

- Increase your credit on charge cards (remember that you will pay high interest rates on these)

- Use personal savings

- Take out a second mortgage or home equity loan on your house or other property

- Sell something valuable, like a car, jewelry, real estate, or art

4.5.5   Government Programs

Small Business Administration Loans

The Small Business Administration (SBA) doesn't actually lend you money. However, they have a program called the "7(a) Loan Program" in which they work with banks to provide loan services to small business owners. The SBA guarantees a percentage of the loan that a commercial lender will give you, so that if you default on your payments, the bank will still get back the amount guaranteed by the SBA. Both the bank and the SBA share the risk in lending money to you. As the borrower, you are still responsible for the full amount of the loan.

When you apply for a small business loan, you will actually apply at your local bank. The bank then decides whether they will make the loan internally or use the SBA program. Under this program, the government does not provide any financial contribution, and does not make loans itself.

The SBA also provides a pre-qualification program that assists business start-ups in putting together a viable funding request package for submission to lenders. They will work with you to help you apply for a loan up to a maximum amount of $250,000. Once the loan package has been submitted, studied, and approved by the SBA, they will issue a commitment letter on your behalf that you can submit to lenders for consideration.

In essence, the SBA gives lenders the reassurance that they will pay back the loan if you don't. They provide the extra assurance that many lenders need to get entrepreneurs the financing they need. You can read more about the process at **www.sba.gov** (click on "Services" then on "Financial Assistance").

The SBA also has a "Micro-Loans" program, which offers loans to start-up and newly established businesses through non-profit entities at the local level up to a maximum of $35,000. The average loan is about $13,000. Interest rates for these small loans vary between about 8 to 13 percent. You can find out more about these loans at the SBA website.

Government Programs in Canada

If you are planning to open a retail business in Canada, you might be interested in the Business Development Bank of Canada (BDC) or the Canada Small Business Financing Program (CSBF). The BDC is a financial institution owned by the federal government that offers consulting and financing services to help get small businesses started. They also have a financing program aimed specifically at women entrepreneurs. You can learn more about the Business Development Bank of Canada (BDC) and its financing resources at **www.bdc.ca**.

The Canada Small Business Financing Program is much like the SBA 7(a) Loan Program mentioned earlier in this section. The maximum amount you can borrow is $500,000, and no more than $350,000 can be used for purchasing leasehold improvements, improving leased property or purchasing or improving new or used equipment. The CSBFP works with lenders across the country to offer loans at 3% above the lender's prime lending rate. To find out more, visit **www.ic.gc.ca/epic/ site/csbfp-pfpec.nsf/en/home** (the links you'll need are on the right-hand side of the page).

4.6 Legal Matters

4.6.1 Your Business Legal Structure

Your business structure affects the cost of starting your business, your taxes, and your responsibility for any debts the business incurs. This section will highlight the several different legal forms a business can have. There are four basic structures: sole proprietorship, partnership, corporation (including the S corporation), and limited liability company (LLC).

Sole Proprietorship

If you want to run the business yourself, without incorporating, your business will be known as a "sole proprietorship." This is the least expensive way to start a business. It is also the easiest because it requires less paperwork and you can report your business income on your personal tax return. All you need to do is apply for an occupational business license in the area where your business will be located. Usually, the license doesn't take long to be processed and you can begin operations fairly quickly.

If you're running the business by yourself, your social security number can serve as your taxpayer identification number. If you have employees, you'll need to request a taxpayer identification number from the Internal Revenue Service.

A sole proprietorship means that you have almost total control of the business and all the profits. The only drawback to this type of business is that you are personally liable for any debts of the business.

Advantages

- Easy to start
- Low start-up costs
- Flexible and informal
- Business losses can often be deducted from personal income for tax purposes

Disadvantages

- Unlimited personal liability: the sole proprietor can be held personally responsible for debts and judgments placed against the business. This means that all personal income and assets, not just those of the business, can be seized to recoup losses or pay damages.

- All business income earned must be reported and is taxed as personal income.

- More difficult to raise capital for the business

Sole proprietorships are extremely common and popular among small business owners — mostly because they are easy and cheap to start with the least amount of paperwork.

Partnership

If you want to go into business with someone else, the easiest and least expensive way to do this is by forming a partnership. Legally, you would both be responsible for any debts of the company and you would enter into something called a partnership agreement. There are two types of partnerships: general partnerships and limited partnerships.

A general partnership is when two or more people get together and start a business. They agree on the conduct of the business and how the profits, risks, liabilities and losses will be distributed between them.

TIP: Partnerships don't have to be divided equally between all partners. However, all partners must agree on how the profit, risk, liability and loss will be divided.

A limited partnership is when one or more partners invest in the business, but are not involved in the everyday operations. Limited partners are investors — partners — but they have limited say in the hands-on operations.

Partnerships usually have more financial clout than sole proprietorships — a definite advantage — simply because they have more in the way of assets than a single person. Another advantage to a partnership is, in an ideal situation, you and your partner will balance out each other's strengths and weaknesses. On the other hand, many businesses have gone bad because of an ill fitted partnership.

Below are some of the advantages and disadvantages to partnerships:

Advantages

- More initial equity for start-up costs
- Broader areas of expertise can lead to increased opportunities
- Lower start-up costs than incorporation
- Some tax advantages

Disadvantages

- All partners are equally liable for the other's mistakes with the same liability as a sole proprietorship
- Profits and losses must be shared
- The business must be dissolved and reorganized when a partner leaves

---

Working with a Partner

Beyond any legal issues, before going into business with a partner you should spend many hours talking about how you will work together, including:

- What each of you will be responsible for.
- How you will make decisions on a day-to-day basis.
- What percentage of the business each of you will own.
- How you see the business developing in the future.
- What you expect from each other.

> During your discussions you can learn if there are any areas where you need to compromise. You can avoid future misunderstandings by putting the points you have agreed on into your written partnership agreement that covers any possibility you can think of (including if one of you leaves the business in the future).

Corporation

Whether you are working alone or with partners, if you want a more formal legal structure for your business, you can incorporate. Incorporation can protect you from personal liability and may make your business appear more professional.

However, it usually costs several hundred dollars and there are many rules and regulations involved with this type of business structure (among other requirements, corporations must file articles of incorporation, hold regular meetings, and keep records of those meetings). Many new business owners consult with an attorney before incorporating.

Here is a list of some of the advantages and disadvantages to incorporating your business.

Advantages

- Protect personal assets and income from liability by separating your business income and assets from your personal.

- Corporations get greater tax breaks and incentives

- Ownership can be sold or transferred if the owner wishes to retire or leave the business

- Banks and other lending institutions tend to have more faith in incorporated businesses so raising capital is easier

Disadvantages

- Increased start-up costs

- Substantial increase in paperwork

- Your business losses cannot be offset against your personal income

- Corporations are more closely regulated

S Corporation

The IRS offers a provision, called an S corporation, where a corporation can be taxed as a sole proprietorship. An S Corporation is similar to the corporation in most ways, but with some tax advantages. The corporation can pass its earnings and profits on as dividends to the shareholder(s).

However, as an employee of the corporation you do have to pay yourself a wage that meets the government's reasonable standards of compensation just as if you were paying someone else to do your job.

Unless you want to wind up paying both a personal income tax and a business tax, you will probably want to create an S corporation. This saves you money because you are taxed at an individual rate instead of a corporate rate.

Limited Liability Company

A Limited Liability Company, or LLC, is a relatively new type of business legal structure in the U.S. It is a combination of a partnership and a corporation, and is considered to have some of the best attributes of both, including limited personal liability.

A limited liability company is legally separate from the person or persons who own it and offers some protections that a partnership does not. Partners in a limited liability company get the same personal financial protection as those in a corporation.

The LLC business structure gives you the benefits of a partnership or S corporation while providing personal asset protection like a corporation. Similar to incorporating, there will be substantial paperwork involved in establishing this business structure. LLCs have flexible tax options, but are usually taxed like a partnership.

Here are some of the advantages and disadvantages of LLCs:

Advantages

- Limited liability similar to a corporation

- Tax advantages similar to a corporation

- Can be started with one (except in Massachusetts) or more members like a sole proprietorship or partnership

Disadvantages

- More costly to start than a sole proprietorship or partnership

- Consensus among members may become an issue

- LLC dissolves if any member leaves

  NOTE: Regulations regarding limited liability companies vary from area to area. Make sure you do your homework if this interests you.

In the end, choosing a business legal structure for your company is a personal choice, and the advantages and disadvantages should be considered thoroughly. Many small business owners begin their independent venture as a sole proprietorship because of the low costs, and incorporate as the business grows and becomes larger and more complex.

For more on business structures take a look at the resources available at FindLaw.com (**http://smallbusiness.findlaw.com/business-structures**). For some additional government resources to help you decide which structure to choose, try the SBA Small Business Planner at **www.sba. gov**. In the "Start Your Business" section, open the "Choose a Structure" link. In Canada, you can find more information about business structures at the Canada Business Services for Entrepreneurs website (**www. canadabusiness.ca**). Click on "English," then on "Starting a Business," then on "Choosing a Business Structure."

4.6.2   Business Licenses

Regardless of what form of legal structure you choose for your business, you'll need to obtain business licenses. This is not a difficult task. All it normally entails is filling out some forms and paying an annual license fee. Contact your city or county clerk's office for more information about registering your business. Contact information can be found in your phone book or online through resources such as the Business. gov website at **www.business.gov/register/licenses-and-permits**.

There may also be a number of other permits and licenses you will need:

- EIN (Employer Identification Number) from the IRS or a BN (Business Number) in Canada. All businesses that have employees need a federal identification number with which to report employee tax withholding information.

- Retail businesses that collect sales tax must be registered with their state's Department of Revenue and get a state identification number. In Canada, you will need to register to collect the Goods and Services Tax (GST), as well as provincial sales tax (except in Alberta), or Harmonized Sales Tax (the HST blends provincial sales tax and GST together in one tax).

- If you are putting up a new building for your salon, you will need to ensure you have appropriate permits and comply with any requirements for zoning or access for people with disabilities (see section 5.1.2).

- For state, county and local licenses required for salons in your area, you'll need to contact your Department of State. The exact requirements will vary from city to city, county to county, and state to state. Generally speaking, however, salons require many licenses, including an establishment license from the Board of Health. Part of the reason for this is that there are many hygiene and health issues involved in beauty and personal care services. For salons renting out booths or space, there are a greater number of licenses required, as each renter is an independent contractor, and thus technically a separate business with its own licensing.

- Aside from the myriad of business licenses required, every barber or cosmetologist working in the salon must possess a valid cosmetologist's or barber's license. All cosmetologists and barbers performing any personal appearance service must be licensed by the state they practice in, with the exception of shampooers and makeup artists.

- To sell retail items, you will likely also need a seller's permit, as will anyone in your salon who sells retail items.

- You may also need a permit for any signage you use.

Keep in mind that any business in the U.S. or in Canada that offers services that could potentially affect the health of its patrons is subject to laws and regulations regarding hygiene, sanitary practices, environmental and product safety hazards, and other health hazards. Following state and provincial guidelines on sanitation and hygiene is vital, as surprise health inspections are a constant possibility that can cost your business money in fines and even threaten to close your business.

Many municipalities require health department approval before a business license is granted to certain types of service businesses. Check with your local town hall's business licensing division to find out what is required when you submit your business license application. For more information on hygiene codes, see Section 6.2 ("Hygiene and Cleanliness").

For information about local, state, and federal requirements in the U.S. visit the SBA Small Business Planner (**www.sba.gov**) and choose "Get Licenses and Permits" in the "Start Your Business" section.

In Canada, business licenses are issued at the municipal level so check with your local municipality for help with acquiring a business license. For a province-by-province list of Canadian municipalities and their websites, visit the BizPal website at **www.bizpal.ca/part_partners.shtml**. Many municipalities offer business license applications right on their websites.

4.6.3 Taxes

If you are properly informed and prepared you won't have to face your tax responsibility with a feeling of dread. In fact, once you are organized and you have enlisted the help of a good tax professional, taxes become just another regular business task.

Get Informed First

The best thing you can do to be sure of your personal and business tax obligations is to find the information you need before you start your new salon. The Internal Revenue Service (IRS) has a number of informative documents online that you can look at today to learn the basics about everything you need to prepare for your taxes as a small business owner. If you read these documents and understand them, you will have no surprises at tax time.

One helpful document is the Tax Guide for Small Business that outlines your rights and responsibilities as a small business owner. It tells you how to file your taxes, and provides an overview of the tax system for small businesses. You can find this document at **www.irs.gov/pub/irs-pdf/p334.pdf**. For more general information for small business owners from the IRS visit their website at **www.irs.gov/businesses/small/index.html**.

For Canadian residents, the Canada Revenue Agency also provides basic tax information for new business owners. This includes information about the GST, how to file your taxes, allowable expenses and so on. You can find this information and more helpful documents at **www.cra-arc.gc.ca/tx/bsnss/menu-eng.html**.

It is also important to be informed about your tax obligations on a state and local level. Tax laws and requirements vary on a state-by-state basis and locally, too. Make sure that you find out exactly what you are responsible for in your state and city. In addition, it is important to find out about sales tax in your area.

The Tax Foundation provides information on a state-by-state basis for personal, sales and other taxes at **www.taxfoundation.org/taxdata**. The Canada Revenue Agency has a linked directory of government websites at **www.cra-arc.gc.ca/tx/bsnss/prv_lnks-eng.html** where you can find tax information on a province-by-province basis.

Getting Assistance

If you decide you would prefer a qualified tax professional to help you handle your taxes, you will find you are in good company. Many small business owners decide to have a professional handle their taxes. An accountant can point out deductions you might otherwise miss and save you a lot of money.

One resource that may assist you in choosing an accountant is the article "Finding an Accountant" by Kevin McDonald. It offers helpful advice for finding an accounting professional whose expertise matches your needs. The article is available at **www.bankrate.com/brm/news/advice/19990609c.asp**.

Once you've determined what your accounting needs are you may be able to find a professional accountant at the Accountant Finder website (**www.accountant-finder.com**). This site offers a clickable map of the United States with links to accountants in cities across the country. Alternatively, the Yellow Pages directory for your city is a good place to find listings for accountants.

You will also need to understand payroll taxes if you plan on hiring employees. Each new employee needs to fill out paperwork prior to their first pay check being issued. In the U.S. this will be a W-4 and an I-9 form. In Canada, the employee will have to complete a T-4 and fill out a Canada Pension form.

Both the W-4 and the T-4 are legal documents verifying the tax deductions a new employee has. The amount of tax you will withhold as an employer varies and is based on the required deductions an employee has as specified by the federal government. Make sure you retain the forms in a folder labeled with their name and store them in a readily accessible place such as a filing cabinet in your office.

Check with your state or province's labor office to make sure you are clear about all the forms employees must fill out in order to work for you. The sites below give more information on legal paperwork, including where to get blank copies of the forms your employees will need to fill out.

- *SmartLegalForms.com*
  (Sells employee forms online.)
  www.hrlawinfo.com

- *GovDocs Employee Records and Personnel Forms*
  (Click on "Employee Records".)
  www.hrdocs.com/Posters/hrproducts

- *Canada Revenue Agency*
  (Download and print forms you need.)
  www.cra-arc.gc.ca/forms/

4.6.4   Insurance

Insurance can help protect the investment you make in your company from unforeseen circumstances or disaster. Types of insurance for a retail business include:

Property Insurance

Property insurance protects the contents of your business (e.g. your computer, your merchandise, etc.) in case of fire, theft, or other losses. If you lease space, you may need property insurance only on your own merchandise and equipment if the owner of the building has insurance on the property.

Liability Insurance

This insurance (also known as Errors and Omissions Insurance) protects you against loss if you are sued for alleged negligence. It could pay judgments against you (up to the policy limits) along with any legal fees you incur defending yourself. For example, if a client is upset because she claims she was nicked with scissors during her haircut (even though she didn't bring this to your attention until several days later) and wasn't satisfied with the refund and gift certificate you offered.

> **TIP:** For some small businesses, getting a Business Owner's policy is a good place to start. These policies are designed for small business owners with under one hundred employees and revenue of under one million dollars. These policies combine liability and property insurance together. Small business owners like these policies because of their convenience and affordable premiums. You can find out more about these policies at the Insurance Information Institute (**www.iii.org/commerciallines/whatitdoes/types**).

Car Insurance

Be sure to ask your broker about your auto insurance if you'll be using your personal vehicle on company business.

Business Interruption Insurance

This insurance covers your bills while you are out of operation for a covered loss, such as a fire. This type of insurance covers ongoing expenses such as rent or taxes until your business is running again.

Life and Disability Insurance

If you provide a portion of your family's income, consider life insurance and disability insurance to make certain they are cared for if something happens to you. If you become sick or otherwise disabled for an extended period, your business could be in jeopardy. Disability insurance would provide at least a portion of your income while you're not able to be working.

Health Insurance

If you live in the United States and aren't covered under a spouse's health plan, you'll need to consider your health insurance options. You can compare health insurance quotes at **www.ehealthinsurance.com**, which offers plans from over 180 insurance companies nationwide.

Canadians have most of their health care expenses covered by the Canadian government. For expenses that are not covered (such as dental care, eyeglasses, prescription drugs, etc.) self-employed professionals may get tax benefits from setting up their own private health care plan. Puhl Employee Benefits (**www.puhlemployeebenefits.com**) is an example of the type of financial planning company that can help you set up your own private health care plan.

Association Member Policies

Some insurance companies offer discount pricing for members of particular organizations. When you are looking for organizations to join, whether your local Chamber of Commerce or a national association, check to see if discounted health insurance is one of the member benefits.

The National Cosmetology Association at **www.ncacares.org/join/ benefits.cfm** offers discounts on health insurance for salon owners and their families and employees, disability insurance, life insurance, prescription drug plans, discount dental plans, and business and liability insurance for salons and independent contractors. The Salon and Spa Association also offers group discounts on insurance, including business insurance and health and dental plans. Visit **www.salonspaassociation. com** to learn more. In addition, the Spa Association offers group health insurance and professional liability insurance to its members. You can learn more on their member benefits page at **www.thespaassociation. com/index.php?pr=Benefits**.

Workers' Compensation Insurance

Another type of insurance to consider if you plan to hire employees is workers' compensation insurance. Most states in the U.S. and provinces in Canada require businesses to have workers' compensation insurance to help protect their employees in case of injury on the job.

To find what workers' compensation laws govern your business in your state check out the Southern Association of Workers' Compensation Administrators' site (**www.sawca.com/workerscomplinks.htm**). Scroll down below the map to find links to the various states' workers' compensation sites. In Canada you should visit the Association of Workers' Compensation Boards of Canada website where you can find information about the WCB for your province. Visit them at **www.awcbc.org/ en/linkstoworkerscompensationboardscommissions.asp**.

More Information

There are other types of insurance and different levels of coverage available for each type. An insurance broker (check the Yellow Pages) can advise you of your options and shop around for the best rates for you. You might want to check out the SBA's in-depth risk management guide that covers most aspects of insurance planning for small business. You can read it on their website at **www.sba.gov/tools/resourcelibrary/ publications** (click on "Management and Planning Series", then scroll down to #17).

5. Setting up Your Hair Salon

Your business plan is written, you have your financing, the legal issues have been dealt with, and all the licenses are in place. You're ready to set up your salon. In this chapter, we'll look at the various aspects of putting it all together, from finding a location through how to finish off the interior of your salon, to the equipment, supplies and inventory you will need.

5.1 Finding a Location

"Location is the most important consideration for any business, so you must choose wisely. Salon owners must take a look at their target market and the image they want to project. When they know this information they need to

find an area where these customers already go. Remember that salons draw most of their customers from a five mile radius."

> — Jill D. Miller, Business Development Consultant, Creative Solutions

You have probably heard it before and it's true: location can make or break your salon. Finding a space that suits you can take a little work, but once you have the perfect location, the thrill of opening your own salon will be that much closer!

5.1.1   Possible Locations

Traditional Retail Space

Retail space can be found in numerous locations throughout any community. Options for salon stores include shopping malls, strip malls, downtown areas or centrally located storefronts, stand alone buildings, and in or near hotels and resort areas.

If you're considering locations within a large metropolitan area, owner Derrick Diggs of Layers Hair Salon advises choosing a central location, because "if the city is more spread out, having a central location allows clients from the metro area to easily access the salon." Locating your salon in a busy area and looking for ways to promote yourself is an important part of this strategy. Ronnie Pryor, owner of Source Salon in Wilton Manors, Florida, agrees: "If you need to build a salon from zero, it's best to be near the action and aim for high visibility." On the flip side of large metropolitan areas, quaint villages that have stand alone retail buildings can also offer excellent locations.

Another tip from Michael O'Rourke for selecting a good location is to find a corner location with lots of windows. His advice for taking advantage of the obvious visibility to attract new clients is to "put the most animated stylists in the windows. Passersby will stop and stare and eventually come in to see what is going on." However, if you are accustomed to servicing fewer clients in a high-end location, a salon in a busier, lower-priced location might not be your best choice. With the higher traffic volume, you would need to increase your productivity rate to one much higher than you are accustomed to.

Budget Considerations

While location can mean the difference between success and failure, you also have to consider your budget. How much rent can you afford? Prime locations often have a prime price tag on them as well. You may have to start smaller and work your way up to the store you can afford.

Larry Dunlap, operating partner of Haircolorxperts maintains that your salon's location "should be based on the way you hope to acquire your clientele and the business model you're using." He offers this advice: "If you plan to make the most of your money from walk-in traffic, then a mall or very busy shopping center is your best choice. A salon that is focused on acquiring long-term clients should determine what the demographic for their ideal client is and seek out a convenient location with a high density of that demographic within a three mile radius." A further consideration is whether you plan to hire salon employees or rent space to stylists. You'll need to consider where your stylist contractors' existing clientele come from. "Booth rental salons are driven by the stylist's established clientele and should focus on a reasonably convenient location balance with cost per square foot," advises Dunlap.

An important consideration in large metropolitan areas is whether to rent on a higher level versus a street level floor where your shop will be seen by people driving or walking by. Federico Calce, owner of the upscale Federico Salon in Manhattan, explains why he would advise a salon owner to consider a higher floor-level location even though this lowers street visibility: "On a higher floor, you pay less rent and you are more exclusive and have more privacy. Because people perceive you as being more exclusive on a higher floor, you can charge more."

Client comfort and rent or lease costs are also factors to consider in choosing street- or higher-level locations. As Calce explains, "On the ground floor, you pay more rent and have less privacy, which is important to many clients. People can just stop in to look around, ask about price and generally bring down the level of the surroundings."

Malls

Depending on your business model, a mall location can be an ideal location for your salon. According to Michael O'Rourke, founder of the Carlton Salons (with several locations in southern California) and co-creator of the Sexy Hair™ product line, a mall location is never a bad choice. However, he adds that "rents are almost always higher" in malls, so you should try to negotiate when the economy is bad. On the plus side, busy malls provide high traffic and visibility.

When considering a mall location, you need to check the terms of the lease carefully, and consider all the rules and limitations the lease imposes. There can be limitations on signage, for example, or other crucial restrictions, such as mandatory mall hours. According to Tony Promiscuo, owner of Godiva Salon in the prestigious Buckhead area of Atlanta, "Most indoor malls require you to be open when they are. This means 7 days a week, for example, 9:00 a.m.-9:00 p.m. and Sundays 12:00 p.m.-7:00 p.m. This creates scheduling challenges unless you have a large staff."

Strip Malls

Strip malls usually have high traffic and can make ideal locations for salons. "Although it comes with higher overhead expenses," notes Michael Peter Hayes of the Michael Peter Hayes Art Salon in Long Island, "your business can be predicated on your neighbors in the center." Finding a location where your salon complements nearby businesses (and vice versa) can help you and your fellow tenants draw in customers. For example, as Suki Duggan, Owner, Donsuki Townhouse Salon notes, "Opening a salon near the hottest new boutique, hotel or restaurant gives you visibility to a higher-end clientele who share new finds with like-minded peers." Johnathan Breitung, co-owner of the Johnathan Breitung Salon & Luxury Spa in Chicago, who also advises getting to know the trendy areas when scouting for potential locations, adds that it's a good idea to "actually stand there and count the walk-bys."

Basement or In-Home Salon

If you have extra space in an easily accessible basement or another area of your home, you may want to consider starting your salon there. You should be able to deduct a portion of your utilities on your taxes but consult with your accountant to be sure.

Operating out of your home raises a number of issues you'll need to consider. For example, you'll need to know if you can legally operate a retail business out of your home (your city's zoning department can advise you), you'll need to arrange for proper liability insurance (covered in section 4.6.4), and you also have residential neighbors to consider.

Many business owners talk to their neighbors before starting a home business. If there is any opposition from neighbors, you can see if there is anything you can do to change their minds, perhaps by keeping particular business hours. Particular disturbances to neighbors can include noisy dryers and the smells of chemicals used in hair services.

Keep in mind that a home salon will be inspected like any salon business, since it's still a public service. You still need the same permits and licenses and need to follow the same hygiene and health codes as you would with any location. On the other hand, if you otherwise have an appropriate space and entrance in your home for a salon business, a home location will save significantly on start-up expenses, such as rent and electricity. This way, you can charge less than businesses with greater overhead expenses and still make a profit.

Travel/On-Location/TV and Film Sets

Some salon business owners travel to television and movie sets, fashion shows, and other off-site events such as weddings, either exclusively or in conjunction with a brick-and-mortar salon location. These stylists are very experienced at their craft and in high demand in the fashion and/or show business world. This business still requires you to have equipment that you can pack and take with you, as salon owners who travel to locations are expected to bring along the tools of their trade.

Notes Heaven Padgett, owner of the Hairem Salon in Houston, Texas, "When doing off-site shoots it's imperative that you are fully prepared for anything. Specify the reason for the shoot or the event. If it's a wedding you should have already decided what the styles would involve. But if you are stepping into a fashion shoot or catalogue you need to be prepared for any texture, length, or style."

5.1.2   Points to Consider

"The ideal location has street frontage with ample parking and easy access to the highway or major route. Signage is also a concern; many people seek out conveniently located salons so you want passers-by to take note."

— Dalgiza Barros, owner,
Creative Energy Hair Studio

You probably have some idea about where you envision your salon's location and what sort of a space you are looking for. But to make sure that you don't get stuck with something you are unhappy with, be as definite as possible about all the particulars you are looking for in a space before you begin your search. As you begin to consider what you need in a space, think about three things:

• Things you must have

• Things you would like to have but can live without

• Things that you definitely want to avoid

Very likely, the first "must have" will be a particular amount of space.

How Much Space Do You Need?

"Choose a salon location with the absolute minimum amount of space required to meet your needs. Empty, non-income producing areas in your salon cost the same as productive space. Retail display area should be kept to the bare minimum."

— Larry Dunlap, operating partner,
Haircolorxperts

"The majority of space should be usable for clients. This makes the salon feel more spacious and not cramped. You only need a very small office, break room, laundry area, supply room, and kitchen."

— Derrick Diggs, Owner,
Layers Hair Salon

Generally speaking, a small salon just starting out should probably allow a minimum of 300-500 square feet and contain two chairs. As Michael Peter Hayes of the Michael Peter Hayes Art Salon explains,

"As a rule of thumb, there should be 100 square feet per chair, plus 50-100 square feet for seating and another 50-100 square feet for the appointment desk, so a two-chair salon should have 300-500 square feet for overall comfort and design." Derrick Diggs, owner of Layers Professional Hair Salon in Richmond, Virginia points out that, "A smaller space feels cozy, especially if you have a few employees starting out. You want to also have room to grow because as you grow your business your revenues will also increase."

The smallest space Diggs would consider would be 1,200 square feet. On the other hand, larger spaces become more difficult to manage. "A salon that has 4,000 square feet would be as big as I would consider manageable, " he says. One salon owner we interviewed mentioned a 25,000 square foot salon in the Seattle area and an 11,000 square foot salon in a mall on Long Island. Obviously, successful salons can come in small spaces as well as large, so keep in mind there are no hard and fast rules.

Ultimately, the right size for your salon depends on many factors, such as the type of salon you envision and its geographic location. In fact, some salon owners have found great success in very small spaces. For example, celebrity stylist DaRico Jackson's Amiri salon "is a very unique 150 square feet studio that is a 'one man show', just me and my assistant, it has a styling station and a preparation station." The key is not to rent more space than you need but to rent enough space so that your salon will not start to feel too cramped for your customers' comfort.

You may also find once you open your salon that your original layout or the mix of services offered within your space does not work. You need to be vigilant and analytical and make any necessary changes to increase profitability. Explains Take Source Salon owner Ronnie Pryor, who purchased his 1,000 square foot salon from a previous owner, "It was originally a three-chair salon with two spa rooms and a nail area. It was cramped and lacked flow. After reviewing the numbers, I decided to remove the spa and nail areas to focus on hair – the salon's major revenue generator by far. For us, it was a profitable move." (Tips on using space are covered in section 5.2.)

Several owners we spoke with indicated that they would have preferred to choose a space that required less construction or building out to open a salon there. "This is my second salon location, and this time I knew I didn't want the hassle of construction, permits, licenses, etc.," says DaRico Jackson, owner and celebrity stylist of Amiri. "I found a place in an artist building this time around. This way, all of the permits and construction were already done. All I had to do was get a business license, make it esthetically beautiful, and start working."

> *"Next time, I would do it differently. I would get an architect involved, as they not only can help you design an attractive and well-functioning salon space, they can make sure everything falls into place. Certain considerations, like plumbing and electrical codes, are extremely important, not only for safety, but for practical reasons. For example, you need to be sure your dryers, which have a high voltage, can be run at the same time as several other appliances without constantly overloading your circuits and causing a breaker to shut it off. To ensure your salon is in compliance with local regulatory and building codes in addition to being a workable and attractive space, it's a good idea to consult with an architect."*
>
> — Lisa DeStefano, Owner,
> DeStefano's Salon

Legal Requirements

Another vital issue is ensuring the space meets all the legal requirements for running your salon. Consider the following issues as you begin your search for your new salon location.

Permits and Zoning

If you are going to make improvements to your space, you will need to make sure that you check your local city, county, and state regulations and get the proper permits to proceed.

Another thing to ask your potential landlord or your local government's zoning department is whether or not the space you are considering renting is zoned as a retail space.

The difference between zoning and the need for a permit is relatively simple. Zoning indicates where a business is allowed by local law to be set up, while permits designate whether a business can operate or not. (For example, many municipalities allow retail pet shops in areas that are zoned for retail, but one selling prohibited exotic species would never get a permit to operate.)

Many jurisdictions also require new business owners to obtain a Certificate of Occupancy. The requirements vary from area to area but many cities require inspections before issuing the certificate.

Access for People with Disabilities

As part of the Americans with Disabilities Act (you can read about the requirements of this legislation at **www.ada.gov)**, businesses are required to provide access for people with disabilities. Similar laws exist in Canada (check with your local municipality). Accessibility requirements may include:

- Floor aisles wide enough for wheelchairs

- Wheelchair ramps

- Wheelchair elevators if steps are present

- Rails in handicapped restrooms

Make sure to discuss this with any landlord you are considering renting space from.

Other Points to Consider

Here are some additional questions to ask:

- In what part of town would I like to locate my salon?

- Are any nearby salons similar enough to my salon to be direct competition?

- Are any large discount, or big box retail stores, that would affect my business close to the area where I would like to locate my sales?

- Are there other businesses or services nearby that might attract customer traffic to my salon (for example, a good location for a children's hair salon might be near schools and daycare centers)

- Have I observed car traffic near my salon at different times of the day?

- How much foot traffic does this location get?

In addition to these questions, you should consider the following points when looking for your retail space:

- *Parking:* Make sure the parking is close enough to your shop for customers to carry their goods to their cars. If they need to pay for the parking, can you offer a validation service?

- *Price:* Sure that spot on Main Street is ideal, but how much will you have to sell in order to afford it? Don't put yourself in financial distress right out of the starting gate; be realistic.

- *Projecting costs:* Calculate how much this space will actually cost. Ask about utilities, taxes, any extra fees you might have to pay.

Considering all these issues should help you narrow down the list of places to consider. The checklist below has a longer list of questions to help you assess the places you decide to check out.

Keeping Track of Places You've Seen

As you look at properties for the perfect potential space for your new salon, keep track of where you have been, what each potential space looked like, and the positives and negatives of each space.

Consider taking along a digital camera on your space-hunting trips to take a picture of each space's exterior and interior so you can more easily remember details of each location later.

To make the process easier, use the checklist provided on the next few pages for each of your space hunting excursions. This checklist, along with a picture or two, will help you to be really clear about each potential location you visit so you can make an informed decision.

Finding Your Perfect Space Checklist

Date: _____   Location: _____

Pictures

- ❑ Exterior front

- ❑ Interior

- ❑ Notes on pictures

Space Location Checklist

- ❑ Does the space have easy freeway access? Which ones?

- ❑ Does the space have handy public transportation? Where and what?

- ❑ Is the quality of the neighborhood good?

- ❑ What possibly helpful businesses are nearby?

- ❑ What possibly detrimental businesses are nearby?

Exterior Checklist

- ❑ How is the overall appearance of the building exterior? Does it need any obvious work? What?

- ❑ Is the building a storefront location?

- ❑ Is there a garden or parking strip area? Who maintains it?

- ❑ Where is the trash area? Is trash pick up included as part of the lease agreement?

- ❑ Is the tenant responsible for sidewalk maintenance? Shoveling snow? General clean up of trash and debris?

Interior Checklist

❑ How is the overall appearance of the building interior? Does it need any obvious work? What?

❑ What is the square footage of the space? Is there any room to grow?

❑ Are the windows functional? Are there enough windows?

❑ Is there adequate light?

❑ Are the air conditioning and heating systems shared or private for each tenant?

❑ Is the ventilation system shared or private for each tenant?

❑ Is the space technology-ready?

❑ Will you be able to use your own already existing Internet Service Provider if you have one?

❑ Is the space wired for cable modem or DSL?

❑ Is the space wired for phone lines? How many?

❑ Does the space have private or shared restroom facilities? What is the overall state of the existing restroom facilities? Are they wheelchair accessible?

❑ Does the space have hot and cold running water?

❑ Are there existing janitorial services and is the cost for this service part of the lease price?

❑ Does the space have a workroom or break room?

❑ Does the space have a kitchen?

Extra Charges

- ❏ What services and utilities are included in the lease price?

- ❏ What services and utilities are provided by the landlord for a fee?

- ❏ What services and utilities are the responsibility of the tenant?

Shared Tenant Services, Spaces, Costs, Responsibilities

- ❏ Are there any shared tenant spaces?

- ❏ Are there any shared tenant responsibilities?

- ❏ Is there a mandatory tenant association?

- ❏ Are there any costs that tenants are required to share?

Extra Benefits and Features

- ❏ Are there any extra benefits or features that make this space especially desirable?

Notes:

_____

_____

_____

_____

_____

_____

_____

_____

5.1.3 Signing Your Lease

Signing a lease for your store space is quite a bit more than putting your signature at the bottom of a legal document. There are a variety of different lease options you can have and a number of things to consider when putting together the details in your lease.

Be sure the following things are clearly stated:

- Who is responsible for what repairs?

- What types of signs can you use? Are there any restrictions on sidewalk sales or signs to draw customers into the store?

- Can you change the colors and décor of the store? (Some malls have very specific rules.)

- Can you make alterations to suit your needs?

- Is there any security?

What to Include in a Lease

Your lease is the legal agreement that makes it clear what each party will do (or won't do). Therefore it is vital that you get everything you expect regarding your store space written into the lease. For example, once you have located a space you really like there still may be a number of improvements that you want to have happen before you move in.

Regular Improvements

Regular improvements are the things that a landlord will do for any prospective tenant — no matter what their business. These are the things that need to be done to prepare the space. Some of the things you should expect (although you should check just to be sure) include:

- Having the space prepared and cleaned by a professional janitorial service

- Painting the interior or exterior of the building as part of normal wear and tear

- Replacing worn bathroom fixtures, mini blinds, or broken fixtures

- Replacing worn or damaged carpet or flooring

Specific Improvements Requests

Specific improvements are the things you want to see done to your space to make it the way you dream it should be. This might include:

- Adding partitions

- Installing a door or a window

- Creating storage or office space

- A break room for employees

In short, these improvements are the things you might hire a contractor to do.

Based on the term of your lease (a longer-term lease makes a landlord more willing to help fund improvements), your landlord will need to agree to the specific improvements that you want to make to the space and all of this will need to be included in the lease agreement. You must determine what the landlord will let you do, what the landlord will fund, what you will need to fund, and who will do the work.

> TIP: If the space you are considering needs too many improvements, maybe you haven't found the right space. Consider looking for a space that fits more of your needs before you commit to a long or complicated improvement plan.

Types of Leases

First you will need to consider the type of lease that will work best for your salon. Your lease will most likely fall into one of these categories:

Month-to-Month Lease

A month-to-month lease is the most flexible kind of lease agreement you can have. If you think you might want to get out of your lease quickly, all that is necessary to do so is 30 days notice. Naturally, there is a downside to this sort of a lease. With a month-to-month lease, you aren't locked into a price for a reasonable length of time, plus the landlord can ask you to leave with 30 days notice.

Short-Term Fixed Rate Lease

While a short-term fixed rate lease has all the benefits of a shorter month-to-month lease, it also locks you into a fixed price for the length of the lease. This sort of commitment might be wise if you are truly concerned about giving up your current job to open your store and want a short amount of time to see if it will really work. With a short-term lease, you can add verbiage in the lease to determine what happens after the lease ends. What happens next is up to you and the landlord to negotiate.

Long-Term Lease

A long-term lease is a lease with a term of a year or more. Long-term leases that are for several years or even longer are called "multi-year leases." The best thing about a long-term lease is that once you find a great space, you can stay there for as long as you want.

Negotiating Leases

Be very careful when negotiating a lease. If you commit to paying $1,200 a month for two years, that is nearly $30,000. Try to get the shortest term lease available, especially as you start out. There is a possibility this could backfire and you could lose your space, but finding a new space is a better alternative than owing thousands of dollars on a store that is not thriving.

Some business owners don't realize that a lease document prepared and presented by a potential landlord is a negotiating tool. You certainly don't have to accept the terms of a lease that you are uncomfortable with, and you can negotiate for the things you would like to see either added to or removed from the lease.

The lease written by a landlord is written in the landlord's best interests, not yours, so look for what you feel needs to be changed or amended to make the lease fit your requirements. Remember, the process of signing a lease is a negotiating experience. Both you and your landlord will probably need to bend a little to come up with a document that works well for both of you.

Don't feel pressured into signing a lease as soon as it is handed to you. Plan on taking the document away with you so you can read it carefully, and, if you wish, show it to a qualified attorney for advice. Good advice on leasing, including an article called "Commercial Leases: Negotiate the Best Terms" can be found at **www.nolo.com/legal-encyclopedia/article-29754.html**.

Sample Lease with Comments

In the sample lease below, we will point out potential problem areas. Note that the comments are simply suggestions about some matters you may want to consider. These are opinions based on our research, and do not come from a lawyer or a commercial real estate agent. As your own situation is unique, make sure you have a lawyer who is familiar with business leases look over any lease before you sign it.

Opening Section

This lease is made between Big Commercial Landlord, herein after called the Lessor, and Stella Stylist, hereinafter called the Lessee.

This is a pretty standard clause in any contract and simply states who are the parties to the lease agreement. If you are a corporation, then you may want to try to use your corporate name as the Lessee. Sometimes, this clause will include your home address.

Lessee herby offers to lease from Lessor the premises located in the city of Greenfield, in the County of Hancock, in the State of Indiana, described as 197 State Street, Suite C, based upon the terms and conditions as outlined below.

This clause outlines the specific space you are agreeing to lease. Things to watch for would be any mistakes in the address. If it is a building

---

with several store spaces, double check that the suite number is correct. You could wind up leasing more square feet than you wanted or losing a prime location.

1. Term and Rent

Lessee agrees to rent the above premises for a term of two years, commencing July 1, 2010, and terminating on June 30, 2012, or sooner as provided herein at the annual rental of 7,200 dollars ($7,200.00), payable in equal monthly installments of 600 dollars ($600.00) in advance on the first day of each month for that month's rental, during the term of this lease. All payments should be made directly to the Lessor at the address specified in paragraph one.

Some of this information is a little hard to break down, but section 1 basically outlines how much rent you will be paying. Double check that the monthly rent matches the yearly sum. Be sure the day you have agreed to is the day that the rent is due and not sooner. Also, you might want to try to get a shorter term on the lease, if possible. Many landlords will negotiate on this point. Two years is standard.

2. Use

Lessee shall use and occupy the premises for a hair salon operation called Enchanté. The location shall be used for no other purpose. Lessor represents that the premises may lawfully be used for the purpose stated above.

This simply states what your business will be. The thing to be most cautious of here is making sure that all things are listed. One thing that jumps right out in the above description is that it does not allow for retail sales of other items besides the main retail sector merchandise. You may want to add additional complementary lines of merchandise that aren't directly related to the main retail business you're in. You should ask to have this added before signing the lease.

3. Care and Maintenance of the Premises

Lessee recognizes that the premises are in good repair, unless otherwise indicated herein. Lessee shall, at the Lessee's own expense and at all times, maintain the premises in good and safe order, including plate glass, electrical wiring, plumbing and heating and any other equipment on the premises. Lessee shall return the same at termination of contract, in as good condition as received, normal wear and tear excepted. Lessee shall be responsible for all repairs required, excepting the roof, exterior walls, and structural foundations.

As you can probably see already, there are many potential problems with this clause. You may have a hard time getting a landlord to change some of these requirements. While it is acceptable for them to ask you to fix any problems you may have caused, such as damage to walls, the idea that you are responsible for heating and cooling systems is a bit troublesome. This could run into very costly repairs. In addition, the lease does not state what responsibility the landlord has to fix such problems. Ask that this section be made much more specific, with phrases such as "normal wear and tear" defined explicitly.

In addition, you might want to double check with your insurance company to be sure that if the roof leaks you would be covered under their policy. If not, will you be covered for any loss under the landlord's policy and what is the system for recourse?

4. Alterations

Lessee shall not, without first obtaining written consent of Lessor, make any additions, alterations, or improvements to the premises.

Again, this is way too vague. What is their definition of an addition or alteration? If you put in slat walls to display your merchandise, is that considered a violation of the contract? Ask for some more specifics here. The inability to add display fixtures could really hinder your business. Do not wait until after you have signed the contract to find out you can't create the store you have envisioned because of a clause in the lease agreement.

5. Ordinances and Statutes

Lessee shall comply with all ordinances, statues and requirements of state, federal and local authorities.

This is pretty much a given and you really have no choice but to do this anyway.

6. Subletting

Lessee shall not assign or sublet any portion of this lease or premises without prior written consent of the Lessor, which shall not be unreasonably withheld. Any such assignment or subletting without consent shall be void and may terminate this lease.

This is pretty straightforward and standard.

7. Utilities

All applications and connections for utility services on the stated premises shall be made in the name of the Lessee only, and Lessee shall be solely liable for utility charges as they become due, including charges for gas, water, sewer, electricity, and telephone.

This, too, is standard. It is your responsibility to cover your utilities with most landlords. There are a few who will cover some costs. It depends on the building and the landlord.

8. Entry and Inspections

Lessee will permit Lessor or agents of Lessor to enter the premises during reasonable times and with notice and will permit the Lessor to post "For Lease" signs within ninety (90) days prior to the expiration of this lease.

This is pretty standard, however, try to get a specific statement about what type of notice, how the Lessee will receive the notice and what constitutes reasonable times (i.e. regular business hours). It is also standard to allow them to place "For Lease" signs sixty days prior to the expiration of the contract. This is not a major point, but you may want to request it, if you feel the signs might hinder your business in any way.

9. Indemnification of Lessor

The Lessor will not be held liable for any damage or injury to Lessee, or any other person, or property occurring on the stated premises. Lessee agrees to not hold Lessor liable for any damages regardless of how they are caused.

This section is troubling. What if the Lessor knows there is a structural fault with the building, does not fix it and you or one of your customers are harmed? Get the landlord to strike this clause or have it changed.

10. Insurance

Lessee shall retain public liability and property damage insurance at the Lessee's own cost.

This is standard, and you will want this anyway. Some contracts may go on further and state the exact types of coverage you will need and/or amounts. Some will require proof of insurance.

11. Destruction of Property

Should the premises be destroyed in part or whole, Lessor shall repair the property within sixty (60) days. Lessee shall be entitled to a deduction in rent during the time the repairs are taking place. If there are repairs which cannot be made within sixty (60) days, this lease may be terminated at the request of either party.

You will want this standard clause, as well. If your space is compromised, you want the landlord to repair the defect as quickly as possible. Otherwise, you could lose business indefinitely. If they are not able to make the repairs in a timely manner, you have the option of terminating the lease and moving your store elsewhere.

12. Nonpayment of Rent

If Lessee defaults on regular payment of rent, or defaults on the other conditions herein, Lessor may give Lessee notice of the default and if the Lessee does not cure the default within thirty (30) days, after receiving written notice of the default, Lessor may terminate this lease.

This is pretty simple. If you do not pay your rent, then the landlord reserves the right to ask you to remove your store from the premises. You may want to try to get sixty days instead of thirty but there is not much wiggle room with this clause.

13. Security Deposit

Lessee shall pay a security deposit upon the signing of this lease to Lessor for the sum of 600 dollars ($600.00). Lessor shall keep the full amount of the security deposit available throughout the term of this lease.

Although a security deposit equaling the first month's rent is pretty standard, I would want to see a bit more detail here about how and under what conditions this money will be returned to the Lessee. This is pretty vague and you may wind up not getting your deposit back. Landlords have been known to make up phony repair or cleaning charges so they can keep your deposit.

14. Attorney's Fees

In the event of a suit being brought for recovery of the premises, or for any sum due under the conditions of this contract, the prevailing party shall be entitled to reimbursement of all costs, including but not limited to attorney's fees.

15. Notices

All notices to either party shall be provided in writing at the address listed on this contract.

Both clauses 14 and 15 are standard.

16. Option to Renew

As long as Lessee is not in default of this lease, Lessee shall have the option of renewing the lease for an additional term of twelve (12) months starting upon the expiration of the term of the original lease. All the terms and conditions herein outlined shall apply during the extension. This option can be implemented by giving written notice to the Lessor at least ninety (90) days prior to the expiration.

I would try for sixty days prior on the notice. You may be looking for another place and not quite sure if you are moving out in three months.

17. Entire Agreement

The preceding makes up the entire agreement between the parties and may only be modified by agreement of both parties in writing.

Signed this___ day of _____, 20__.

_____

Stella Stylist, Lessee

_____

Big Commercial Landlord, Lessor

5.2 Salon Design

Once you have chosen your space, you will need to decorate the inside and outside. To help you in this task, you may want to start by choosing a "theme" for your salon. Once you have decided on a theme, you can choose your salon layout, logo, background music, lighting, and even scents that will pull your salon and its theme together.

Will your salon be contemporary or old-fashioned? Will it be hip and young, relaxing, or upscale? It is important to choose an atmosphere that will draw customers into your salon and reflect the type of merchandise you plan to offer.

Don't forget that displays will need to be updated to maintain your "look," so choose something low maintenance. Many customers prefer well-organized stores to trendy ones where they can't move without bumping into things.

5.2.1 Outside the Salon

Remember the external appearance of your salon is the first impression potential customers have of your business. It should be neat but eye-catching.

Does it need a fresh coat of paint? If the landlord is responsible for outside paint but does not seem in a hurry to finish the project, offer to paint it yourself for a discount on your rent that month. Let's say the paint costs you $30, and it takes you two hours to paint. You figure your time is worth $20 an hour. You would ask the landlord to grant you a seventy dollar credit on that month's rent (arrange this before you paint). Many landlords will work with you on this because it saves them money and the aggravation of hiring an outside contractor. Your bonus is a fresh coat of paint to hang your new, bright sign upon.

Signage

After your choice of name and location, your choice of signage is probably the most important aspect of creating interest in your location. Your signage could mean the difference between bringing foot traffic right to your salon or people walking right on by.

Your signs should reflect your style. To create more effective and professional-looking signs you might decide to have a local painter create a wonderful, vintage-looking sign for your storefront. Make sure you can see it from a distance and it shows clearly what your shop is selling.

You will want an eye-catching sign that customers can see from the street. A good sign can actually entice customers into your salon. Your sign should make a statement about your store, have a simple logo, and make the customer want to visit you. If your municipality allows it, you might also put up roadside signs to direct buyers to your salon.

Logo

"One of our most effective marketing tools was the phrase 'Cut Above the Rest', a slogan I and my brother-in-law came up with and trademarked in 1968. We incorporated all of our marketing around it and still use it today."

— Philip Pelusi, creator of P2 hair products;
owner, Tela Design Studio

With some of today's inexpensive graphics software, it is possible to create your own simple logo and use it on your sign and other business materials. People will come to associate your store with that logo. There are companies, such as MyLogoDesigners.com or LogoYes.com, that you can pay to create a logo for you. MyLogoDesigners.com will create a custom designed logo for you for about $129 for a basic package. With LogoYes.com, you design your own logo using their online template that uses standard clip art. They charge about $69 for a logo design or $100 for a logo with 100 business cards.

You could also purchase software that lets you design your logo on your own. There are a number of different programs like Logo Design Studio (**www.summitsoftcorp.com/products/Logo-Design-Studio**), for example, which sell for less than $50. If you decide you want to design your own logo with this type of software, be sure they offer a demo version that you can try out first, so that you know it meets your needs. Most local print shops also offer design services, since they already have the software for it. Keep in mind that, if you have already chosen a theme, your sign and logo can be a good place to tie into that theme again.

> *"One quick way to distinguish your salon from the competition is to have a signature tag line. The one I created for Salon Acote in Boston is "Boston's' Most French Salon." That says it in a nutshell. For another hair salon, also French, I created this tagline: "The hair salon with a French Twist."*

>   — Debbi Kickham, Owner of PR firm
>   Maxima Marketing

Lettering and Fonts

Make sure the letters on your sign are large enough that customers will be able to spot the words from a distance. If your sign will be more than 400 feet from the street front, then you will want to use seven- to ten-inch high letters. If you are located inside a mall, where you will not need to be visible from a street, then you may be able to use lettering between three and a half to seven inches.

Watch the fonts you use for your sign. A fancy script may look nice, but customers might have a difficult time reading the letters. Use both upper and lowercase letters for some variety and to make the sign easier to read. The colors of the sign should contrast with one another — dark and light colors work best (black and white, yellow and navy blue, white and royal blue).

You might find hiring an expert for this particular job worthwhile even though it will cost you a little extra money. Most small towns have stores that create signs for local businesses. Be sure that you get several quotes for your project, as prices can vary widely. Also, do not rule out buying the sign used. You may be able to locate a simple sign without a store name at a store that is going out of business

Be sure to check with your landlord or city zoning board to find out about any ordinances on signs. Some cities have very specific guide-lines about height and other requirements, particularly if you're in a heritage area where local history is used as a tourism draw. It's better to check with your municipality before investing a lot of money in a sign you can't use.

Also, most malls have specific requirements for store signs, such as re-quiring a minimum/maximum letter height, lighted signs, etc. If your location comes with a place to install a sign, you will probably be able to order an appropriate sign with the help of the mall's management. Professional sign companies offer design and manufacturing — check in your local Yellow Pages under the "Signs — Commercial" category. Another option is to order a sign online. Here are a few companies that specialize in signs for businesses:

- *Capitol Design Sandblasted Signs*
  www.sandblastedsigns.com

- *Spring Valley Signs*
  www.springvalleysigns.com

- *American Sign Company*
  www.americansignco.biz

- *Custom Hand-Carved Signs by Sally Claus Focht*
  www.customhandcarvedsigns.com

- *Lincoln Sign Company*
  www.lincolnsign.com

5.2.2   Inside the Salon

Interior design is really one of the most enjoyable parts of opening your own salon. There is nothing like planning and preparing for your salon, and then suddenly seeing it ready, in all its glory, just waiting for the first customer to step through the door. Planning your space helps you create an environment that customers will love and enjoy being in.

Creating a space that customers love will encourage them to buy — and to return again. Your layout will depend upon a variety of factors, such as the space available, the shape of that space and the amount of items you have available.

To design the interior space of your store, imagine your store full of customers. What are their needs? What are their expectations? What sort of design elements will help your customers move through your door, enjoy the process of getting their hair done or shopping in your salon, and have a positive experience purchasing what they want? How can you set up a functional store interior that will help them get what they want and leave, happily anticipating their next return trip?

Customers tend to head to the right when they enter a store. Keep that space open and put special items up front. Think about the possible layouts and how you want the traffic to flow through the store. Be sure to leave plenty of room around the cash register in case you have several customers in the store at once.

How can you utilize wall space? If you have ever been in a clothing store at the mall, you have probably noticed how they use those slatted walls and hang hooks with clothing right on the walls. By utilizing this space, they are able to display a lot more merchandise than if they only used the center of the floor. Think about ways you can use your wall areas most effectively.

Salon Layout

As you will see from the sample salon layouts included on the next few pages, it is important that the traffic in your salon be able to flow from point A to point B. You can print or photocopy the samples below to create a mock-up of your own retail space to help you with designing a layout that works well for your salon.

Sample Salon Layout - Large Salon

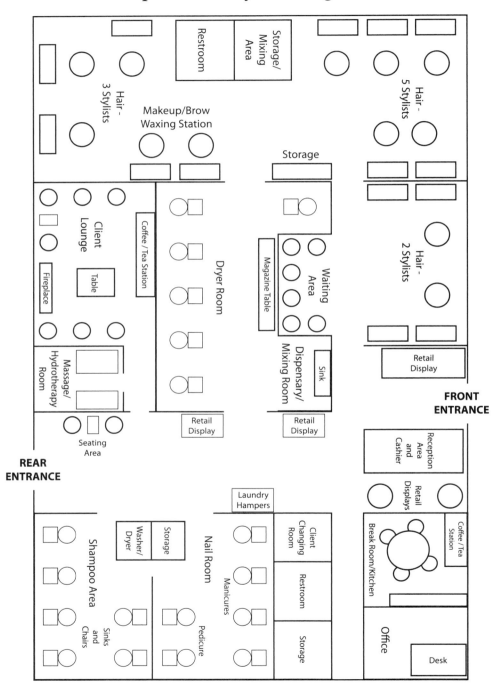

Sample Salon Layout - Small Salon

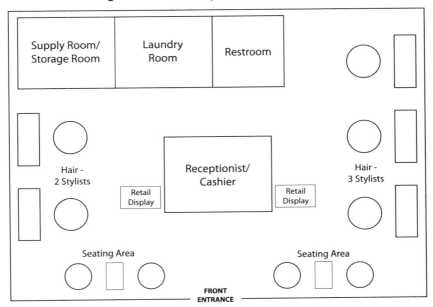

Keep in mind there will be times when more than one person is in your store. If there is a crowd, is there room for them to pass one another? What about wheelchairs or other special needs? The layout of your store can affect how long a customer stays and how many items they purchase. Have you ever been in a large retail store late at night when they are restocking? Boxes are stacked everywhere and you can't move from one aisle to the next. Sadly, some retail stores don't look much better during non-restocking times. Do not let your store become a super center nightmare.

Keep aisles clear and easy to move through. Do not shove displays or racks so close to one another that your customers won't be able to make their way between them. Spend some time considering the flow of traffic. Your main aisle should have plenty of room and be easily accessible from the front entrance. Mark everything clearly with signs so that customers can quickly locate items of interest to them.

Your entry should be open and inviting. Have a mat for the entryway and leave space for deliveries. The sales floor should be uncluttered and clearly organized. It should be clear to customers where various items are located. You can use in-store signs that show customers where to find different categories of merchandise.

If your type of business allows for it, an area for children to play can be a good idea. A play area to keep children occupied is greatly appreciated by shoppers with small children. If there is a play area where parents can keep an eye on the children but still have a little freedom to shop, they will be much more likely to linger in your store and buy more. Is your clientele likely to have children? If so, then you will definitely want a small table and some coloring supplies. Some store owners offer small televisions and appropriate videos in the play area as well.

Cash Register Area

Make your cash desk appealing and functional. Your cash register should be in a spot where you can greet customers as they come into the salon, while allowing you to keep an eye on the rest of the store. Do not overcrowd the checkout area. Keep in mind your customers may have their arms loaded with items and will want a place to set them down. You should have a worktop that allows enough room for placing purchases and also some business cards nicely displayed along with comment cards, leaving room for impulse displays.

Have you ever grabbed an item you hadn't planned to purchase while waiting in a checkout line? This is called impulse buying, and you want your customers to do this in your store, too. Place interesting items near the register, especially smaller, lower-priced items that people might find attractive or that complement other higher priced merchandise. You might even consider selling magazines, books, or other informational materials. Whatever you do display though, keep it tidy and relevant.

You'll learn more about merchandise displays in section 5.3.

Be sure to put out some business cards and brochures for customers to take and share with others. Magnetized business cards are a good investment and remind customers of your store each time they go to their refrigerator.

Another consideration is all the point-of-sale and other equipment and retail supplies you will need at your cash desk. Make sure there is space behind your counter for credit card processing machines, your computer, bags, packing materials and other sales aids. Your cash desk will likely need to have shelving and drawers built into it for storage of supplies.

Indoor Lighting

Harsh fluorescent lighting may sound like something you would worry over in an office building, but it can change the look of items you are trying to sell, too. It can make items look washed out or a different or unappealing color.

Certain types of lighting can also disturb customers and cause them to leave the store sooner than you would like. If you have ever walked into a bookstore with flickering fluorescent lights and tried to read the back cover of a book, you know how irritating this can be. You don't want your customers walking out on you because you chose the wrong lighting.

Be aware of small things like this. You can become so used to them that you are not even aware of the problem. Watch your customers. Be aware of their reactions and ask questions if they seem irritated.

5.2.3   Salon Security

One of the facts of life in retail is that you can become the target of shoplifters. While you may be concerned about theft of costly items such as flat irons, shoplifters can make off with shampoos, conditioners, hair accessories, or any other products they want.

How you lay out your retail area is an important component of deterring shoplifting. Try not to stack items too high in the center of your store. Keep displays low enough that you and your staff can see over them. Another good tip is not to keep small items in areas where you have difficulty keeping an eye on them.

You should also learn and teach any staff you hire about how to be on the lookout for suspicious behavior. Place a security mirror to reflect corners you can't see from your cash desk. A security camera is also a great idea to aid in apprehending anyone you think might be shoplifting.

Ways to Spot a Potential Shoplifter

- Carries a slightly open umbrella (especially if there isn't a cloud in the sky) to use to drop or push small items into, as they "browse."

- Wears a coat too heavy for the season

- Two shoppers come in and one distracts you while the other goes to a hard-to-see area of the store.

- A single shopper comes in and sends the only clerk to the back of the store to find something.

- A group of shoppers comes in and they all separate making it difficult to watch them all.

- Carefully watch customers who are carrying bags, large open purses, or have an arm in a sling.

- Be suspicious of customers who seem to be walking funny, tugging at their sleeves, or holding their coats closed.

- Shoplifters often engage clerks in describing items, but don't appear to be interested in the answers.

- Often, shoplifters will quickly scope the store. Real shoppers tend to seem genuinely interested and less erratic.

- Be wary of people who drop things; this might be a ruse to hide an item.

You need to deter burglars as well and your business insurance policy might require you to install an alarm system. A good alarm system can pay for itself in reduced rates and thwarting would-be thieves.

There are many security companies who can provide you with the equipment and support you'll need to keep your store secure. Check out your local Yellow Pages to find security companies in your area. To learn more about security for your store you can check out ADT Security Services (**www.adt.com/small_business**) who offer a variety of services for surveillance and alarms systems for small business owners. Broadview Security is another trusted name in security systems. You can find out about the many services they offer for small businesses at **www.broadviewsecurity-business.com**.

> **TIP:** Check with your landlord to see if they will cover the cost of installation if the alarms are not already provided (you can purchase basic alarms at any hardware or department store).

5.3 Displaying Merchandise

While there are many different theories on how a store should be merchandised, the most important thing is to arrange your items to give an organized and clean appearance.

> **TIP:** Books and magazines about interior design may give you ideas for displays and help you create a style for your shop. Additionally, most community colleges offer night classes in decorating that would help you understand the principles needed to create eye-catching and pleasing displays.

5.3.1 Maximizing Sales

Where to Place Items

Merchandise with the highest margin of profit should be placed at the front of your store. This way the customer passes it twice—once on the way in, and once on the way out. You want these to jump out and grab customers as they walk in the door and as they walk out. Display these goods in special ways so that they attract attention quickly.

Popular items that most people are looking for (whatever the current trend is) should be placed at the back of the store. That way, people will need to walk through almost your entire inventory in order to get to those pieces. This is exactly why milk is always at the back of the supermarket.

Most stores place their clearance racks in the back of the store. This is a good idea because your profit margin is much smaller on these items. This is not where you want your customers to fall in love with the items they just have to have. Instead, you want them to browse through the main selections first (which will bring you more of a profit), and get through to the clearance racks last. If they spend all their money on clearance merchandise you have at the front of the store, they will not have any left for your high profit items.

Impulse Displays

Think about the checkout area of your favorite big name stores. "Oh, yes," you say as you stand there waiting for the cashier, "I really need batteries, a book light, and some air freshener." This is called impulse displaying and you can do the same thing. Think about placing some special groups of items that people might overlook normally, such as small bottles of hair products or hair accessories. You could move any number of smaller items closer to your cash area, or perhaps items that tweak your customers' interest and trigger an impulse purchase. Try displaying different items week by week to see what sells best.

Also try not to stuff too much merchandise onto a display rack. This is an occupational hazard. It is better to leave some items in the back room and pull them out a little at a time than to have racks so full the customer can't see what you have in stock.

Displaying on the Sidewalk

This is a tough one. While you should not put your cheapest things out front, there is something to be said for enticing customers to visit the salon. You might build customer loyalty and get repeat customers. A sidewalk display is the perfect way to accomplish this. Make sure you are allowed to have items on the sidewalk. Read your lease carefully. Some malls (even strip malls) will not allow this.

So, should you sidewalk display or not? The final decision is up to you, but you should at least try sidewalk displays to see if they improve your sales. For example, you could have a sidewalk sale on your high profit items with 10% off (you still make a good profit but still offer a sale). Many merchant associations, especially in downtown areas, regularly host sidewalk sales to encourage shoppers who normally would only visit the local mall to shop in their area.

The effectiveness of this type of promotion may also depend upon the type of items you are selling and the area where you are located. You may want to test the waters. One weekend have your discounted clearance items on the sidewalk and the next keep them inside. Compare the sales for each weekend (they need to be comparable weekends and not when a special event is in town or on a holiday weekend).

5.3.2   Creating Window Displays

If you are fortunate to have a great window with a view to a well-traveled sidewalk, be sure to take advantage of it to make your salon irresistible to passing customers. Think of creating little vignettes with similar items. Whatever you do put in the window, make sure that it won't be ruined by exposure to sunlight.

Window displays are a good place to let your creativity shine. You'll want to put your best items on display. Your goal is to draw customers into your salon Exciting window displays will encourage customers to come in and check out your services. Some things to remember:

- Make sure the glass is clean with no streaks. You may have to clean the windows often, particularly if your clientele includes children, but it will be worth the effort.

- Even when you aren't open, you may want to light the window displays to attract new customers who will see the items and come back during regular business hours.

- A few props can go a long way. Think thematically, and try to incorporate things like holidays, special local events or the passing seasons into your displays.

Here's a list of basic ideas to tie in the season with merchandise in your window display (let loose your creativity and imagination from there):

Autumn:	Brightly colored leaves and a few large branches with a couple of large pumpkins in the center.
Spring:	Flowers and greenery suggest spring. A strategically placed fan can create the impression of a breeze.
Summer:	A beach theme is easy with some inexpensive sand, sea shells, and beach balls. (The sand cleans up easily with a shop vacuum.)

Winter: Christmas trees and lights create an eye-catching display. Create a snowy scene using cotton batting or even a white sheet.

Window Design Basics

There are a few design basics to keep in mind when you are designing a window display.

- You should have one item that is your focal point.

- Arranging odd numbers of items on various levels is more pleasing.

- Group items in threes, fives, and sevens.

- Use boxes under lovely fabrics to create more levels, or better yet, a variety of stands, small tables and chairs.

Remember that you need to be prepared to sell items out of your window displays. When you do, you'll have to think of new items to add to the mix that will work as well or perhaps redesign the display a little to incorporate something new into it.

An example of a simple yet elegant display concept is that of the upscale Salon Acote in Boston. First, the salon is located right on Newbury Street in Boston. The front windows, which measure approximately 12 by 13 feet wide, pivot open and have window boxes. Every Wednesday, Alison Safar goes to the fresh flower market and chooses the flowers to use for the week, which keeps the changing flower displays looking fresh and new. These displays vary seasonally with the fresh flowers that are available.

Using flowers she has carefully chosen, she creates six-foot tall arrangements to place in the windows. Behind these striking floral arrangements are simple placards bearing the shop's name and logo. This beautiful display is complemented by soft music that is piped throughout the salon as well as onto the street, serenading and drawing the attention of people as they pass by. Inside the two-story salon, which features an outdoor patio area with furniture where clients can relax while their hair processes or their nails dry, she places three additional floral arrangements on the first floor, and two on the upper floor and out on the patio.

5.4   Business Equipment and Supplies

5.4.1   Items You'll Need

In addition to the fixtures you'll need to display merchandise, there are a variety of other items you will need to equip your salon. This section begins with suggestions for various areas of the salon, followed by information about suppliers. Check what your salon already has, or what your landlord provides, and make your shopping list.

In addition to the items below, section 6.3.1 has advice on computer equipment and supplies. For information about how to find manufacturers and wholesalers who can supply you with inventory for your store, see section 5.5.

Special Equipment and Supplies

General Salon Supplies

- Camera System: In some large salons, having a good camera system makes it easier for a busy owner overseeing many employees and salon areas to keep tabs of things during business hours.

- Capes and Drapes: These are important for protecting clients' clothing from chemicals and keeping them from getting covered with hair.

- Chairs: Salon chairs should be comfortable for both clients and stylists. Stylist station chairs are usually adjustable in height.

- Computer Systems

- Mirrors: You will need large wall mirrors for each work station as well as hand-held mirrors to allow clients to view the backs of their heads.

- Schedule Book/Program: You'll need a schedule book or computer program with good visibility that is easy to use and is easy to make changes in.

- Towels, Washer, Dryer, Washing Supplies: You will need many towels for your salon, and thus will likely need a washer and dryer on the premises to keep up with the constant chore of laundry. Even those salons that outsource some of their laundry generally do at least some of their own laundry on site.

Hair Styling Equipment and Supplies

- Blow dryers and diffusers: You will need powerful professional quality blow dryers with good UL ratings. Be careful to plug them in away from water sources to avoid electrical hazards and keep cords where people will not trip over them and they will not become tangled.

- Brushes: various types to handle all types of hair.

- Clamps, clips, rubber bands, bobby pins, clear elastic bands

- Coloring Supplies (gloves, foil, processing caps, neck strips, skin cream, etc.)

- Combs (pick, rat tails, etc.)

- Curling Irons and flat irons

- Hair Extensions, bonding glue, braiding hair (synthetic or natural), nylon thread (for weaves)

TIP: DaRico Jackson, owner and celebrity stylist of Amiri in Beverly Hills, recommends pony yaki hair instead of kankaleon because "it's soft, easy to use and does not cut through the client's natural hair in the braiding process."

Jackson suggests bonding glue that is free of rubber "so the natural oils don't soften the glue and it holds up through a good moisturizing shampoo and conditioner."

Consider using nylon instead of cotton for a natural looking weave. "Nylon is more secure," explains DaRico Jackson, "and after so many shampoos it doesn't expand or dissolve, this way your weave lasts longer and stays secure."

- Hair Styling Products: shampoos, conditioners, perm chemicals, chemical hair relaxers and straighteners

- Pressing Combs (for straightening hair)

- Razors: (handheld, straightedge and electric)

- Rollers and perm rods, in a variety of sizes and types.

- Scissors: regular hair cutting scissors, thinning shears, trimming scissors

- Spray bottles

- Timers

General Business Supplies and Equipment

- Bags

- Boxes

- Blank gift certificates

- Signs ("Sale", "Open/Closed", "Store Hours", etc.)

- Cash register

- Credit card machines

- Office Supplies

- Filing cabinets

- Desks

- Chairs

- Office supplies (pens, paper, stapler, scissors, tape, markers, clips, etc.)

- Phones

- Answering machine or voice mail

- Internet connection

- Computer

- Software

- Printer (consider a combination fax/printer/copier/scanner)

- FAX machine

- Copier (optional)

TIP: If you watch closely, you can sometimes catch free or almost free telephones after rebate. OfficeMax, Office Depot, and Staples have all offered these at one time or another. Watch your Sunday circulars and you may be able to find a great deal on some of the items you will need.

Price Labels

Most retail stores use either simple labels with neat, handwritten prices or printed price stickers from a pricing gun or computer printer. If you're starting out on a shoestring budget, you might consider self-adhesive labels, but be very careful. Some labels leave glue residue on items, and will sometimes cause a permanent mark when removed.

Many retailers use string tags that they can tie onto their merchandise. Use these for larger, more visible items because some people might be tempted to remove a higher price tag and replace it with a lower price one from other items. You might be aware of the price of items in your store, but your part-time staff might not.

Some store owners use bar code tags that work with whatever type of software and scanner they are using. It sounds expensive, and initially it might be, but if you get very busy the time you save keeping track of your inventory might pay for it. (You can read more about inventory systems, pricing and labels in section 6.3.2)

TIP: Worn tags make customers aware that an item has been around for a long time. When you're dusting, take the time to replace worn tags.

Overall Salon/Retail Area

- Paint

- Wallpaper

- Window treatments (e.g. blinds)

- Wall decorations

- Carpeting or area rugs

- Trash cans and trash bags

- Broom and dust pan

- Mop

- Vacuum cleaner

- Cleaning supplies

- Air filters

- Light bulbs

- Fire extinguishers

- Fire alarm

- Burglar alarm

Break Room

- Tables

- Chairs

- Refrigerator

- Microwave

- Time clock

- Bulletin board for employee laws and other postings

- Coffee maker and coffee supplies

- Stationery

If you plan on sending out mailings to clients or suppliers, you may wish to consider having your own stationery printed up. This can include business cards, letterhead, envelopes, and any other special items you can think of. Section 7.1.4 provides detailed information about stationery and suppliers.

5.4.2   Suppliers

Many suppliers can be found simply by checking your local Yellow Pages. However, we have included some links in this guide to help you with your search for suppliers. Office supplies and equipment are readily available and office supply chains offer competitive prices.

General Business Supplies

Office supplies are easy to find and can be purchased at a variety of locations. Office supply chain stores are competitively priced, and may deliver if you buy in quantity.

- *Office Depot*
  www.officedepot.com

- *OfficeMax*
  www.officemax.com

- *Staples*
  www.staples.com

Retail Supplies

To find supplies for retail (such as bags, gift certificates, etc.) you can check the Yellow Pages or do an online search for retail supplies. Here are a few suppliers to get you started. You may need a copy of your retail license to get the wholesale rate or to avoid paying sales tax.

- *NEBS*
  www.nebs.com

- *Paper Mart*
  www.papermart.com

- *Bags & Bows*
  www.bagsandbowsonline.com

- *Shopping Bags Direct*
  www.shoppingbagsdirect.com

Cash Registers

You will need a safe place to keep your cash. You may decide to use a common lockbox, or you may want something more advanced. You can purchase cash registers that can be programmed to work with your computer or you can purchase freestanding systems. You may want to start simple and then upgrade to a deluxe model as your business grows. As with other types of equipment, there are a number of places you can find cash registers (including eBay) for used and your local office supply store or cash register supplier for new.

- *eBay*
  www.ebay.com

- *Cash Register Store*
  http://cashregisterstore.com

- *Cash Register Sales, Service and Supply, Inc.*
  www.cashregisterman.com

Display Fixtures

To find shelves and fixtures for displaying the merchandise you are selling, you can check the Yellow Pages or do an online search for retail fixtures. The Yahoo! Business Directory at **http://dir.yahoo.com/Business_ and_Economy** lists a large number of companies that sell store fixtures. To find these, choose the "Business to Business" link and then scroll down to the "Retail Management" link, where you'll find a "Fixtures" link.

Here are a few additional sites to get you started:

- *Display Warehouse*
  www.displaywarehouse.com

- *Franklin Fixtures*
  www.franklinfixtures.com

- *Victory Display Equipment*
  www.victorydisplay.com

- *Eddie's Hang-Up Display Ltd.*
  www.eddies.com

You might also consider building the fixtures yourself or hiring someone to do so. For used displays, try publications like The Trader (**www.traderonline.com**), and check out the classifieds in your local newspaper. Do not overlook auction sites like eBay for additional opportunities to pick up display racks at a reasonable price. Also be on the lookout for stores going out of business. You can approach them and offer to purchase their display fixtures.

5.5 Obtaining Your Inventory

Without a doubt, the most important items you will purchase for your retail store are the products you will sell. The online encyclopedia, Wikipedia, defines inventory as "a list of goods and materials held available in stock that also brings associated costs for space, for utilities, and for insurance to cover staff to handle and protect it." These are important concepts to keep in mind when purchasing your inventory.

You'll want to match your inventory to your clientele and make sure that you know how to choose the right products as well as where to find them. You don't want your inventory collecting dust in your store and tying up your valuable space and resources.

How much do you need at first? That is a personal preference. Some retail store owners want to have a large quantity of items before opening, and others take things on consignment and only need a few items to get started. Below are some tips to help you develop a starting inventory and where you can find merchandise to sell.

5.5.1 Wholesalers

A wholesaler buys products from the manufacturer, usually in large quantities, and resells them in smaller lots to retailers. As a result, the wholesaler is sometimes referred to as the "middleman" between retailers and manufacturers.

You will get the best deal if you can buy directly from the manufacturer. However, some may not be willing to sell to you because of their arrangements with their current wholesalers. In those cases, you will need to go to the wholesaler.

The best wholesale supply sources for your salon will vary by state. Distributors generally serve different areas of the country, and distributors do not carry all product or color or retail lines, so it's best to decide what product line(s) you want to use and then figure out which suppliers that service your area carry those products.

Deciding on Product Lines to Carry

"I think the product lines you choose depend on your core demographic. Are you appealing to youth; upper middle class; professionals, or families on a budget?"

— Michele Wright, General Manager,
Haircolorxperts

Deciding what hair product line or lines to offer in your salon is one of the most important initial decisions you should make as a new hair salon owner. Derrick Diggs of Layers Hair Salon in Richmond, Virginia, advises, "Professional hair care lines would include shampoo and styling products as well as hair color and other chemical services. Once you decide on the lines you want to offer, you can call or visit their websites and get the information that will connect you with local distributors."

For other items that do not hinge as much on personal preference (such as foils, cotton, drapes), you may want to go with the company that charges the least for these items. In addition, some salons stick with one line of hair care products, while others use several. For these reasons, some salon owners get all of their supplies from one source, while others get their supplies from a variety of distributors.

Hair Products Wholesalers

The following are some companies that come highly recommended from successful salon owners around the country. These distributors generally carry both hair products and salon equipment.

Sally Beauty Supply

One of the largest beauty supply companies (which owns other beauty supply distributors under a variety of other names) is Sally Beauty Supply, which distributes in both the United States and Canada. They carry a complete line of salon and spa supplies. Their website is located at **www.sallybeauty.com**.

Cosmoprof

Another well-respected name in the beauty supply industry (and a holding of Sally Beauty Supply) that distributes to several mid-western and western states in the U.S., as well as Florida, Alaska, Hawaii, and Canada is Cosmoprof (known in the west as West Coast Beauty Supply). You can visit their website at **www.cosmoprofbeauty.com/redmain.aspx**.

Other Suppliers

Another major beauty supply company in Canada is Beauticians Supply, located in Kitchener, Ontario, (800) 265-8987. In the mid-west and west coast of the United States try Maly's, (800) 446-2597, which carries liquid hair care products, tools, and salon equipment.

An excellent wholesale salon furniture and equipment source in Mississauga, Ontario, is Beauti Shape, (905) 564-5267. On the East Coast of the U.S., one reputable beauty supply company that carries a large line of beauty supplies from hair care products to furnishings is Columbia Beauty Supplies, **www.cbslink.com**, which has been in business since 1920. For a wonderful 300 page catalogue of wholesale beauty supplies, you can't beat The Industry Source (**www.theindustrysource.com**).

Trade Shows

An excellent way to meet wholesalers is by attending conferences and trade shows dedicated to your industry. You can look for trade shows by industry across North America at BizTradeShows.com (**www.biztradeshows.com/trade-shows-by-industry.html**) or check wholesale conventions and tradeshows where you can connect with manufacturers and wholesalers at **www.wholesalecentral.com/tradeshowcal.htm**. Section 3.6.2 has links to industry trade shows recommended by our salon owner experts.

You can also find wholesalers in the Yellow Pages under whichever category you are looking for. Another option is to check directories at your local public or university library, such as the American Wholesalers and Distributors Directory published by Gale.

5.5.2   Salon Supplies and Furnishings

Manufacturers are companies that make products, usually in large quantities. Most manufacturers sell to wholesalers, and will not sell directly to individuals.

Thomas Register (**www.thomasnet.com**) is the most comprehensive online resource for finding manufacturers in the United States. You can do a search by company, brand, or product. Each manufacturer's information includes the head office address, phone number, fax number and product descriptions. For salon furniture and equipment suppliers, try typing "salon" or "beauty" into the search box on the home page. For hair care product suppliers, try typing in the type of product, for example, "shampoo: hair", or "conditioners: hair".

The American Manufacturers Directory includes detailed information on over 600,000 U.S. manufacturers. While you could purchase it yourself for $795, you will probably be able to find it at a local university or public library. Many libraries carry directories for specific industries as well. You can find a directory of Canadian manufacturers and distributors online at the Canadian Trade Index website (**www.ctidirectory. com**). Or try Industry Canada's website at **www.ic.gc.ca/epic/site/ic1. nsf/en/h_00070e.html**.

Depending on your salon's niche, you may eventually want to purchase that industry's directory of manufacturers. However, directories typically cost several hundred dollars so you may want to view them at the library first, if possible.

There are many fine hair product lines available, so many that a decision about which ones to buy may be daunting for new salon owners. Following are some suppliers and manufacturers of salon product lines you can take a look at to help you decide.

Salon Furniture and Fixtures

- *Belvedere*
  Belvedere is a long-established leading manufacturer of salon furnishings and furniture, from desk work spaces and cabinets to sinks and chairs.
  www.belvedere.com

- *Takara Belmont*
  Manufacturer and international supplier of salon fixtures and equipment for salons, spas and barber shops
  www.takara-belmont.com

- *Kaemark Salon Furnishings*
  Manufacturer of salon furnishings and fixtures.
  www.kaemark.com

The furnishings and furniture are available directly from the manufacturers and through distributors such as those listed in the Wholesalers section, above.

Hair Product Lines

Keep in mind that most specialty hair product makers whose products are sold only in salons, require salons to register as a member salon and purchase a minimum of retail products throughout the year.

- *Aveda*
  http://aveda.aveda.com/grow/partner_with_us.asp

- *Bumble and Bumble*
  www.bumbleandbumble.com

- *Goldwell Professional Haircare*
  (Highly recommended for coloring)
  www.goldwell-northamerica.com/site/salon-alliance/benefits-&-requirements

- *Mizani*
  (Contact them using their "Professional Stylist Customer Service" phone number: 888-322-1142.)
  www.mizani-usa.com

- *Paul Mitchell*
  www.paulmitchell.com

- *Sebastian International*
  www.sebastian-intl.com

The following are smaller but top-quality hair product lines developed by some of the top stylists in the United States. These are worth investigating when deciding which specialty hair care product lines to use and carry in your salon.

- *Donsuki*
  Products include Seaweed Shampoo, Seaweed Hair Moisturizer, Seaweed Hair Masque, Seaweed Styling Gel, Donsuki Conditioner and Texturizer, hair sprays, and 62nd Hair Treatment, a spray on and comb-out detangling formula. Contact **sales@donsuki.com**.
  www.donsukisalon.com

- *Sexy Hair*
  Products include Big, Curly, Healthy, Strong, Short, Silky, Straight, and Simply Sexy, Color Me Sexy, Sex Symbol Aero Tan™, and Sexy Bath and Body™.
  www.sexyhair.com

- *Barry Fletcher*
  Hair products designed especially for African American hair
  www.barryfletcherproducts.com/1113530.html

- *Justin Hickox Studio Hair Products*
  www.hickoxstudio.com

A reputable source for hair extensions, wigs and hair pieces is distributor Hair U Wear, **www.hairuwear.com/huw.aspx?pgID=968**. In Canada a great supplier of hair extensions, wigs and hair pieces is Euro Naturals at **www.euronaturals.ca**.

5.5.3   Prices and Terms

Manufacturers and wholesalers typically have suggested retail prices and offer discounts based on quantities purchased. Here are some questions to consider when considering their prices and terms:

- Are the prices and terms the company is offering acceptable? Ask the vendor to tell you all the charges that will be involved with a purchase. In addition to the price of the product, there may be taxes, delivery charges, duties for items coming from another country, rush charges, etc. If you are dealing with a wholesaler, you should ask about "up charges" (a fee on top of the manufacturer's price).

- What discount will you receive off the retail price? Typical discounts when buying wholesale (i.e. from the manufacturer) are 20-50%. You may need a copy of your retail license to get the wholesale rate or to avoid paying sales tax.

- When is payment required? If you do not have a business history, most vendors will want to be paid for items before they ship them. Many times you will not be able to purchase wholesale using your credit card, so you will need to have funds readily available to cover your purchases with a check.

- What about over-runs or under-runs? While manufacturers normally do their best to ensure they deliver exactly what you have ordered, many include in their contract that they can ship 10-15% over or under the amount ordered.

TIP: Make sure you read any sales contracts carefully and have them reviewed by your lawyer to ensure you are protected.

Your wholesaler may offer different shipping rates, as some use a flat rate system and others charge by total weight of the products ordered. Paying shipping based on weight can often be less costly to the purchaser because flat rates sometimes allow a seller to profit on the shipping rates as well as the products purchased. A few distributors may offer a line of credit for an initial purchase. C.O.D. and credit cards are almost universally accepted. "The standard we met from distributors when we first opened was generally a 30-day invoicing," Cindy Feldman of Progressions Salon Spa Store told us. "We chose to do a lot of COD and this served us well. Currently we do use credit cards for purchases as it makes bookkeeping much more simplified."

Always check out and clarify a vendor's prices and policies before placing an order. "Agreeing to terms with your vendors ahead of time is a tremendous advantage," says Anne Marie Sheeley of Salon Diva, "as you will not have time to worry about signing a check when your products arrive. As an owner, the interruptions are overwhelming and frequent. Anything you can do to save time is crucial." When dealing with suppliers, it never hurts to negotiate to try to get the best terms possible, although many wholesalers will not extend volume discounts to smaller salons.

However, says Dalgiza Barros of Creative Energy Salon, "If you are a consistent and valued customer you can often get samples of products more regularly. You can also take advantage of discount days at your local beauty supply stores to stock up, as well as purchasing in bulk at hair shows where you can get especially great deals on the last day of the show when suppliers look to get rid of the inventory rather than packing it up and shipping it back." Ronnie Pryor, owner of Source Salon in Florida adds that, "When dealing with wholesalers, always remember that the squeaky wheel gets the discount or even the freebies. I've found this to be true more of equipment than products. "

Another tip from Larry Dunlap of Haircolorxperts in North Carolina is to try to negotiate your best deal when your business is new and sales representatives are trying to land your business as a new account. "I've found that as soon as you have signed the deal on your location the sales reps come streaming out of the woodwork like ants. It's your best time to leverage one against the other and get your best deals. You can often bundle your equipment and products from one supplier and save on everything."

As for returns, Anne Marie Sheeley, president of Salon Diva in New York advises checking with your supplier for their return policy as well as their education policy. "Salon products should have a money back guarantee," explains Anne Marie. "If your supplier's return policy is not straightforward, do not buy from them. You should be able to return a product to your vendor for a full refund, no matter what the reason. If they cannot guarantee that, find another distributor or manufacturer." Many manufacturers also offer free education to teach stylists about the product and ways to market the product effectively, which can save small businesses money.

6. Running Your Business

6.1 Salon Operations

6.1.1 Developing a Procedures Manual

As you move through the process of opening your salon, you will begin to notice that you are starting to develop routines around how you do various things. These routines will fall eventually under the more official business term — operations. One of the great things about owning your own salon is that you are in charge of deciding the routines of your operations, and you can plan how things run in your salon to satisfy your needs and desires.

Every time you do something new, keep a record of how you did it. As you go along, take accurate notes about what works, what doesn't work, and what will need to be done a different way. Over time you will begin to see an organized system emerge — this is the beginning of the development of your operational procedures.

Having written records and instructions of important salon procedures and tasks makes it possible for your employees to complete tasks more efficiently by themselves. Also, salon procedures aren't necessarily things that you can (or even want to) store in your head. It is hard to remember all the passwords and codes for things, the procedures for receiving merchandise, or the steps in taking a check from a customer. The best thing to do is to make a guide for employees (and for you) to keep this information organized and accessible.

Putting together an operations manual for your salon will help you get all of your procedures and instructions for every little task organized and in one spot for you and your employees to refer to. Follow the simple directions below to make your own Salon Operations Manual.

A procedures manual will be more appropriate in some salon settings than others. For example, in a complex salon set-up such as a large salon or a chain of salons with several departments and many different employees, an operations manual may be essential to keep things operating smoothly. In a small salon with only one stylist, however, a procedures checklist might be helpful to the owner, but a more involved procedures manual would likely be overkill. Operations manual advocate, Valery Joseph of Valery Joseph Salons, notes that it is " a fantastic way to keep organization and unity in a salon. Each employee receives one once they start work at either Valery Joseph salon. It keeps the business running smoothly by constructing codes, appearance, coming on time, always saying 'yes' and accommodating the client, leaving attitude at home, always taking that extra step, etc."

In a salon setting with booth (chair) rentals, while an operations manual or an operations checklist may help you keep track of all the detailed duties you need to cover on a daily basis, it might not be warranted for your renters. As Dalgiza Barros of Creative Energy in Massachusetts, explains, "A general manual outlining general operational issues would be helpful, but one that is more specific might not apply to a booth rental salon, as these types of salons try to let renters set their own standards."

Some salons such as Tony Promiscuo's Godiva Salon in Atlanta use both a policies and procedures manual as well as an operations manual. Some salons also provide their receptionists with standard scripts to help them deal more effectively with situations that can come up.

What You Need

Here are the things you'll need to create your manual:

- Checklists for each area of the salon (see below for some sample checklists)
- Three-ring binder or folder with clear plastic insert space on cover and spine
- Three-hole punch
- Binder dividers with section labels
- Checklist forms
- Task forms
- Special reminder forms
- Emergency forms

What to Do

Once you have gathered your materials, follow these steps:

- Carefully consider each area of your operations. Make divider tags for the binder with the following labels: Opening Tasks, Closing Tasks, Daily Tasks, Weekly Tasks, Monthly Tasks, Quarterly Tasks, Annual Tasks. Place these labeled dividers in the binder.
- Make a checklist for each area. Use the checklist examples on the following pages to get started. List the tasks that you can think of for each area. Remember to write down important reminder information like where things are located, which lights to turn on, etc.

Think about how you would instruct someone unfamiliar with the task to do it. Sequentially ordered steps work the best.

- Fill out a separate sequential form or reminder sheet for each specific area of operations in your store.

- Make a list of emergency numbers and other emergency information for the first page of the binder. You might want to place a copy of every employee's emergency information card inside the binder directly behind the emergency number and procedure page.

- Label the binder clearly and make a copy of all the contents to store in a safe place away from your store.

TIP: Remember that this operations manual will be fluid and will change over time. As you change your procedures, remember to change the corresponding task page.

Here are some areas to consider in creating the operations manual for your business:

- *Job descriptions for each position:* Knowing what is expected of them is a major factor in employee satisfaction, according to a recently released study based on Gallup poll research.

- *Cleaning and maintenance schedule:* If staff is expected to perform routine maintenance on the equipment they use, they need to know this. If you hire someone or assign someone to this task, they need step-by-step instructions of what needs to be done, and how often, and have a chart they can fill in upon completion. One particular task that needs to be done in a salon is keeping up with the laundry. Whether you have a particular person assigned to this task or everyone in the salon pitches in, this is something that should be made clear so that it is done in a timely and proper fashion.

- *Procedures:* for day-to-day operations such as opening and closing cash registers, answering the phone, shutting down computers, lights to be left on, retail displays that need to be checked or restocked, reception area duties such as answering the phones, scheduling appointments, checking clients in and out, etc. Be very detailed in this regard, and pay attention to seemingly obvious or insignificant tasks. Even something seemingly insignificant as, for example, cleaning the lint screen from the dryer after every few loads of laundry can be important, because the build up of lint near a heat source in a dryer can pose a potential fire hazard.

- *Employee behavior and dress codes:* to set the proper tone and atmosphere for your salon. For example, dress codes may be more lax in a salon that caters to young hip urbanites seeking edgy hairstyles than in a salon catering to an upscale business crowd. Also, it's a good idea to cover certain behavioral procedures, such as no gum chewing, chatting with other employees while with a client or discussing controversial, personal, or potentially offensive topics in front of clients. While it may seem obvious, you may also want to make clear that salon employees should avoid discussing a client, especially negatively, in front of anyone.

- *Troubleshooting manuals:* If you have to call a repair person every time something malfunctions, you are going to be paying out unnecessary money. Make a troubleshooting guide for each piece of salon equipment that is based on the manual that came with the machine. Add to it with every incident so that when someone says, "What did we do last time this happened?" you'll know.

- *Work schedules:* They don't need to have employee names yet, but you should know how many hours a week you want each stylist on site, and how many of them at a time. You also want to develop a system that allows you as the manager to check for unfilled appointments quickly and easily so you or your receptionist can try to fill those spots.

- *Company policies:* Do employees get sent home if things are slow? Do they get written up if they are late twice? What about three times? Do they have to purchase and wash their own smocks? These are the kinds of things your staff will resent not knowing if it comes as a surprise, so make a list that details your policies on these matters. Being inconsistent or making things up as you go along can make you seem indecisive and can also lead to poor policy-making. Try to think ahead as much as possible; however, if and when a new situation arises that calls for creating or implementing a new policy, be sure to inform all employees promptly of any changes or new policies.

- *Record-keeping:* Do bills get filed away or tossed? How long are they kept for? Do you need to fill in all the information in the client information database, or is a name and phone number sufficient? Whoever maintains your filing systems (both electronic and paper) will need to know how you want your salon records kept. Even if you do this yourself, it's a good idea to create a procedure list. If not, this can cause problems if you need someone to cover your record-keeping duties in the event of illness, vacations, or another occasion arises that causes you to be away from the business for a significant time period.

- *Sales goals:* These will initially be based on your sales projections from your business plan, and eventually on last year's sales. You can post your progress to date for management to see, or everyone, so they can all feel involved.

- *Hierarchy:* Knowing the staff hierarchy and who should report to whom is important. Keeping everyone's roles clear from the beginning will make communication a lot easier during those critical early stages. Creating an organizational chart early on also makes it easier to understand new roles that get added once the business grows.

- *Safety and hygiene policies:* In most states the OSHA will require that you develop a plan for safe practices in the workplace, related to equipment, hygiene, etc. They will provide you the details of what they require. The website **www.oshafastfix.com** will sell you ready-made and custom materials to help you develop these. While many salon employees, especially those who are licensed barbers or cosmetologists, will be trained in health and hygiene practices mandated by the state, it's crucial that all employees who are responsible for these practices be thoroughly trained in them and that a copy of all standard procedures be included in your procedures manual. Lisa DeStefano, Owner of DeStefano's Salon in Carlsbad, California, adds that, "It takes a salon owner to be proactive and to reinforce health and safety rules to his or her staff at all times, and to stay up at all times with any rules and regulations that may change from year to year." Again, unannounced health inspections are an inevitable part of running a salon, so making sure these regulations are followed is crucial. Also, because these regulations are intended to protect your clients — your business's most important resource — from potentially harmful bacteria and illnesses, this is a critical part of running your business.

Keep in mind that as your business operates and grows, you may need to alter or add to your operations manual. As John Stevens, owner of deNovo Aesthetics Center in Dallas, Texas, states, "We have an operations manual and it evolves daily. As often as possible, you should deal with any given situation only one time. Take the time to develop the process and put it down on paper. Ask yourself: If I had 25 offices and 500 employees, how would I deal with this situation and how would I develop the policy to keep it simple?"

6.1.2   Areas of Operations Checklists

Here are some examples of various areas of the salon and some issues in each area that you might want to address in your operations manual:

Opening/Closing

- ❏   Door locks
- ❏   Lights — both indoor and outdoor
- ❏   Security systems and codes
- ❏   What to do if the alarm goes off accidentally
- ❏   Turning on/off the air-conditioning and heating units
- ❏   Turning on/off computers/fax/postal machine/copier
- ❏   Mail sorting and opening
- ❏   Brewing coffee and/or heating tea pots; purchasing and putting out refreshments
- ❏   Email
- ❏   Check and fill any online orders (if applicable)
- ❏   Answering machine
- ❏   Cleaning break room and staff kitchen area

Work Stations

- ❏ Stocking work station with proper supplies

- ❏ Keeping all work areas tidy and sanitized

- ❏ Properly cleaning and sterilizing all implements between clients

- ❏ Offering clients refreshments

- ❏ Performing styling or other salon services in a timely and skillful manner

- ❏ Handling clients efficiently to avoid unnecessary delays and wait times

- ❏ Consulting with clients regarding service to be provided

- ❏ Making sure all laundry is properly washed, dried and stored in a timely fashion

- ❏ Checking restroom regularly for cleanliness

- ❏ If appropriate, recommending additional services to client

- ❏ Documenting client services performed for future reference

- ❏ Being attentive and friendly to client throughout service

- ❏ Avoiding chatting with other employees while handling clients

- ❏ Avoiding personal, controversial or potentially offensive topics with clients

- ❏ Advising and teaching clients how to use hair/skin products

Reception/Sales Area

- ❏ Phone procedures/scripts for particular situations

- ❏ Scheduling appointments

- ❏ Directions to salon

- ❏ Checking clients in

- ❏ Hanging clients' coats up for them

❏   Giving clients a robe, directing them to changing area

❏   Collecting client tickets from stylists/technicians

❏   Operating the cash register

❏   Preparing money drawer for opening

❏   Processing credit and debit cards

❏   Processing checks

❏   Accepting and selling gift certificates

❏   Completing a transaction

❏   Keeping track of what is sold/Inventory

❏   Using computers/fax/postal machine/copier

❏   Mailing list

❏   Promotions and sales

❏   Cash deposits and bank deposits

❏   Wrapping gifts

Merchandise and Sales

❏   Procedures for receiving inventory

❏   Pricing merchandise

❏   Putting tags on items

❏   Shelving merchandise

❏   Making displays

❏   Cleaning and organizing displays

❏   Answering customer questions

❏   When to discount prices on merchandise

❏   Handling refunds

Safety/Emergency Procedures

❏ Emergency contact numbers—fire, police, hospitals, etc

❏ Staff and owner emergency contact numbers

❏ Procedures for emergency in-store illness—for both staff members and customers

❏ Evacuation procedures

❏ Emergency or natural disaster plan

❏ What to do in case of shoplifting

❏ What to do in case of robbery

6.1.3   Setting Your Hours of Operation

Your hours of operation will depend on whether you are hiring a manager or you are going to try to be onsite as much as possible yourself. This is an area where you will want to start cautiously. You can always add more hours, but you won't make any friends by reducing them.

Salon hours are normally long and cover at least six and more often seven days a week. Most salons open by 9:00 a.m. and sometimes as late as 10 a.m. The key is to remain open late until at least 7:00 p.m. or 8:00 p.m., since many people need to get their hair done after work. Evenings and Fridays and Saturdays are often the busiest times for salons (as well as holiday periods), so plan your hours accordingly.

Depending on your busiest times, you may want to close a little earlier Monday through Wednesday and then be open later in the evenings on Thursdays and Fridays. Again, if you are in a mall or strip mall, your hours may be determined for you. While it is perfectly acceptable to close on Sunday if you desire, you may be losing potential business. You may want to try staying open every second Sunday at first, and see what the demand is in your area. If you find this is one of your busiest days, then by all means, expand your hours to every Sunday.

Alex Safar, owner of Salon Acote in Boston, prefers more flexible hours to meet the needs of the salon's clientele: "Although we officially open at 9 a.m., we have three stylists who come in at 7:30 a.m. for people who want to get their hair done before work. Also, although we officially close at 7:30 p.m., our last appointments begin then, so we are actually here until about 8 or 9 p.m. most evenings."

6.2 Hygiene and Cleanliness

One special area of consideration is hygiene and cleanliness. In order to provide services to your clients that are safe and healthful you must always pay close attention to keeping your equipment and your general work environment spotless and sanitary. Creating a schedule of regular maintenance and cleaning will help you avoid becoming complacent about cleanliness.

General Cleaning

Many salon owners hire a professional cleaning company or hire a staff housekeeper to look after general cleaning. The services provided by the cleaner should include cleaning the reception area, disposing of garbage, vacuuming or other floor cleaning and so on. If you don't want your place of business smelling like pine cleaner you should specify to your cleaner that you prefer that they use a mild disinfectant or one with a neutral odor.

General cleaning is not overly difficult, but it does require care and attention on a daily basis. Try to walk through your salon with the eyes of a customer and pick out things that might need attention. Especially check areas that customers are in constant contact with or where they will have time to sit (such as in a reception area) and notice dust building up on furniture or inventory. If you provide washrooms for your clientele, be sure that they are always spotless. Put together a schedule that includes checking and cleaning such areas several times a day.

Laundry

If you use towels or other items that need to be laundered, you will need to ensure you don't run out of fresh laundry. Many salons have a washer and dryer on the premises and do all their laundry in-house. They either have a staff member whose job includes completing this very important task or salon personnel all pitch in to get it done.

Ronnie Pryor's Source Salon in Florida offers several reasons they take care of cleaning needs on-site:

> "One, I already employ an assistant and desk manager. Between their other duties they easily and efficiently keep up with the laundry throughout the day. Even the stylists help out, so why pay someone else to do this? Two, given the volume of laundry our salon produces daily, I'd have to stock at least four times as many towels and capes as I do now in order to make it until the outside vendor could have our laundry done. And three, water is included in our lease."

Other salons, however, do some of their laundry on-site and have some laundry picked up by a professional laundry service. The service does the laundry and delivers it back to the salon when finished. This can be expensive, but worthwhile in certain instances.

Bob Patrizi's Halo [For Men] spa and salons in the Chicago area uses a combination of on-site laundry and using a laundry service. "At our downtown location we offer a variety of spa services along with straight razor shaves, so we use a linen company to ensure the highest of sanitation for those services."

A third "hybrid" arrangement between doing laundry on-site and out-sourcing it is that practiced by the Michael Peter Hayes Art Salon in Locust Valley, New York. They drop off and pick up their laundry at a local laundromat where their laundry is washed and folded. At the salon, the staff refolds the towels into a roll to make it look better in the cabinets.

Hygiene

This is another area to consider carefully. State and provincial governments, as well as local health departments, have an active role in developing guidelines and regulations that help to ensure businesses are run with customer health and safety in mind. Government inspections are ongoing and not limited to your opening. You can expect inspectors on a regular, and often unannounced, basis, at least yearly or more often.

Train yourself and your staff to follow hygienic practices and learn as much as you can about industry regulations in this area. You may need to send your staff on courses occasionally to update their qualifications.

You will need to follow safe industry practices and only offer products for use or sale that adhere to government guidelines and regulations. In addition, your premises must be clean, sanitary, and free of environmental and other safety hazards.

The industry association (see section 3.4.2) that you are a member of can help you to learn more about the requirements for businesses like yours. They can also help you to find information specific to your location. Contact your local health department for general guidelines.

Here are some general hygiene tips to consider:

- If you're using off-the-shelf products in delivering your services, don't "double dip". That is, if a product has come into contact with a previous customer, don't use it again on your next customer. This also goes for things like towels, facecloths, and so on.

- Clean furnishings and equipment that come into contact with clientele immediately after use. In other words, once the first customer has gone, clean any furnishings and equipment you or your staff has used in delivering the service with an antibacterial solution and wipe it down thoroughly.

- Ensure that your staff members practice personal hygiene. This includes no nail-biting, keeping shoes and clothes (uniforms, too) clean, making sure they wash their hands regularly (especially after using the washroom), and so on.

- Check with vendors and suppliers for advice on the proper use of products and equipment. They can also advise you on the safe operation of any equipment you use in your business for delivering services.

In addition, there must be ample toilet paper and paper towels in the bathroom. As for scissors and combs that are constantly used in salons, hygiene regulations require them to be washed and scrubbed using soap and hot water. They must then be additionally soaked in a sanitizing solution such as Barbicide for ten minutes, washed thoroughly with water again and dried. All counters and surfaces must also be disinfected using special anti-bacterial solutions.

You must make sure your salon and all personnel who perform services there are in compliance with these codes at all times. Remember that random health inspections are a constant factor of salon ownership. As Federico Calce of Federico Salon in Manhattan explains: "The Board of Health and other licensing agencies state regular inspections every six months or so. It could be seven or eight months. It is always done without warning so you cannot prepare. It's always a surprise so you must always be ready."

Also, adds Federico, "Usually they come to inspect one time a year. However, if they find something wrong, they can come back as many times as they like during the year."

Another thing to be aware of if you choose to have any nail work done in your salon is that nails are an area covered by many hygiene and health rules and that poses a high risk of potential violations. As Lisa Destefano of Destefano's in Carlsbad, California adds, "You must be especially careful with nail technicians and make sure they follow the rules and regulations to the letter. If you don't, you can be taken down quickly by the health department."

For more information about rules and regulations for your business, visit your state's cosmetology and barber licensing board website, or in Canada, go to Health Canada for more information, **www.hc-sc.gc.ca**. Any industry association you are a member of (see section 3.4.2 for more about associations you can join) will have literature available that outlines safe business practices for its membership. Also, all states issue a booklet of the health and hygiene rules and regulations you must adhere to.

6.3   Managing Appointments and Inventory

6.3.1   Salon Software

Client-tracking software allows you to keep track of hundreds of appointments and keeps you from becoming over-booked. You can also include notes about clients, such as any special needs or likes and dislikes. You want appointments to go as smoothly as possible with little or no error.

There are a wide variety of options available to salon owners. Which software works best is often a personal choice and depends on the type of salon, the size of salon, and how many customers you have. Most offer the capability to book appointments, track inventory, emailing capability and other features to make running a salon easier.

This can be a big investment, so take your time. Fortunately, many of these software programs offer a free demo trial period, so you can try out several different versions before deciding which one you would like to purchase. Try the various demos. Find out which program works best for you before using up valuable hours punching in information, only to realize the software you purchased is not working to meet your needs.

Here are just a few of the choices available to you in a range of prices:

- *Salon Iris*
  This company was established in 1983 and is a favorite among many shop owners. The software has a wide variety of features and starts at about $799. Try the demo to see if this software is right for you.
  www.saloniris.com

- *Spa/salon Manager*
  This software is an interface for an online database for your salon. It is priced based on the number of employees your salon has. Prices start at $595 for one employee and go up to $795 for 4 employees, $1095 for ten employees, on up to $2095 for the deluxe version for very large facilities. You can also try a 45 day trial package for $195.
  www.spasalon.com

- *Leprechaun Spa and Salon software*
  Leprechaun is a low-cost and user friendly subscription-based software service. The software is designed specifically for salons and spas. The current monthly full package fee is $59. This includes all support, training webinars and live telephone support. This ongoing subscription avoids the potentially costly upgrade purchases and customer support plan fees.
  www.leprechaun-software.com

- *Pro Salon/Pro Solutions*
  Pro Solutions software offers several software programs geared towards salons and spas. The basic Essential software package costs $399, while the Professional version costs $2,299. Both versions include an appointment book, inventory tracking and client database. Additional features are available. A demo is available. They also offer a financing program. **www.prosolutionssoftware.com**

6.3.2   Inventory Tags and Labels

To keep track of inventory some stores use simple tags they label by hand, while others use bar code tags that work with whatever type of software they are using. You should use whatever system makes the most sense for your store.

If your store is organized neatly and your prices are marked clearly, not only will shopping be easier and more comfortable for customers, you will find that keeping track of your inventory is easier. Using inventory systems to keep organized will help you avoid the frustration of not being able to find inventory or a special order.

Most retail stores use either simple labels with neat, handwritten prices or printed price stickers from a pricing gun or computer printer. You might consider self-adhesive labels, but be careful with them. Some labels leave glue residue on items and will sometimes cause a permanent mark when removed. Many retailers use string tags that they can tie onto merchandise. Use these for larger, more visible items because some people might be tempted to remove a higher price tag and replace it with a lower price one.

Some retailers use bar code tags that work with whatever type of software and scanner they use. Although initially more expensive than stickers or string tags, if you get very busy the time you save keeping track of your inventory might easily pay for it. Your choice of which system to use will largely depend on the type of inventory you carry and your inventory turnover.

To find out more about labeling and bar code systems you can visit Motorola Retail Solutions at **www.motorola.com/Business/US-EN/ Business+Solutions/Industry+Solutions/Retail** or **POSWorld.com**, both of which offer labels, inventory management and bar code systems. Most office supply stores like Staples, Office Depot, and Office Max, sell string tags, price stickers, and pricing guns.

6.4 Pricing Services and Products

"One of the biggest mistakes I see new salon owners make is underestimating overhead costs and not be able to stay open due to lack of funding and paying stylists high commissions. Some have no profit margins — they can do a million dollars in business a year and still go broke. Volume doesn't dictate success."

> — Philip Pelusi, owner,
> Tela Design Studio

6.4.1 Guidelines

One main consideration for pricing items is what the local market will bear. If certain items are in high demand then you'll probably be able to charge higher prices for those. This is the "law" of supply and demand and you should pay close attention to any trends you see developing in your customers' buying patterns to take advantage of this.

Here are some basic pricing tips:

- Consider what the market will bear. A store in an upscale area may allow you to price your items a bit higher.

- Consider your competition. Are there any other stores like yours in the area? What are they charging for similar items?

- It is not always best to price items lower than the competition charges. Most people believe you get what you pay for. The key is to price the item fairly but allow yourself a reasonable profit.

- Items in a particular section of the retail industry have a certain perceived value. What are customers willing to pay for the item? What is it worth to them?

Following is more information to help you set prices for your services and products.

6.4.2   Pricing Services

As you saw in section 2.2, there is a range of retail prices you can charge for each type of service you provide. For example, a typical price for hair cuts may range from $15 to $120 depending on the salon.

Setting prices for the services you offer is a balancing act that juggles what your clients are willing to pay, what your own costs are, and how much a particular service is in demand. Few of these factors are constants, so expect that to a certain extent your prices will fluctuate as a result of these shifting market conditions. Of course, the bottom line is not just breaking even, either, but being profitable. Without profit, your business cannot grow. Here are some issues to consider in your pricing your services to be profitable.

Covering Your Costs

"My biggest bit of advice is figure out before you open/buy your salon how much everything will cost, including repairs and at least a small salary for yourself and then decide on prices. You must do it this way, otherwise you will not be profitable."

— Elizabeth Coy, owner,
Indigo Salon

How you determine the price of a particular service should be based on the following costs to you as owner:

- *Your labor costs:* Certain types of labor cost less than others and you will pay less per hour to staff who do not have, nor require, specialized training. Unique services requiring specially trained staff will cost you more.

- *Product costs:* Consider the costs of any products you need to use in order to deliver a particular service. These costs should be factored into your service fee.

- *Overhead costs:* Running your business costs you money, including everything from electricity, heating and cooling, taxes, rent, right down to the pen you write with. If any of these costs are exaggerated by a service you offer, be sure to account for that in your fees.

Many small business owners feel guilty about charging too much more than what they are paying to provide the service, but you should try to achieve the healthiest margin the market will bear. After all, if your cost to provide a service fluctuates your clients won't want to suddenly pay more (just consider the public outcry over increased airline fares as a result of recent fuel price hikes, as an example). If you have a buffer built into your fees against increases in your own costs of doing business, then you'll be better prepared to absorb those costs.

Perceived Value and Your Client

In many businesses, prices need to be very competitive in order for a business owner to be successful. For example, customers know that they can buy milk at one store and it's pretty much the same product at the store down the road. Once they know that the milk is the same, the determining factors come down to cost and convenience.

Service offerings are a bit different from offering milk, though. If your services can set you apart from the competition, then you have a bit more "wiggle room" in setting your prices. Your services can be unique in themselves, or they can be unique in the way they are presented to the public.

Consider adding some unique feature that your competitors don't have. Maybe it's the little "perks" that come with patronizing your business. Maybe it's a fun, lively, or chic atmosphere they find at your business, they don't find elsewhere. Adding something original to your service offerings in this way will give your services a perceived value over and above your competition and will keep clients returning to you.

By keeping up with trends in the industry and investing in training for your best employees, you can offer new services just as soon as they come into vogue. If you can keep pace with trend-setting centers in large urban areas, for example, you can bring that cachet home to your clients and they'll love you for it.

TIP: There is a difference between trends and fads. Trends are general directions of consumer preference, while fads are here today and gone tomorrow. Before you invest in expensive products or equipment to meet a new and exciting service, think about whether you are buying into a trend or a fad.

Sample Prices

You can find a range of retail prices for some of the services you might offer in section 2.2. You can use this as a starting point in developing your own prices, taking into consideration the advice above. You can also see a "menu" of sample prices in section 7.1.4.

6.4.3   Product Pricing Formulas

There are different methods that retailers use to arrive at their prices. Many manufacturers have a suggested retail price (MSRP) for retailers to follow. These are found along with their wholesale price to the retailer in their product catalogs. You can choose to follow a MSRP or not. The important questions to ask are whether the MSRP allows you sufficient profit and is it priced too high for your market. If the answer is no to the first and yes to the second, you might want to look for a different supplier.

A more efficient and profitable way to price is using a retail pricing formula. Generally, there are two concepts retailers should be aware of: percentage margin and price markup. Using these formulas will tell you what your percentage of profit is based on the percentage markup above your wholesale (i.e. purchase) price for that item. If the profit percentage is too low, then you'll want to use a different price markup percentage for that item.

As an example of how pricing affects your business, we'll use the break-even point for a fictional business. You may remember the formula for calculating the break-even point from section 4.4.2 as:

$$\text{Break-even point} = \text{Total fixed costs} \div$$
$$(1 - \text{total variable costs} \div \text{revenues})$$

In the example in section 4.4.2, the break-even point for the business was $69,000 in annual revenues. Also, for every dollar of sales, the company had 56 cents in variable expenses. Therefore, to break even, fixed costs can represent no more than 44 cents on every dollar. So if you had an item priced at $1.00, 56% of the selling price would be variable expenses and the rest would be fixed costs, leaving no room for profit. Obviously, nobody wants to run their store like that.

Based on these figures, the store owner might want to increase the profit margin. So for example, instead of selling a product for $1.00 as before, the owner might increase the retail price to $1.25. This would lower the percentage for each of fixed and variable costs as a percentage of revenue, resulting in an increased profit margin.

TIP: A trick most stores use is to price things just under the dollar mark. For example, instead of putting a price of $10 on an item, you would mark it $9.99. Even though there is only a penny's difference between the two prices, customers will perceive one as ten dollars and the other as nine dollars, resulting in better sales.

Standard Markups

According to Jill D. Miller, business development consultant at Creative Solutions, a consulting firm that works with new salons, "Salon products are marked up 'keystone' — meaning the wholesale price is doubled for retail." She also notes that many salon product lines have suggested retail prices from manufacturers. While the vast majority of salon owners we spoke with adhere to this 100% standard mark-up for any retail hair products, a few use a 50% markup (and one Canadian salon owner and manager we spoke with said their markup was closer to 80%). If your distributor or manufacturer charges for breaking a case, adjust your resale prices to reflect that added cost.

For most skincare products, the markup is also 100%. For cosmetics, the standard markup is usually a higher percentage, typically 300-400%. According to Heaven Padgett, owner of the Hairem Salon in Houston, Texas, the markup for cosmetics can be on the higher end if you manufacture your own through a private factory, "but of course, your minimum orders are higher and you have to buy in bulk."

Anne Marie Sheeley of Salon Diva in White Plains, New York, recommends adding another 20% to your markup to cover your shipping and incentive bonuses for stylists. Being actively engaged in retail sales should be mandatory for all stylists in your salon to ensure employees are properly educated about the products. "Don't worry about having too high a price point," Sheeley advises. "If your prices are higher than your competitors, your clients will tell you".

Clearing Items Out

You have to do something with items that do not sell. You will find that some items, even though they seemed like a good choice for your store when you bought them, just won't sell. How long will you wait until the cost of carrying an item on your shelf exceeds what you originally paid for it? Sometimes it's better to cut your losses and get at least something for such merchandise.

Clearance racks or tables are a good place to start. Many retailers also offer slow selling merchandise for sale during sidewalk sales or other similar promotions. Make sure that you're offering good bargains, too, when you do this or customers will see that you're just trying to get rid of tired merchandise. Put new price stickers or tags on the merchandise and dust it if needed.

Your discount schedule is a matter of individual preference. Some owners leave their items at full price until 90 days or longer have passed or until the items are no longer in season. They then discount the items (e.g. by 20%) or offer them as "buy two get one free" or even "buy one get one free."

6.4.4   Profit Margin vs. Percentage Markup

Every business owner needs to understand the difference between profit margin and percentage markup. The profit margin is the amount of the price you charge for your services that represents profit for you over and above the cost of providing the service. This would include costs such as labor, any products you used in providing the service and so on. This is also true of any products you sell retail; that is, your profit margin represents the retail price you charge minus the price you originally paid for the merchandise you sell. In a more sophisticated model, you would also include your total operating expenses as well, adding in your fixed and variable costs and factoring them into your pricing model, along with cost of goods.

The percentage markup is the percentage amount you increased the service price or the retail price of merchandise over your cost for a given product or service. After you have been in business for a while, you will know what price markup generally works best for you. Pricing by percentage markup is less usual than pricing by profit margin.

Let's look at a specific example. Consider a service you have priced at $100.00. The total cost to provide the service is $40.00.

$$\begin{aligned} \text{Margin} &= (1 - (\text{cost} \div \text{service price})) \times 100 \\ &= (1 - (40 \div 100)) \times 100 \\ &= (1 - .40) \times 100 \\ &= .60 \times 100 \\ &= 60 \end{aligned}$$

So in this example the profit margin is 60%.

If, however, you decided that you would set your prices by marking up everything by 60%, then the percentage markup formula is:

$$\begin{aligned} \text{Price} &= \text{cost} + (\text{cost} \times 60 \div 100) \\ &= 40 + (40 \times 0.60) \\ &= 40 + 24 \\ &= 64 \end{aligned}$$

Using a fixed markup of 60%, the price of a service that costs you $40 would be $64.

Look carefully at these two formulas. Notice that markup pricing and profit margin pricing create two very different prices. In the first example, pricing based on a 60% profit margin required a selling price of $100. In the second example, using a percentage markup of 60% on cost resulted in a price of only $64, a profit margin of only about 38%.

A quick way to calculate a profit margin price is to divide the cost price by the difference between 100 and the profit margin. For example, if you wanted to have a 5% profit margin you would divide your cost price by (100-5) or 95 percent. So if your cost to provide the service is $40 and you wanted a 5% profit margin, to arrive at your price for the client you would use the formula:

$$40 \div (100 - 5) = 40 \div .95 = 42 \text{ cents}$$

Here are some additional examples so you can see the trend:

$$10\%: \quad 40 \div (100 - 10) = \$44$$
$$15\%: \quad 40 \div (100 - 15) = \$47$$
$$25\%: \quad 40 \div (100 - 25) = \$53$$
$$50\%: \quad 40 \div (100 - 50) = \$80$$

Once you know your cost of doing business, you can easily arrive at a minimum profit percentage margin price that will meet your needs. You'll also be able to look at an MSRP and determine if it meets your profit margin requirements.

Keep some of the other pricing concepts in mind as well. Your market may be able to support a higher profit margin in your pricing. Alternatively, you might be able to split margins by pricing higher ticket, lower volume items at a lower profit percentage, and use a higher profit margin on merchandise that sells for a lower price but at a higher volume. Another way to increase your profit margin is to reduce your variable expenses. If you find that your profit margin is too low, you can reduce costs like labor, store supplies, or even look for lower cost wholesale merchandise.

To read more about retail pricing concepts, try the following online resources:

- *Markup or Margin: Selling and Pricing*
  www.buildingtrade.org.uk/articles/markup_or_margin.html

- *Margin Markup/Profit Percentage Table*
  www.csgnetwork.com/marginmarkuptable.html

- *Pricing Your Products and Services Profitably*
  (Click on "Financial Management Series" and look for #7.)
  www.sba.gov/tools/resourcelibrary/publications/index.html

6.5 Getting Paid

As soon as you establish your business you will need to open a business checking account at a bank, trust company, or credit union. You can shop around to find a financial institution that is supportive of small business, or use the same one that you use for your personal banking.

In addition to your checking account, a financial institution may provide you with a corporate credit card used to make purchases for your business, a line of credit to purchase items for your store, and a merchant credit card account enabling you to accept credit card payments from customers.

You have a variety of options for getting paid by your customers.

6.5.1   Accepting Debit Cards

With a debit purchase, the funds come directly out of the customer's account at the bank and are deposited directly into your business bank account. There is no credit involved for customer or merchant. In order to set up debit payment, you will need to ask your bank for an application and you will need a debit machine. The equipment costs about $200 to $500, but some companies offer leases.

There may be a short delay or small charge to you, initially or ongoing, depending on the bank. And you will have to get the equipment to process the payments and print receipts. (Federal law mandates receipts be provided to customers for debit card purchases.) To find out more about debit card services in the U.S., visit the Electronic Transactions Association directory of member companies at **www.electran.org** (click on "Information Resources" then "Links"), or in Canada, visit the Interac Association at **www.interac.org**.

6.5.2   Accepting Credit Cards

American Express and Discover cards set up merchant accounts nationally and internationally. MasterCard and Visa are local. To become a merchant accepting MasterCard and Visa, you will have to get accepted by a local acquirer (a financial institution like a bank licensed by the credit card company). Because yours is a new business, you may have to shop around to find one that gives you good rates (you may be charged between 1.5 and 3 percent per transaction for the service, and often an initial setup fee and perhaps ongoing fees for phone calls, postage, statements, and so on).

You might also have to provide evidence of a good personal financial record to set up an advantageous rate, at least until you've become established in your business and have a good track record for them to look at. Remember, the bank is granting you credit in this instance, "banking" on the fact that your customers will not want refunds or that you won't try to keep the money if they do.

These days, although the acquiring bank will be a local bank somewhere, it need not be in your hometown. Numerous services are available online to help you set up a merchant account. MasterCard and Visa accounts, as well as American Express and Discover, can all be set up through your local bank or by going to the websites of each of these companies.

- *MasterCard Merchant*
  www.mastercard.com/us/merchant
  www.mastercard.com/ca/merchant/en/index.html

- *Visa*
  http://usa.visa.com/merchants/merchant_resources/
  www.visa.ca/en/merchant/

- *American Express*
  https://home.americanexpress.com/homepage/
  merchant_ne.shtml?
  www10.americanexpress.com/sif/cda/page/0,1641,14821,00.asp

- *Discover*
  www.discovernetwork.com/discovernetwork/howitworks/
  howitworks.html

6.5.3   Accepting Payment Online

If you have a website you can accept payments online through services such as PayPal (**www.paypal.com**). Typically, these services charge a greater "discount rate," which is what the 1.5 to 3 percent the banks and credit card companies hold from your payments is called. And the purchase must be made online. Still, there may be instances when you are doing business online with some of your clients, and it may be useful then. Also, it provides a safe route for conveying financial information over the Internet.

6.5.4   Accepting Checks

When you accept checks, especially to cover big-ticket items or major corporate purchases, you may want to have a back-up system for getting paid if the customer has insufficient funds in their checking account. It's important to get a credit card number, driver's license number, and full phone number and address (you might even want to check it online quickly to insure they are legitimate). If you have any doubts as to their honesty, it might be a good idea not to accept the check and let the sale go.

You can accept checks from customers with greater assurance by using a check payment service such as TeleCheck. TeleCheck compares checks you receive with a database of over 51 million bad check records, allowing you to decide whether to accept a check from a particular client. The company also provides electronic payment services, from telephone debit card processing to electronic checks. You can find out more about TeleCheck at **www.telecheck.com**.

6.5.5   Tips and Gratuities

Since most service-oriented businesses accept tips and gratuities from their clientele, you should have a policy in place regarding these. For one thing, this will clearly delineate how these are accepted and how they will be divided up among your staff. For another, having a policy in place when you open for business will prevent conflicts over the issue from occurring in the future.

Depending on your business, you may want to allow tipping as a part of the payment process. You can purchase point of sale equipment (credit and debit card readers) that allows people to choose a tipping option when they pay with these types of cards. This option allows the customer to input the amount of a tip the way they enter their PIN or at the time a credit card is used. This is a discrete and efficient method.

Another method sometimes used by service-oriented companies is to provide envelopes for tips. These have the caregiver's name on them, so that when the customer places the tip in the envelope and seals it, there is no doubt to whom the tip should go. Again, this respects the customers' privacy and they can choose to use the envelope or not.

A third option is to include a mandatory tip in the form of a "service fee." This is common in the hotel and resort industry, and many other service businesses make use of the practice, too. If you choose to charge such a service fee, you should make it clear in your promotional literature (including menus, brochures, and your website) that tips are included in this way.

In some industries, tips are an assumed source of income for employees. Government rules allow certain types of companies to pay a wage that is lower than the minimum wage in other types of businesses because the employee is expected to earn a percentage of the company's sales revenues as tips. If you plan to do this, first check employment regulations to be sure this is allowed, and then don't withhold tips from employees or you'll soon find yourself without a staff.

A final consideration is how to divide up the tips. You can choose to pool tips and divide them up among staff equally at the end of the day, or once each week. Most companies also divide up tips into "staff" vs. "house", meaning employees draw from the pool at a certain rate and the owner draws a portion as well. Keep in mind that you may have employees who are not in direct contact serving customers. You should have a fair and even-handed policy to include these employees in the tip pool. They are also valued members of your staff.

6.6   Financial Management

6.6.1   Bookkeeping

We did not speak to a single salon owner who enjoyed keeping books, but all of them stressed the importance of doing so. Maintaining accurate, up-to-date records can help you run your business more cost-effectively and efficiently. By keeping track of how much everything costs, you'll quickly know what marketing efforts don't pay off, and what types of pieces are not worth bringing in.

Keeping your books includes tracking two things:

- How much money you have coming in

- How much money you have going out

Bookkeeping Systems

Some people prefer to keep track of everything manually. Many business owners simply buy a few journals, write their accounts across the top and enter each month's expenses by hand. This method works well if you are organized, and love the feel of pen on paper. But if you have employees, several sources of income, and a steady flow of traffic through your store, you'll soon forget a few months, and it will become a monster lying in wait for you in your desk's bottom drawer.

Luckily for small business owners, there are several fairly inexpensive software systems that can easily guide you through the bookkeeping process. Intuit offers different types of financial software for different types of businesses. Intuit's Quickbooks, one of the most popular bookkeeping systems, can run about $800 with point of sale functions, but will quickly pay for itself in the savings of not hiring a full-time bookkeeper. Intuit also offers a basic program, Quicken Home & Business, which is a good option for new businesses and costs about $99.

Another maker of business management software is Acclivity. Their "AccountEdge" suite allows you to track revenues and expenses, record bank deposits, generate reports, track customers and more. There are several other financial programs, including Simply Accounting that you can find at your local office supplies store.

- Acclivity
  http://acclivitysoftware.com/products

- Quicken
  http://quicken.intuit.com

- QuickBooks
  http://quickbooks.intuit.com

- Simply Accounting
  www.simplyaccounting.com

Even though software can make most of the work easier for you, you might consider taking a beginning accounting or a bookkeeping class at a local community college. Accounting basics are vital information that all store owners need, but sometimes neglect to learn. Even if you hire someone to do your books, you'll need to know the basics so that you can understand what is going on in your accounts.

You might consider hiring a part-time bookkeeper on a contract basis if you find yourself so busy running your salon that you don't have time to do your books yourself. Depending on how busy you are, it may take the bookkeeper a few hours per week to get your books up-to-date and balance them with your bank statements. You can find a bookkeeper through word of mouth or the Yellow Pages.

Even if you plan on having a full-time bookkeeper or accountant, you should know enough about your salon's books to be able to do them yourself if you need to, and certainly to be able to check the accuracy and honesty of those whom you employ. You should know how to:

- Make a daily sales report of how much money you take in every day

- Make accounts payable and accounts receivable reports

- Make and read an income statement (also called a profit and loss statement)

- Make and read a cash flow statement

- Understand a balance sheet

The following sections will help you to understand more about these business basics.

6.6.2 Financial Statements and Reports

"Based on all the salon business classes I've attended, you can generate a 10% profit if you are diligent about your financials."

— Ronnie Pryor, Owner,
Source Salon

The Daily Sales Report

Every day you take in money. You get cash, you take credit cards, and possibly debit cards for payment, and you may even accept checks. A daily sales report logs all of this information. It will also help you ready the monies you take in for your bank deposit. Most accounting software will allow you to enter this information. Some booksellers do this by hand—they create or buy a form to use and put the daily proceeds in an envelope. You will want to check your cash register receipts against what you actually have in your cash drawer to make sure it all matches at the end of each day.

Most accounting software will provide this type of report or you can do the report by hand. Here is an example of a daily sales tracking report.

Sample Daily Sales Report

Date: October 13, 20__

	Today	Month to Date
Cash	$1,319.10	$18,000.00
Checks	515.85	7,200.00
Master Card	180.04	2,400.00
Visa	$70.26	1,200.00
Other	0	400.00
Store Credit	0	0.00
Subtotal	**$2,085.25**	**$29,200.00**
Starting Float (Subtract)	(-250.00)	(-250.00)
Deposit Total	**$1,835.25**	**$28,950.00**
Returns	0	178.75
Voids	0	43.92
Pay Outs	0	250.00
Other	0	0
Total Cash Paid Out	**0**	472.67
Deposit Total Less Total Cash Paid Out	**$1,835.25**	**$28,477.33**
Sales Tax Collected	91.76	1,447.50
Cash Register Reading	$1,834.25	$28,477.65
Difference (+ or -)	$1.00	$0.32

> **TIP:** Balance your cash register float every day to your sales tracking report. (The "float" is the cash you start your day with in order to make change.)

Your Sales Pace

A good way to determine if your sales for the month are on track on any given day is to follow your sales pace. At any time during the month, this will tell you what you can expect to earn for the remainder of the month. Perhaps a big snow storm has caused a sales slump for several days during the week. How much will you need to earn for the rest of the month to meet your revenue target?

The basic formula for calculating sales pace is:

Sales Pace = (Total Sales ÷ Number of Business Days so far for the month) x the number of business days in the month

From the Daily Sales Report above, the salon did $18,000 up to the 13th business day of the month. The sales pace is calculated using the preceding 12 days of sales as: $18,000 ÷ 12 x 31 = $1,500 x 31 = $46,500.

So, for the entire month at the current sales pace, the store can expect around $47,000 in sales. If the store owner had projected $45,000 in sales for this month, then the sales pace is well on track. If the projection was $50,000, then sales are a bit behind.

Another point to consider is that sales on the 13th day of the month were above the average daily sales ($1,835 as compared to $1,500). The store owner can figure out now what the sales pace for the rest of the month will need to be to maintain the target pace.

Let's say the store owner had projected $50,000 in sales for the month. To calculate the sales pace that is needed for the remainder of the month, use the formula:

Sales pace = ($50,000 – ($1,500 x 12)) ÷ 18 = $1,778

The store will need to produce $1,778 in sales each day for the remaining 18 days of the month in order to reach the $50,000 sales target for the month. Based on the preceding 12 days of sales, the store is a bit behind in its daily and month-to-date target sales.

Income Statement (Profit and Loss Statement)

Your income statement (also called a profit and loss or P&L statement) will tell you how much money you have in expenses and how much money you have in revenue for a given period. A number of things are necessary for an income statement.

You'll need to know:

- Your revenues for the period (gross sales minus returns and discounts)

- The cost of goods sold (what it cost you during the period to purchase merchandise for your store for the period)

- Your gross profit (revenues minus cost of goods sold)

- Your operating expenses (everything you must pay for to operate your store, including non-cash items like depreciation)

- Your net profit before and after taxes (revenues minus your operating expenses, and then subtract your tax liability)

The end result will tell you how much money your store is making — what is commonly referred to as "the bottom line."

You will want to decide which method of accounting you want to use, accrual method or cash method. In the accrual method, income is reported in the month it is earned and expenses reported in the month they are incurred (even if they have not yet been paid).

The cash method tracks actual money received and actual money spent. You do not consider any outstanding bills or invoices. The Business Owner's Toolkit website has an article entitled "Cash vs. Accrual Accounting" at **www.toolkit.cch.com/text/P06_1340.asp** that you can read as an introduction to this topic.

Here is an example of a typical income statement:

Sample Income Statement

Income Statement [Company Name]
for month ending July 31, 20__

REVENUE ($)

Cash sales	5,250
Credit card sales	1,600
Online sales	150
Total Sales	**$7,000**

COST OF GOODS SOLD

Inventory and material purchases	1,800
Shipping	50
Supplies	150
Total cost of goods sold	**$2,000**

GROSS PROFIT

	$5,000

EXPENSES

Lease	1,850
Insurance	75
Licenses & taxes	250
Office supplies & postage	100
Interest	95
Utilities	225
Wages	550
Telephone and Internet	115
Depreciation	55
Vehicle expenses	220
Repairs & maintenance	65
Total Expenses	**$3,600**

Net Income for the Month   **$1,400**

Cash Flow Statement

The cash flow statement allows you to quickly see whether more cash is coming in than going out, or vice versa, at the end of each month. It also allows you to make projections for certain periods of the year (such as the summer months when you might have increased sales due to larger numbers of tourists in your area at that time), or project cash flow year-over-year, and budget accordingly. You can also use it to track monthly cash flow and make projections for the coming month. This is handy if you're planning to make a large equipment or inventory purchase and need to know if you can afford it.

Cash flow is an important element of your financial picture. Monitoring cash flow lets you see how well your business is doing from day to day. Are you paying expenses with the money you take in from your operating revenues, or are you paying for expenses with other business funds such as banked working capital? If you are doing so with the former, your business is self-sustaining.

To keep track of expenses, you will need to keep copies of all receipts. This can be a challenge for new business owners who might have a habit of tossing out receipts for small items or not asking for receipts in the first place. However, you are likely to have numerous small expenses related to your business, and these can add up over time. These expenses should be accounted for so you can minimize your taxes. And, of course, knowing exactly where your money is going will help you plan better and cut back on any unnecessary expenses. So make it a habit to ask for a receipt for every expense related to your business.

On the next page is a sample six-month cash flow worksheet for the first six months of operation.

Accounts Payable/Receivable Reports

Accounts payable are those accounts that you must pay — the money or bills your store owes. Accounts receivable are any accounts that are owed your store — the money that others owe you. Accounts receivable reports can vary widely depending on how you do business. For instance, accepting credit cards or selling over the Internet will affect how this report looks. And you may sell more at certain times than at others. If you have a layaway plan, this will affect your accounts receivable as well.

Sample 6-Months Cash Flow Worksheet

Month	1	2	3	4	5	6	Total
Starting Cash							
Cash Receipts							
Cash sales							
Layaways							
Credit card receipts							
Debit card receipts							
Total							
Cash Disbursements							
Start-up Costs							
Advertising							
Bank Charges							
Fees & Dues							
Fixed Assets							
Insurance							
Loans-Principal							
Loans-Interest							
Licenses & Taxes							
Purchases for resale							
Office Supplies							
Professional fees							
Rent							
Repair & Maintenance							
Telephone & Internet							
Utilities							
Wages & Benefits							
Owner's Draw							
Monthly Surplus or Deficit (Cash less Disbursements)							
To Date Surplus or Deficit*							

[Monthly surplus/deficit to date is calculated by carrying through any deficit or surplus from month to month]

Accounts payable reports will tell you what bills you owe and when they are due. It's important to know clearly what you owe before you make any additional purchases. You have to be able to pay all your incoming bills and still have enough money for the other things you need to purchase for your business. An accounts payable report will help you to schedule when you will pay your bills, and will help you make sure nothing is neglected or forgotten.

Balance Sheet

A good metaphor for a balance sheet is that it is a snapshot, like a photograph, of your business taken at one moment in time. A balance sheet is the quickest way to see how your salon is doing at a glance. It shows you what you own and what you owe. In other words, it is a balance of your assets against your liabilities.

The balance sheet consists of:

- Assets (the items you own including your inventory)

- Liabilities (what you owe)

- Owner's Equity (what you've put into the business)

Types of assets are current assets and fixed assets (long-term and capital assets). A current asset is something that is acquired by your business over your business's fiscal year and will probably be used during that period to generate more revenue. Inventory, prepaid expenses such as rent already paid, and accounts receivable are examples of current assets. A fixed asset is an item that doesn't get used up quickly such as land, buildings, machinery, vehicles, long-term investments, etc., whose value is depreciated over time.

There are two types of liabilities: current and long-term. A current liability includes all those bills waiting for you to send a check out, such as utilities, short-term loans, or anything else payable within twelve months. A long-term liability is something that will be paid over a period of time longer than twelve months, for instance, a mortgage, a long-term equipment lease, or a long-term loan.

Owner's equity is anything you've personally contributed to (invested in) the business or any profit that remains in the owner's account that you have not drawn out in wages for yourself. If you used money from your personal accounts, or put your own assets into the business's inventory, the business "owes" you and it is recorded in this section of the balance sheet.

On the next page is what a typical balance sheet will look like. Note that assets balance exactly against liabilities + owner's equity. Also note that owner's equity equals assets minus liabilities.

6.6.3   Building Wealth

The following excellent advice on building wealth is adapted from the *FabJob Guide to Become a Coffee House Owner*, by Tom Hennessy.

Sometimes we get lost in the adventure of building a business and forget that on top of the perks of being our own boss, we can also make money in our venture. However, like all things, success doesn't just happen — you have to create it.

Even when you are making a good net profit each month, if you don't have a system for managing that profit, it can leak out during the course of a year. Then you will have nothing to show for your labor come New Year's Eve. In order to build wealth, you need to know how to squeeze all the value out of each and every dollar through budgeting, saving and investing.

Through these practices, you can build up a substantial amount of money without having a huge business. That is because time goes by very quickly. Five or ten years can slip away fast, and if you have a plan to carry you through those years, you will be amply rewarded. The two magic ingredients of time and compound interest are very valuable allies indeed.

Compound Interest and Debt

Think of compound interest as a steep hill. People are either on one side of this hill or the other. On one side of the hill, you have compound interest that you pay. On the other side is compound interest that is paid to you.

Sample Balance Sheet

Balance Sheet [Company Name]
As at June 30, 20___

ASSETS
Current Assets

Cash	12,200
Accounts Receivable	1,000
Inventory	80,000

Total current assets 93,200

Fixed Assets

Furniture	3,500
Vehicle	20,000

Total fixed assets 23,500

TOTAL ASSETS $116,700

LIABILITIES
Current Liabilities

Accounts Payable	5,000
Taxes Payable	2,225
Loan (short-term)	12,500
Current Portion of long-term loan	667

Total Current Liabilities 20,392

Long-term liabilities

Loan	35,000

TOTAL LIABILITIES   55,392

OWNER'S EQUITY

Capital – Owner's Deposits	90,000
Less Owner's withdrawals	(32,500)
Net Income/Loss	3,808

Total Owner's Equity 61,308

TOTAL LIABILITIES AND OWNER'S EQUITY $116,700

When you first start out in business, you generate a lot of debt. Your $200,000 loan may seem like a deal at 9 percent over 7 years, but is it really? By the time you pay off the loan, you will have paid an additional $70,295 in interest. That's over 35% of your loan.

When you are paying off your loan, you are looking up from the bottom of a steep slope towards the debt-free top. Most of the monthly payment is interest—hence the steepness. During the first year of the note, you have paid $21, 486 in principal and $17,128 in interest. That is a lot of interest compared to principal.

By the end of the note, this ratio will level off. In the final year, you will pay $36,795 in principal and only $1,818 in interest. At the top of the hill, you are debt free. You owe no interest and you receive no interest.

A business can't really move to the other side of the hill and receive interest because the government punishes businesses that retain profits by taxing them. You need to spend money on capital improvements or pay it out in wages or other forms of compensation, again triggering taxes. A good accountant will help you to minimize paying taxes while maximizing compensation.

Paying Off Debt

Accountants don't like businesses to pay off debt too fast because it creates phantom income. This is because you can only expense interest, not principal, since you never really owned the principal in the first place. It wasn't your money; you borrowed it.

When you wrote that loan payment check every month, the principal you paid back wasn't yours in the first place so it is not considered a legitimate expense. Only the interest that you pay on that loan payment is considered yours and therefore you are allowed to expense that portion of the payment.

In the example earlier, you paid $21,486 in principal and $17,128 in interest during your first year. You expense the interest on your income statement, but where does the principal go? You'll find it in the bottom line as profit. Only you gave that profit back to the lender and you get taxed on it, even though you don't actually have the cash anymore. That is why it is called phantom income. A good accountant can help you deal with this issue and at the same time help you to pay down your loan quicker and minimize taxes on phantom income.

If you can pay off your loan in 5 years instead of 7 years, you can save $21,197 in interest payments. That is significant. To generate the cash to do this, though, you need to learn the value of money.

Here is a good math lesson for you and your employees. Let's assume that you are netting 8% profit before taxes. Every time you spend money on expense items, that is money that normally would go straight to the bottom line in the form of net profit (except you spent it).

Suppose you bought a box of mechanical pencils for $9.95 at the office supply store. How much in the way of sales do you need in order to produce enough profit to pay for them? The easiest way to figure it out is to divide $9.95 by your net profit percentage, which is 8%.

$$\$9.95 \div .08 = \$124.37$$

Looking at it another way, on $124.37 you would generate net profit of $9.95, which is 8% ($124.37 x .08).

You need to sell an additional $124.37 in merchandise to produce enough profit to cover your pencil purchase. Every time you spend a dollar, a corresponding sale is needed to pay for it. That's over and above your regular sales. You'll need to generate an additional $124.37 above your usual sales in order to pay for your pencils.

Thinking about the value of a dollar in these terms can have a drastic effect on your bottom line. When you think about the amount of related sales needed to offset expenses, you'll consider your purchases more carefully.

Forced Savings Account

In a forced savings account, you automatically transfer a specific amount of money from your checking account into an interest-bearing account on a certain day of each month. It follows the old rule "Pay yourself first." If you don't do this, the year will slip by and you will have nothing to show at the end of it for all your efforts.

Even $100 a month is easy to do for most businesses. At the end of the year you will have $1,200 plus interest to do whatever you like with. Use it to pay for a vacation, employee bonus, or a new piece of equipment (that you didn't have to borrow the money for, saving even more money in paid interest).

Your bank can set this up for you. Your interest is better if your money is invested in treasury securities. Talk to a stockbroker or investment advisor about different options. For example, $2,000 per month invested in an index fund averaging 10% per year will grow to $412,227 in 10 years. At the same time, you want your money invested in something safe, but you want it to be accessible in case you need to write a check for some emergency.

There is nothing wrong with creating wealth. It is only through profit that you provide capital to grow your business and pay wages. You're taking responsibility for your own financial well being. As you save and invest, you start to live on the other side of the interest hill and you start earning money without actually having to work for it. It's a beautiful thing to watch.

6.7   Employees

"I wish I knew how difficult it is to find talented stylists who are willing to work hard and are also dependable. I also wish I were better at managing staff early on. Make sure you do not promise your staff anything you cannot deliver, because as the owner, your word needs to be trusted and true. Share with your employees future plans, and ask for ideas — as what they help build, they will support, as the saying goes."

— Derrick Diggs, Owner,
Layers Hair Salon

6.7.1   When to Hire Help

Even if you plan to start on a shoestring budget, chances are you will need at least one other employee to help during busy times (weekends, especially), or to give you a day off here and there.

Many business owners prefer to work all the hours their store is open, closing shop a couple of days a week, during holidays and for vacations. This system can work very well, especially if you notify your customers in advance of vacation time so they aren't disappointed with a wasted trip. You can even use the reminder as a selling tool by including a coupon for them to use when you return from vacation.

However, most shop owners reach a point in their careers where they want to make more profit by staying open more days or hours, or the store is so busy on a daily basis that they need the extra help at all times. In addition, malls and downtown business areas may have strict rules or bylaws about operating hours, and they'll fine you if you don't comply. You may not want to be in the store all the hours that it is required to be open, so you'll need to hire someone to be there when you're not.

Many retailers these days have a rule that if there are ever more than three people in line at the express checkout, then they will open another line. You might want to adopt this "three's a crowd" policy, too. If you consistently have more than three people waiting for help, or to make a purchase, then you may need to hire.

Take a look at your finances and make sure you can afford another employee. Are you making enough profit to hire extra help on the weekends and holidays? Will it increase your profits even more? If customers are getting frustrated at the wait time and leaving, then it most definitely will. Perhaps your business has even grown to the point where you need a full-time employee.

There are several types of staff members you can hire, and each has its advantages and disadvantages. All employees should be considered as investments, since you will spend time and money hiring and training them. You will see a return on that investment in increased sales, higher productivity in your store, more free time for you, and even new ideas for running your store based on employee input.

Full-time staff members work 30 or more hours a week. Most people work only one full-time job at a time, so, since they spend so much of their week working with you, they will naturally develop a sense of loyalty to you. In addition, full-time employees become so familiar with your store's routines and procedures that they can assist in training new staff members and run things if you need to take a day off here and there. A particularly competent and loyal full-timer might even become your second-in-command as manager when you take a vacation or open your second location. Keep in mind that full-time employees also come with the extra burdens for you of increased paperwork, health and other benefits, employment insurance, and so on.

Part-time staff members generally work less than 30 hours a week. Many people work more than one part-time job, often because of the unavailability in certain industries for full-time opportunities. (As discussed above, full-time employees cost more to employ.) As a result, loyalty will be less assured from your part-time staff and they are more likely to leave you if they receive a higher-paying or full-time job offer from another employer. However, the advantage to you is that you will save money, time and paperwork by hiring part-timers.

Often, students, seniors, and stay-at-home parents enjoy part-time work, as it allows them some income while not demanding as much of them as a full-time job might. However, you may find that they require more training, as they are less likely to have pursued a career in the beauty or hair salon industry.

Casual or on-call staff can also fill an important niche in your business. A talented cosmetology student studying at a local beauty school or apprenticing for another non-competing business might be interested in earning extra money when your salon is busiest, or when you need a vacation. Also, a family member might want to earn extra money at holidays by filling in at the store working as a shampoo assistant or receptionist.

No matter which type of employees you decide to hire, start small. Hire a part-timer to get a feel for being an employer. If you like the person you hired and they're working out well, you might want to offer them increased hours or even a full-time position. If you hire someone on a full-time basis in the beginning and find that you can't afford to keep them on full-time, you will likely lose that employee and generate hard feelings. Hiring someone part-time also gives you the flexibility to hire someone else if the person you originally hired doesn't work out.

6.7.2   Recruiting Staff

Hiring employees can be one of the most challenging aspects of owning a business. It can be difficult to find an employee who learns easily, is friendly with your customers, is honest, and comes to work on time.

Qualities of Great Employees

Have you ever gone into a store and been treated rudely or without concern by an employee? Everyone has run into a rude salesperson at some time or another. Sometimes store salespeople are so rude and so unconcerned that potential customers leave the store without buying something they fully intended to purchase. A rude employee can hurt your sales and cost you customers.

But if you pick the right employees, you will have other people who care about your store and the customers who come there, and who will work to make your store a success. So it is vital that you choose carefully.

As you think about the demands of your new salon, the niche you are hoping to fill in your community and the customers you hope to have, make a list of the qualities you want in your employees. Think about the type of people who will be easy for you to work with, who will be warm and helpful to the customers, and who will be an asset to your salon.

Consider some of the following qualities of great retail employees:

- Honest
- Hardworking
- Responsible
- Reliable
- Friendly
- Knowledgeable
- Polite
- Good sales ability
- Good customer service ability
- Niche experience (e.g. if your salon attracts a lot of male customers it is helpful to have employees who have experience working in a men's salon or barber shop)

Now that you know the kind of people you want, you have to find them. If you talk about your salon— and you should, because it's a good way to generate excitement — you can ask everyone you come into contact with if they know someone who would be a good employee for your salon. Your regular customers are a good source for referrals, and more than one store owner has hired a customer to work as an employee in their store. Almost everyone knows someone who is looking for a job — it never hurts to ask around.

Types of Employees

Aside from all the normal qualities you would look for in a good employee listed above, you may need to hire some specially trained employees for your business.

These might include:

- Salon and/or Spa Director or Coordinator
- Shampoo Assistant
- Esthetician
- Hair Colorist
- Hair Stylist/Barber
- Housekeeper
- Makeup Artist
- Massage Therapist
- Nail Technician/Manicurist
- Nurse or Doctor
- Receptionist
- Salesperson
- Spa Technician

Consider writing up job descriptions for each of your specialty employees. This will help you determine exactly where each one fits into your overall operations and daily needs. In addition, you can practice writing up schedules for these "virtual" employees in order to see how they would fit into your service offerings and to determine if you have staff enough to cover all the required tasks. You can then use these job descriptions to write up ads for each of the positions you plan to hire for.

Sample Job Description

Salon Receptionist:

Reporting directly to and working closely with the salon owner, the salon receptionist performs general administrative duties, including answering telephone calls, returning emails, as well as assisting stylists when needed. Other duties include helping with laundry, cleanup, and assisting with shampoos.

Duties and responsibilities:

1. Check appointment books regularly and make stylists aware of appointments that need to be filled or rescheduled.
2. Oversee stylists' work schedules, help them set goals and work with owner to resolve scheduling problems or issues.
3. Work closely with owner and keep owner apprised of issues relating to employee relations, scheduling, and other relevant matters.
4. Gather and organize client tickets, gift cards, receipts and payout records for accounting purposes.
5. Manage and oversee vendor deliveries.
6. Work weekly with website manager to update web page.
7. Monitor salon equipment maintenance and building repairs as needed.
8. Performs other related duties as required.

Knowledge, skills and abilities:

1. Advanced knowledge of personal computers, including internet, email and client management programs.
2. Good analytical, organizational and problem-solving skills.
3. Knowledge of good office management practices.
4. Ability to communicate effectively both verbally and in writing with staff, employees, clients and vendors.
5. Ability to operate standard office equipment including photocopier, fax machine, and scanner.
6. Ability to schedule and organize salon tasks effectively.

Advertising

The first place to advertise your job openings is in your own salon. You can put a "Help Wanted" sign in the front window, and another by the cash register.

Also consider placing an ad in your local paper's employment classifieds. Depending on the job market in your community, this can be an excellent way to find good local employees. Make sure your ad is eye-catching and uses just a few words to get the right kind of people through your door. Consider the following ad:

> WANT TO BE PART OF A CUTTING EDGE HAIR DESIGN TEAM?
> If you're an organized and dynamic person who wants to be part of the area's most exclusive hair design team, this is the perfect opportunity for you! Enchanté, a busy, upscale salon located in downtown Rancho Largo seeks a full-time receptionist. Duties include scheduling, working with stylists, and managing vendor deliveries. Must be available to work Tuesdays through Saturdays 11AM - 7PM. Previous salon experience a big plus. Please fax your resume to 555-1234 or call 555-1000 and ask for Stella Stylist.

Make sure the ad gets the point across quickly. Classified advertising is expensive and is priced by the word. Therefore, it is important to get your point across as quickly as you can. The ad above is about 80 words long.

Make sure all the vital information is included. Potential applicants need to know how to contact you or where to fax their resumes. Also, in order to save you lots of time with applicant questions, remember to include the basics about the job in your ad, including any benefits. One important thing to mention is whether the opportunity is full-time or part-time.

Make sure your ad is correct before it runs in the paper. When you work with an ad rep from your local paper, always ask them to give you a copy of your classified ad as it will appear, so you can check for mistakes. When your ad appears, check it again and make sure it is correct — especially your contact information.

Make sure that you include words or phrases that quickly help potential applicants find themselves in your ad. In the example advertisement above, the title includes the important question "want to be part of a cutting edge hair design team?". The reader knows immediately that this is a salon-related position. Potential applicants who have never worked in a salon setting will know immediately that the job isn't for them. People who do know the salon industry will be drawn to the ad and will know they should send you a resume.

When you run an ad, decide ahead of time if you are too busy for phone calls and would prefer the first round of submissions to be sent by fax or email. Taking prescreening phone calls from applicants is time consuming. Decide what works best for you and your hiring schedule.

6.7.3   The Hiring Process

"We try to hire staff fresh out of school or new to the area and train them thoroughly ourselves. This way, we can teach them our methods and it's easier for them to adapt to our way of doing things than, say, someone who already has an established client base or has worked at another salon for five or ten years."

— Alex Safar, owner,
Salon Acote

The selection process starts with the prospective employee filling out an application. Here are some other things to look out for when prospective employees come in to fill out an application or drop off a resume:

- Are they dressed nicely? Well-groomed?

- Are they polite or do they say, "Gimme an application"?

- Are they alone? Chances are that if the potential employee can't come to fill out an application without their best friend, they can't work without their friends either.

- What does your gut instinct tell you?

The Interview Process

The purpose of an interview is to get to know potential applicants as much as you can in a short period of time. It is therefore important that most of that time be spent getting the applicants to talk about themselves. Most employers with limited interviewing experience spend too much time talking about the job or their store. And while that is certainly important, it won't help you figure out to whom you are talking and if that person is a good match for your salon. A good rule of thumb to follow is that the applicant should do 80% of the talking.

To make the best use of your time, have a list of questions prepared in advance. This will keep the process consistent between applicants. You can always add questions that pop up based on their answers as you go along. Possible questions to ask include:

- Why did you apply to work here?

- What is the ideal schedule you would like to work?

- When can you absolutely not work?

- What sort of experience do you have that you feel qualifies you for this job?

- Tell me about your last job and why you left.

- What was the best job you ever had-the one you had the most fun in?

- Who was your best boss and what made them so great?

- If I talked to someone who worked with you, what would they say about your work habits?

- Describe an instance in which you went "beyond the call of duty".

- Name three trends in the industry today and explain why you like or dislike each.

- Where would you like to be five years from now?

- Give me three adjectives that describe your personality at work.

- What creates stress for you? What do you do to eliminate stress?

- Tell me about when one of your weak qualities caused a problem at work.

- Why should we hire you?

Any negative comment about a previous job or previous employer should make you wonder if they will have the same negative feelings toward you some day. Be wary of candidates who bring up wage/salary and benefits questions too early in the interview. Likewise, be suspicious of job seekers who talk about "needing" rather than wanting the job, and of those who never look you in the eye or use constricted body language. Other flags include "yes" people, argumentative types, someone who tries to control the interview or doesn't listen to you, someone who gives confusing or contradictory answers, and people who are rude to other applicants or your staff.

To get a sense of how an employee will actually behave on the job, it is also a good idea to ask "behavioral questions." Behavioral questions ask applicants to give answers based on their past behavior. An example is "Tell me about a time you had to deal with a difficult customer. What was the situation and how did you handle it?" Instead of giving hypothetical answers of what someone would do in a particular situation, the applicant must give examples of what they actually have done. While people's behavior can change, past performance is a better indicator of someone's future behavior than hypothetical answers.

You can also ask questions that communicate your store policies to discover if the applicant will have any issues in these areas. Some examples are:

- When you are working, I expect your full attention to be on my customers. I do not allow private phone calls unless it is an emergency. Is that a problem?

- It is important that we open on time. I expect my workers to be punctual. Is there anything that could keep you from being on time for every shift?

By being clear on specifics and details in the interview, you can hash out any potential problems right then and there or agree to go your own ways because it is not going to work.

What You Can and Can't Ask

You should be aware that there are some things you simply cannot ask about during a job interview. Some are illegal and others are insulting and open the door to charges of discrimination. They include questions about:

- Age
- Race
- Religion
- Marital status
- Family status or pregnancy
- Disability
- Workers Compensation claims
- Injury
- Medical condition
- Sexual orientation

References

Once you have found an applicant who appears to be a good fit, you can learn more by checking their references. The best references are former employers. (Former co-workers may be friends who will give glowing references no matter how well the employee performed.)

Many companies will not give you detailed information about a past employee. They are only required to give you employment dates and sometimes they will confirm salary. But many times you will be able to learn a lot about a potential applicant from a reference phone call. A good employee is often remembered fondly and even asked about by a former employer. An employer may not be able to tell you much about a bad employee for liability reasons, but they can answer the question "Is this employee eligible to be rehired?" Here are some other additional questions from Tom Hennessy, author of the *FabJob Guide to Become a Coffee House Owner*:

- How long did this person work for you (this establishes the accuracy of their applications)?

- How well did they get along with everyone (looking for team skills)?

- Did they take direction well (code words for "did they do their job")?

- Could they work independently (or did they sit around waiting to be told what to do next)?

- How did they handle stressful situations (this is important, especially if you are busy)?

If the references make you feel comfortable, call the employee to let them know they have a job and to come in and fill out the paperwork.

Auditioning the Talent

In a salon setting, you will need to do more than simply see a resume and ask questions of your potential employees, from stylists, manicurists and other technicians to receptionists. An initial interview and resume review is a good idea, as is a reference check (see below), but once you are interested in possibly hiring a person, you need to "audition" them to evaluate their artistry and skills thoroughly before hiring them.

Alex Safar's upscale Salon Acote in Boston, for example, does a thorough check of its potential employees.

> "I don't love resumes, although I will call some references, but the most important step if someone appears to be a potentially good fit is to have them work a full day. We need to make sure they are talented, as we will provide through training if the potential is there. But there are many other important qualities not found on a resume, such as, do they smile? Are they friendly? Are they willing to put coins in a meter for a client, and do they enjoy going that extra mile?

> You need to look at each case individually and from a manager's viewpoint. You may, for example, have an employee who simply wants to work 35 hours a week and then go home to their family, no matter what comes up. As a manager, you need to decide whether that works for your business or not. If not,

you need to be able to replace that employee with someone who can work the hours you need them to. Or, if that employee is indispensable, you need to accept that and move on and make up for any gaps elsewhere.

A management course is extremely important, because it will help you learn to deal with different types of employees who have different goals from yours. Your basic goal as a salon owner is to make money. Your employees' goals will naturally be different from yours, so you need to look at things from their perspective and find ways to motivate them so that they are happy and your goals are ultimately achieved."

Safar adds, however, that in the case of stylists, exceptional talent can occasionally override these other considerations. He cites the example of a very shy stylist whose artistry was so beautiful that "not hiring him was simply not an option," and an appropriately trained assistant was able to compensate for his social shortcomings.

This thorough hiring test is carried out with all employees, including even receptionists. Because customer service is so crucial to a salon, they are not placed in this role unsupervised or even hired on a permanent basis until thoroughly tested "on the job". At Salon Acote, potential receptionists (who have already been screened and interviewed) are trained and observed under close supervision for a day. If they seem right for the job, they will then work with a senior desk person for an initial period, similar to "job shadowing" until they are able to handle the reception desk adeptly on their own.

6.7.4 Paying Your Staff

"I wish I had known that the absolute maximum for your total labor costs can't exceed 54%. That percentage should include your front desk costs, management, commissions and all social security and benefits costs."

— Larry Dunlap, Haircolorxperts

Another area to be clear about is what the pay is. Some employers will tell you not to talk money until you make the actual job offer, but that is really your choice. You do not want to go through the interview process, agonize over your decision, choose Johnny Good, offer the job and find out he does not want it because he thought it paid more and included health and dental benefits.

The government establishes a minimum wage that workers must be paid. Whether or not you want to pay over this amount is up to you. However, if you want the best candidates, then you'll need to offer them a competitive salary. To learn more about minimum wages in your area check out the U.S. Department of Labor website at **www.dol.gov/esa/minwage/america.htm**. You can also use web based surveys and services such as Salary.com, which allows you to narrow the survey to your local geographic area.

For wage information in a variety of occupations in Canada, visit the Services Canada website at **www.labourmarketinformation.ca** (click on "English", and then choose "Wages & Salaries" in the left frame menu). Visit **www.hrsdc.gc.ca/eng/labour/employment_standards** for Employment Standards in Canada, including information about minimum wage.

Ask your accountant to set up a payroll for your salon and maintain it for you. That way, you can be assured that you are making the correct amount of deductions for taxes and other benefits.

Employees are paid either weekly, bi-weekly, or on the 15th and last day of each month. You should have sufficient funds in your business checking account to ensure payroll checks will be covered. You may offer employees direct deposit paychecks (in which their pay is deposited into their bank accounts) or regular checks (which they may take to the bank themselves).

> **TIP:** It's often best to pay bi-weekly, after the credit card charges and checks have cleared the bank.

Pay Structures

"We live in an age of 'benefits'. I feel that a critical part of an employee package must include benefits such as vacation and health insurance at a minimum, in order to entice successful stylists for employment. While benefits are

expensive to a salon owner, having a full, booked, and happy staff will ease the pain of the cost and in the long run produce much more revenue."

— Derrick Diggs, Layers Hair Salon

Salaried Wage

Paying your employees a set salary usually means more profitability for you, so long as you can arrive at a number that both you and your new employee are happy with. You must also take into account additional payroll premiums paid to the government such as workers' compensation, social security, and medical benefits. Salaries are generally offered to management and other specialist employees.

Here are some ballpark salary ranges for different positions in the salon industry:

- *Stylist:* Average salary $55,000

- *Barber:* Average salary $16,000-$37,000

- *Manicurist:* Average salary $16,000-$32,000

Hourly Rate

Most entry level positions are paid hourly in the salon industry. Some of your employees will likely prefer this option to commission only, especially when they are just starting out, since this guarantees them a basic wage, regardless of how many clients they deal with. Many salons may also offer a commission (e.g., 10%) on all salon products sold. Note, however, that in the case of salons with rented booths or chairs, the rental fee will usually be a flat monthly rate so the cosmetologist keeps all earnings including tips and commissions on retail products sold in excess of this rental fee.

Here are some basic hourly rates for different positions in the salon industry:

- *Salon Manager:* $12 to $25 per hour

- *Spa Manager:* $16 to $20 per hour, depending on experience

- *Stylists' assistants:* $8 to $15 per hour (they often aspire to become stylists and seek this as an entry level position)

- *Receptionist:* from minimum wage to $15 per hour, depending on skills (this position is often filled by aspiring stylists fresh out of beauty school looking for an entry level position)

- *Shampoo Assistant:* $7.50 to $10 per hour plus tips

- *Esthetician:* $8 to $15 per hour plus tips and commissions

Straight Commission

A straight commission pay basis means that your staff are paid a percentage of the fee charged to each client they serve. Typical straight commission rates start at 50 to 60% of the cost of the service, and range up to 70% for experienced employees who supply their own products and equipment. Again, the point is to find a percentage that works for both of you. Although the commission split varies somewhat as mentioned above, many of the salons we spoke with who use a commission system use a 60-40 split.

While having contractors instead of employees may seem like a great cost-cutting plan to reduce labor expense and to motivate staff to work hard, this setup can also backfire. First, it may be hard for you to attract talented staff when you are just starting out. They won't want to work for a low rate while you grow the business; they want to step into a business with a huge clientele so they can maximize their earnings.

In addition, when all your staff are on commission, you lose a sense of the team in your business. Staff may not want to promote each other's services as complementing each other because they don't want to risk losing a client to another staff member. In some businesses, commission is the norm, though, so it generally works well in a situation like that.

Commission is also subject to withholding taxes and vacation pay, so be sure to put it through your bookkeeping system correctly. If you have any questions, it's wise to call your accountant. Additionally, you might want to have a lawyer draw up a commissioned sales staff contract. It's always better to be clear at the outset before any miscommunications occur.

Hourly Plus Commission

If you decide that you're going to offer only a commission and not an hourly wage, bear in mind that this can lead to overbearing sales staff.

However, a guaranteed wage might mean that as soon as you leave they whip out their favorite novel. Perhaps a mix of commission and guaranteed salary might work best for you.

In this scenario, employees agree to a combination of an hourly wage and commission, both of which are paid at a lower rate than if they were being paid one or the other. This gives employees the chance to benefit from developing a loyal and consistent client base. It also takes into account slow days when employees still earn some money and aren't sitting around "on call." In this type of arrangement, commission is closer to 30% or 40% and the wage is reduced to the low end of the hourly rates mentioned earlier.

A similar form of compensation ties commission into the performance of all staff members. Each employee receives a base pay plus a commission that reflects the sales and services of the spa that month. This profit-sharing arrangement often gives employees a better team attitude and more motivation to perform well and work harder.

Also, most salon employees or renters receive a commission on any sales of retail products, which encourages them to help sell retail products.

Bonuses and Benefits

Offering health benefits, extra paid days off, or occasional cash bonuses to your employees may cost you money, but they may also keep your employees loyal to your business in a competitive job market. Many business owners underestimate the cost of hiring and training new employees and forget to factor in the lost revenue from losing experienced employees and their satisfied clients (who may follow your employee to a new place of employment).

Also, keep in mind that not all payment comes in the form of dollars and cents. You can think about ways to make your employees happy that cost relatively little, such as premium coffee in the break room or an occasional after-hours staff party.

> **TIP:** Allowing your employees to bring in guests occasionally for free services benefits both of you. You get a new client and the employee gets to brag about what they do or trade for other services they want.

6.7.5 New Employees

After you shake hands and say, "The job is yours!", you have to know how to work with the new employee to make sure it is a positive experience for everyone.

New Employee Paperwork

When a new employee is hired there will be paperwork they must fill out. In the U.S. this will be a W-4 and an I-9 form. In Canada, the employee will give you their social insurance number; you must also have them fill out a TD1. The U.S. W-4 and Canadian TD1 are legal documents that will determine the amount of tax that is to be deducted from an employee's wages. The U.S. W-4 and Canadian T-4 forms are legal documents verifying how many tax deductions a new employee has. The amount of tax you will withhold as an employer varies based on the amount of deductions that an employee has. Have the employee fill out the forms, and then file them in a folder labeled with their name which you will keep on file.

Check with your state or province's labor office to make sure you are clear about all the forms employees must fill out to work. The sites below give more information on legal paperwork, including where to get blank copies of the forms your employees will need to fill out.

- *SmartLegalForms.com*
  Sells employee forms online
  www.hrlawinfo.com

- *GovDocs Products - Employee Records and Personnel Forms*
  Sells blank forms by the pack
  www.hrdocs.com/Posters/hrproducts/

- *Canada Revenue Agency*
  Download and print any form you need
  www.cra-arc.gc.ca/forms/

Employee Emergency Contact Card

If the unexpected happens, as it sometimes will, you want to be prepared. Having employees fill out an emergency card for their file will help you contact their doctor, spouse, or other friends or family members in case of an emergency. Besides being the most rational and human thing to do, being prepared in this way can safeguard you against liability.

Make sure every employee's emergency card contains the following:

- Their correct and updated address and phone number

- Their family doctor and choice of hospital

- Any medications taken

- Allergies or special medical conditions

- The name and phone number of a family member emergency contact

- The name and phone number of an alternate emergency contact

Make sure that the emergency cards for staff, including one for you, are filled out and placed in alphabetical order in a filing cabinet or another location, and that everyone who works with you knows where this information is kept. Ask employees to verify that their emergency information is correct and updated as soon as it changes.

New Employee Orientation

Showing up on the first day of a new job is stressful for any employee. The new employees you hire are full of hope and anxiety, and are trying their best to make a good impression and be successful in your eyes. You should do your best to make them feel welcome and appreciated.

Here are some tips to help them succeed:

- Make definite orientation plans for your new employee. Develop a list of what you will show and tell your employee, and go through each point. (This is where it helps to have a procedures manual as described in section 6.1.)

- Plan for the employee to have lunch with you or a friendly co-worker on the first day.

- Don't expect your brand new employee to be able to do everything on the first day. Realize that the first few days in your salon will be a time for your new employee to learn and become comfortable with procedures.

- Don't throw your new employee into the fire. Starting them out on the day of the biggest sale in your salon's history is a bad idea. Choose a time that is relatively slow-paced to let your new employee learn in a calm environment.

- Once your employee has been working for a few days, schedule an informal meeting to check in. Ask them to voice questions, comments, and possible concerns. Offer some positive feedback about your new employee's performance.

Taking the time to make sure your new employee feels comfortable and positive working in your salon will pay off in the long run. Happy employees who feel positive about what they are doing often become long-term assets for your business.

Training, Motivating, and Retaining

"We don't rent chairs at the salon; all the stylists are our employees. Stylists spend more time at the salon than they do at home, so technically they are family. Treat your employees well and make sure they are always happy. Give them an environment they truly want to work in each day."

— Valery Joseph, Owner,
Valery Joseph Salons

It costs less to retain the staff you have than to recruit and train new staff, so make sure you keep open lines of communication with your employees. Take the time to ask them how things are going. Listen intently to what they say. Perhaps they are spending more time in your shop than you are and can offer valuable insight to problems you might not have noticed.

Encourage, and if you can, pay for staff to take courses to help them be the best they can be at their jobs. This not only helps them feel good about themselves, but will solidify their attachment to you and your business.

Think of interesting ways to motivate your sales staff. Could you offer a discount on items? An incentive bonus for hitting a sales target? Find out what motivates them, and create a sales incentive program that suits them.

Stay Informed

The government has many laws that protect workers in the workplace. It is important to be aware of these laws and to make sure that your salon abides by them. The U.S. and Canadian governments have websites which provide information on almost any issue concerning employment law. Make sure to check how these laws affect your salon and how you can abide by them. The U.S. Department of Labor website is located at **www.dol.gov**. In Canada, you'll find employment law information at the Human Resources and Skills Development Canada website at **www.hrsdc.gc.ca**.

7. Getting and Keeping Clients

"A salon owner needs to have great hair service from head to toe, as well as fabulous customer service, to always accommodate and never make them wait."

— Valery Joseph, Owner,
Valery Joseph Salons

7.1 Marketing Your Business

"First know your brand. What makes you unique and better? Say it in every way you can. Everyone who works at your salon needs to know your brand and breathe it when they are working there. Get a lot of PR. Be a celebrity.

Everyone wants to go to the salon that the newspaper is talking about; the one that is on TV all the time."

> — Nancy Trent, Founder of PR firm
> Trent & Company, Inc.

Assuming you have a good location, you will get some foot traffic off the street. People will walk into your salon out of curiosity and some of them will buy from you. While this walk-in business can certainly contribute to your success, you can achieve even greater success by attracting customers to your salon through effective marketing.

If your salon is located in a shopping mall, the mall administration will have a calendar of promotional events that you can participate in. Likewise, if you have a salon in a popular shopping district, there will likely be a local merchants association that you can join for cooperative advertising and events. In addition to any marketing you do through your mall or merchants association, you will likely need to do additional promotion on your own. This section outlines a variety of techniques you can try.

7.1.1   Your Grand Opening

> *"The only thing I wish I had done was plan a big grand opening the first day I opened my doors. While it likely wouldn't have driven additional business, it would have provided a means to thank all of those involved in making my dream a reality — from clients, to chair renters to friends and family."*

> — Dalgiza Barros, Owner,
> Creative Energy Hair Studio

Holding a grand opening can be a great way to introduce yourself and your new business to potential clients. If planned carefully, such an event can make your target market aware of your presence in a big way. The goal is to generate curiosity and interest in the services you have to offer, as well as to make people aware of how you differ from the competition. If you're taking over an existing business you may want to let people know that the business is under new ownership and let them know how you plan to keep existing customers happy and serve the needs of new customers.

If you are opening a franchise operation (as explained in section 4.2.2), your franchisor actually may require you to hold a grand opening. Usually they will provide you with guidance as to how they would like it to be conducted. Also, your franchisor may require you to have a certain amount of available capital on hand in order to pay for the event. For information about holding a grand opening for a franchise, you should consult with your franchisor. In this section, we will look at how a non-franchise business owner can host a grand opening event.

Some of the elements to consider when planning your grand opening are:

- *Budget:* how much money can you put toward the event?
- *Timing:* When is the best time to reach the most people?
- *Publicity:* How do you make people interested in attending your grand opening?
- *Invited guests:* Who can help to attract people to your event (local celebrities, for example)?
- *Advertising:* What are the best ways to get the message out to your target market?
- *Promotions:* How will you reward people for attending?

Budget Considerations

There are a number of factors you should consider when planning your grand opening budget. First, you should put aside a certain amount of money in your start-up budget (see section 4.5 for more about start-up financial planning) for the event. Whether your start-up capital comes from your own cash resources or a loan, your plan for a grand opening should be clearly stated in your business planning documents.

Some of the grand opening budget items include extra staffing, advertising, printing invitations, brochures or flyers, promotional items, hiring a master of ceremonies, a remote local radio broadcast from your salon, hiring a guest speaker or celebrity look-alike, hiring a D.J. or band, hiring a caterer to supply refreshments, etc. You should find out the costs for all of these things well in advance and then figure out how much of your start-up cash you can devote to each.

Timing Considerations

When to hold your grand opening is also a major consideration. If you are in a downtown location, then the best time to hold your grand opening might be through the week when traffic is high in the area. If you are opening in a mall or strip mall, then the best time might be on the weekend when these locations usually are busiest.

Another consideration is the season. You shouldn't plan a grand opening close to any major holidays, since people are too busy to give much attention to a new salon opening. Worse, many people travel during holiday times and this can have a negative impact, too.

Time of day is important, also. According to one Chamber of Commerce source, the best time of day for a grand opening is from Tuesday through Friday, from 10:00 a.m. to 12:00. This is the best time to get media attention and maximize attendance. You can informally survey local businesses where you plan to open to determine the highest traffic periods in that area.

Be sure that people are aware of the grand opening well in advance. You should start any advertising several weeks or more before the actual event. Send out your invitations to any guests you plan to invite in advance, too. You want to give them time to respond, and perhaps find someone else to come should one turn down the invitation.

Publicity and Advertising

There are a number of ways to get publicity for your event. You might want to consider a press release; distributing brochures, flyers or menus; contacting your local radio or television station to ask them to do an interview with you; paying for a remote on-location broadcast and so on. Section 7.1.2 has more advice on how to generate publicity, as well as tips for effective advertising.

Invited Guests

Who you invite to your grand opening can also have an impact on attendance. You might want to have the mayor or other high-profile citizen cut the ribbon to officially open your business. Perhaps you know someone famous who wouldn't mind helping out for the event.

Another consideration is to invite people who have a wide network of contacts. They can help to spread the word about your business. Other people to invite include:

- Local Chamber of Commerce members

- City or town council members

- Other government officials

- Local business owners

- Any contractors who worked on remodeling your store

- Business Improvement Area representatives and members

- Any other person or group who you know has a wide sphere of influence

- Any of your existing clients

- Others who were instrumental in helping you open your salon (friends, family, business associates, employees and/or renters)

Promotional Considerations

In promoting your grand opening, you'll want to give people a reason to attend. Put yourself in the place of your hoped-for clientele and answer for them the question: "What's in it for me if I attend?" The answer might be something like a 10-20% discount on products or services, a free sampling of your services, free refreshments (some businesses offer coffee and doughnuts or a barbecue), gift merchandise (give-aways) and so on. The chance to meet a highly regarded celebrity can also be an incentive.

You should also put together a schedule of how you would like events to proceed during the grand opening. This will help you manage the logistics of the event, such as when to start setting up, when to hold the ribbon-cutting ceremony (if you plan to have one), when to serve refreshments, and so on.

On the next page, you will see a sample Grand Opening Plan that includes an event budget and a proposed schedule of events.

A Sample Grand Opening Plan

Grand Opening Budget

Extra staff (4 hours).. $100.00

Master of Ceremonies.. $500.00

Advertising Costs... $600.00

Printing Costs... $450.00

Catering service... $500.00

Balloons... $50.00

Ribbon... $30.00

Remote on-location broadcast...................................... $500.00

Giveaways (at cost) $200.00

Total Grand Opening Costs.................................... $2,930.00

Schedule

9:00 a.m.	Meet with staff and go over the plan
9:15 a.m.	Start setting up, local radio crew to arrive to set up for on-location broadcast
9:30 a.m.	Caterer to arrive with refreshments
9:45 a.m.	Master of Ceremonies and Mayor to arrive
10:00 a.m.	Invited guests to arrive; greet guests and the public in front of the store
10:15 a.m.	Mayor to cut ribbon; invite guests and public inside
10:20 a.m.	Refreshments to be served
10:20-11:30 a.m.	Meet and greet; interviews with local radio talent
11:30-11:50 a.m.	Hold draws for door prizes
11:50 a.m.	Thank everyone for coming. Final words from M.C.
12:00 p.m.	Start clean-up

7.1.2 Advertising

There are many places you can advertise your salon, including the Yellow Pages, newspapers, magazines, radio, television, and the Internet. It is wise to combine two or more of these media, but you will want to consider several factors before you decide for sure which you choose. You'll want to know how much a particular advertisement costs, how long it will last, and most importantly, what consumers it will reach.

Cost

"Advertising is one of those necessary evils. Ads are expensive, but empty chairs are much more costly in the long run. A proper advertising budget need not break the bank, but a steady top of mind awareness in consumer's minds is one of the most solid ways to create demand."

— Susie Galvez, beauty industry expert and author

Your advertising dollars go towards supporting the media organization you're buying an ad from. The more expensive the media, the more expensive its ads are likely to be. A high school yearbook will be able to offer much lower rates than a daily newspaper, and a college radio station (if it takes ads at all) will be cheaper than the area's hottest new music station. And television ads are the most expensive of all.

To find out how much various ad types cost in your area, call your local media outlets and ask them to send you a rate card. Rate cards list all the advertising options offered by the media outlet, and they often include other useful information such as demographic statistics (age, gender, income level, etc.) about the target audience — the type of viewers, listeners, or readers the outlet tends to reach.

Before you make any decisions, read the rate card and target audience information carefully. Is this the media outlet where most of your customers will hear your message? Sixty percent of your advertising budget should be aimed at existing customers, so keep that in mind when you're looking at the rate cards.

If advertising in a local magazine is really inexpensive, but you know most of your customers prefer to listen to the radio, you might want to try the magazine ad as an experiment to see what kind of new customers you might get from it. On the other hand, if you know your customers read the local daily newspaper, you should plan on doing most of your advertising there, and perhaps even forego the expensive television ad that targets people unlikely to shop at your store.

Yellow Pages

Yellow Pages ads can help you attract people from outside of your immediate area, particularly if you have a unique niche. Take a look at Yellow Pages ads for other salons like yours to get ideas (look under categories that match your type of business).

You can either design the ad yourself, have the Yellow Pages design it for you, or hire a designer. If you are interested in advertising, contact your local Yellow Pages to speak with a sales rep. Check the print version of your phone book for contact information. To find the Yellow Pages online, go to **www.yellowpages.com** (U.S.) or **www.yellowpages.ca** (Canada).

Newspapers and Magazines

"Advertisers want to work with owners. Lots of times they have creative ways to incorporate a salon ad along with a complimentary company in which both would benefit and yet the cost would be minimized. Also, editorial is an excellent way to get the word out. Let the press know what you are doing. Every day newspapers, local magazines, television and radio stations have to fill the slots, and if you can offer them a good story, you will make it easy for them to do their job, and you benefit from free recognition."

> — Susie Galvez,
>   beauty industry expert and author

Consider specialty magazines for your area that pertain to your salon's niche. Read a magazine or newspaper carefully to see if an advertisement for your salon would fit with the theme of the paper, the articles, and the other ads.

Also consider advertising in newspapers with classified ads for merchandise like yours. These might be known locally as a bargain, trader, or shopper newspaper. For example, one major advertising newspaper in the U.S. is **www.traderonline.com**, and a similar paper in Canada is **www.buysell.com**.

Many publications will provide you with a free media kit with lots of information about their readership. This information will help you determine if their readers are the sort of customers you are looking for and if it is the right publication for your ad. Some publications will design your ad for free, while others will design it for an additional cost and give you a copy of the ad that you can then run in other publications if you wish.

Creating Effective Ads

"The major professional hair care lines provide you with lots of opportunities to grow your business. They can and will help you with advertising, link your salon on numerous websites, as well as provide any signage that may help attract potential clients."

> — Derrick Diggs, Owner,
> Layers Hair Salon

Some people spend years learning how to create the most effective ads. Since we do not have years, we're going to focus on a couple of key points. For additional tips on creating effective ads read the article entitled "How to Run Effective Advertisements" at **www.usatoday.com/small/ask/2001-07-30-ask-ad.htm**.

Most people need to see an advertisement several times before they buy, so running an ad only once may not give you as much business as you hope. A small ad that you run every week for a couple of months can generate more business than a single full page ad.

You can test a variety of ads, relatively inexpensively, by buying local ads on Google at **http://adwords.google.com**. Try different offers and wording to see which ones are most effective. You can set a maximum daily spending limit which keeps your costs down if lots of people click on your ad without buying. The offers that result in sales might also be effective in your other advertising as well.

One of the most effective ways to draw people into your salon – and to test the effectiveness of each ad – is with some sort of incentive. An incentive can be anything from a discount coupon to a free gift.

To measure advertising effectiveness with coupons, it's a good idea to put a time limit or expiration date on it. Make sure this date is clearly printed on the coupon. It should allow customers enough time to get themselves to your salon – maybe a week or two – but not so much time that they forget about the coupon, thinking they can use it well into the future. Tie the coupon to a date that's easy to remember, such as the end of the month.

The coupon offer should be simple, but with high perceived value — a buy one, get one free offer, or perhaps "This coupon good for 30 percent off your entire purchase," or "Redeem this coupon for a free cosmetic travel bag with every purchase." Above all, it should require that customers come into your shop to redeem their coupons. The idea is to get them to pay you a visit, see what other things you have for sale, and maybe buy something besides what they came for with the coupon.

Giveaway items include key chains, fridge magnets, pens — you name it. Of course, giveaways should be cost-effective, so decide on a budget before you start looking into ordering any. There are numerous companies that can supply you with promotional items. Check the Yellow Pages or do an online search for "advertising specialties" or "promotional products."

7.1.3   Free Publicity

One of the best ways to market — with potentially excellent results for minimal cost — is to get free media publicity. While you don't have the final say over what gets reported, the exposure can give a boost to your business.

Public Service Announcements

If you are working with a charity, you may be able to get a Public Service Announcement aired on local radio stations. Write a 15 second or 30 second announcement and send it to "Public Service Announcements" at local radio stations. It probably will not be prime time, during the drive home, but every bit of exposure helps. Also, contact your local cable company to find out how to submit Public Service Announcements to the community channel.

Press Releases

"Call local editors and invite them or their family members to get hair cuts. Give discounts to the local newspapers or TV stations and encourage them to cover your salon. Always let them know by email or phone what you think the latest hair trends are. And treat journalists like rock stars when they come to your salon."

— Nancy Trent, founder of PR firm
Trent & Company, Inc.

Another way to get free publicity in local newspapers or magazines is by using a press release. Press releases typically announce an event. They should be a page or less, encompass the main points, and be put together as though they were going to be printed verbatim in the newspaper (they sometimes are). A sample press release appears on the next page. You can find additional tips at **www.publicityinsider.com/release.asp** and **www.xpresspress.com/PRnotes.html**.

While you can self-promote, you do need to tie it into the community somehow. Try to brainstorm ways your activity benefits the community. If you donate to charity, then this should be an easy tie-in for you.

Donations

Donations are a good way to get your shop's name and services into the public eye. You'll probably be approached for donations by churches, community centers, non-profit or not-for-profit organizations, schools, sports teams, and more. They might ask for a cash donation but, more often, will want a service or product such as a free haircut or shampoo and blow-dry or free manicure/pedicure that they can use as a prize in a raffle or drawing.

You don't, by any means, need to donate to every organization that asks. But ones that offer charitable tax receipts are worth considering, as are causes you believe in. Ones that you know will reach a large number of people are always worth supporting, because you'll have your shop name recognized by a large group of people as a donor. Be sure to ask for acknowledgment in any programs or posters made for the event.

Sample Press Release

FOR IMMEDIATE RELEASE

Date: January 9th, 20__

Contact: Stella Stylist
           (555) 555-1234

ENCHANTÉ HOLDS VALENTINE'S WEEKEND
BENEFIT TO HELP FIGHT DOMESTIC ABUSE

This Valentine's Day weekend, Enchanté will hold a special "Helping Hearts" event to raise money to help fight domestic abuse. Proceeds from this event will go to the "Cut It Out: Salons Against Domestic Abuse Fund." This fund fights domestic abuse and trains hair stylists to spot victims of abuse and refer them for counseling and other crucial services.

As local District Attorney Frances Meyers explains, "Women often confide and open up to their hair stylists, as going to the salon is a social event where lengthy and often personal conversations take place. This puts hair stylists and other beauty professionals in an excellent position to spot victims of domestic abuse and to refer them to the appropriate services to get the help they need." Enchanté has been a long-time supporter of the Cut It Out: Salons Against Domestic Abuse program.

The "Helping Hearts" weekend event to be held Saturday and Sunday, February 13th and 14th during salon hours will feature a Valentine treats bake sale, a Valentine card, candy, and balloon sales, face painting for children, special makeup and up-do hair demonstrations and tips (just in time for that romantic Valentine's Day dinner), and 10% off all retail products and gift certificates during this event. Owner Stella Stylist will also be on hand all weekend to provide information about the Cut It Out program as well as referral information for victims of domestic abuse.

Enchanté is open weekdays from 10 a.m.- 9 p.m., Saturdays from 11 a.m.-7 p.m. and Sundays from 12 p.m.-6 p.m.. The salon features top local stylists and colorists, manicures, massage, and offers quality hair and skin care products as well as jewelry and accessories. Enchanté is located on Newman Street in Rancho Largo.

When donating, it is nice to donate a basket of hair or skincare products or certificate for a free haircut that will catch the eyes of those who will see it. But consider donating coupons instead – something that will bring people into your salon to collect their service – and possibly encourage them to buy something else besides.

7.1.4   Printed Promotional Tools

When you start a new business you will have to invest in some printed promotional tools at the outset. These tools should be designed in a way that promotes your salon and shows people the style of your salon. Fonts on business cards, letterhead, ink colors, and even your advertising should all be designed to reinforce that style.

If you have a computer with a high quality laser or ink jet printer, you may be able to inexpensively print professional looking materials from your own computer. Free templates for any of the print materials you are likely to need for your salon can be found online. HP offers templates for a variety of programs at **www.hp.com/sbso/productivity/office**. For example, you can create a matching set of stationery (business cards, letterhead, envelopes) in Microsoft Word or a presentation in PowerPoint. The site includes free online classes and how-to guides to help you design your own marketing materials. Another excellent resource is the Microsoft Office Online Templates Homepage at **http://office.microsoft.com/en-us/templates**. At this site you can search a database to find templates for:

- Business stationery (envelopes, faxes, labels, letters, memos, etc.)

- Marketing materials (menu of services brochures, flyers, newsletters, postcards, etc.)

- Other business documents (expense reports, invoices, receipts, time sheets, etc.)

Your Menu of Services Brochure

Your menu of services is a brochure (also called a menu of services pamphlet) that invites people to use your salon's services. Your menu is often the first introduction of your business to potential customers, so take the time to make your menu a powerful tool.

Inspiration for your menu of services can come from any number of places. Chances are you have amassed a collection of them as you pondered opening your own salon. If not, visit the websites of companies similar to yours, and check out their menus (if you have access to actual physical menus, so much the better). Note the similarities and differences in each. Finally, note the unique features that set each menu apart. What is most appealing to you about your favorites? Remember, it's very important that, whatever your menu ends up looking like, it should be anything but bland and unexciting.

What to Include

Your menu will convey information about each of the services you plan to offer, including a description of each, a price, and why the reader will enjoy the service. Think in terms of the overall theme and feel of your business and how that appeals to new clientele. Build on those themes in your menu.

Before writing your menu text, consider the term menu: it evokes the idea of dining out. The language you use in your menu will be similar to what you are used to reading in a restaurant. The peas are never just "peas"; they are "mouth-watering, juicy bursts of sweetness." This is the kind of language you want to emulate, as you'll see in the sample menu in this section.

When you choose your service offerings, make sure that each service is unique, and different enough from your other service offerings to warrant listing as a separate service. If you find that two services seem to be too close in nature, choose the one that best suits your business, is most economical to offer, or is the best fit with the products you'll use and offer for sale.

TIP: Plan to reprint your menu from time to time. Reprinting the menu is an opportunity to remove services that don't do well and maybe add something more marketable.

Many menus include a brief section that explains company policies. This can include the types of payments you accept (cash, credit card and debit card, for example), hours of operation, your cancellation policy and so on. This should be included in an unobtrusive, but clearly visible location.

Service Packages

Packaging your services together for a reduced price is a great way to sell your clients additional services they might not otherwise purchase. You can link your packages to the changing seasons, holidays, or just about anything that inspires a common theme.

Take the time to come up with names for your service packages that convey a particular mood or feel. Match your package names to your target clientele. The names should evoke a certain emotional response from your customers and entice them to purchase your service package.

To encourage retail sales and add more value to your packages, consider offering a credit towards any retail purchase of products you sell to go along with customers' package purchases. This encourages people who otherwise would not purchase your products to do so rather than "wasting" their credit.

A Sample Menu

A sample menu apears on the next few pages.

Design and Printing

Your menu should have visual appeal, too. Where appropriate, you may want to include pictures or artwork that conveys the ambience of your salon. The colors you choose should evoke the image of your business that you wish to convey to the public (although black and white can be effective, too). You may also want to use the logos of any brand-name products your salon is affiliated with in order to inspire consumer confidence.

When you have your written content and an overall look planned out for your menu, take it to a graphic designer. If you don't have a graphic designer, any full-service print shop can help you with design. Expect to pay a minimum of $50 an hour for professional design and several hundred dollars or more to have your menu professionally printed. Some print shops include design work free of cost when you print a certain quantity with them.

Sample Menu - Front

Services & Products

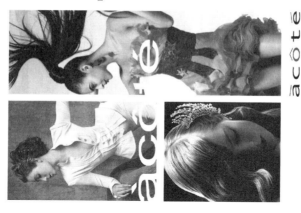

ācôtē
www.salonacote.com
Tel. 617-262-5111 | Fax. 617-267-3686
132 Newbury Street, Boston, MA. 02116

Located on Newbury Street, in Boston's prominent Back Bay, acôté was founded in 1998 by Gaston Safar. Owner of Safar Coiffure also located on Newbury Street. Gaston's vision for unsurpassed client satisfaction, has made salon acôté as well known as it's owner's reputation in the beauty industry. acôté offers comprehensive services, from the signature haircut & color services and bridal party accommodations, to the new protein bond cinderella hair extensions and Bio-ionic thermal reconditioning. Our salon maintains an internationally trained staff and a breathtaking outdoor terrace where you can enjoy a cappuccino or a glass of wine to insure the ultimate experience. Gaston Safar will be extending his insight to Miami with the introduction of his new salon in late 2006

Brochure from Salon Acote, Newbury Street location, Boston.
Copyright © Salon Acote, reprinted with permission. Prices are current as of October, 2008.

Sample Menu - Back

acôte PRODUCTS

evokativ

KÉRASTASE
PARIS

ghd
thermodynamics

STYLING SERVICES

WOMEN'S HAIRCUT & BLOW OUT	*$55
MEN'S HAIRCUT & STYLE	*$45
BLOW OUT	*$35
UP DO	*$70
CONDITIONING TREATMENT	*$30
CONDITIONING TREATMENT & BLOW OUT	*$60
CONSULTATION	Complimentary

COLOR & PERM SERVICES

SINGLE PROCESS	*$75
SEMI-PERMANENT COLOR	*$70
HIGHLIGHTS FULL HEAD	*$145
HIGHLIGHTS PARTIAL	*$115
PERMS	*$100
RELAXERS	*$100
JAPANESE STRAIGHTENING	*$350

acôte

GIFT CARDS ARE AVAILABLE

WEDDING SERVICES

HAIR CONSULTATION (ONE HOUR)	*$70
MAKE UP CONSULTATIONS (ONE HOUR)	*$70
BRIDES HAIR (IN SALON)	*$100
WEDDING PARTY (IN SALON)	*$70
BRIDES HAIR (ON SITE)	*$145
WEDDING PARTY (ON SITE)	*$115

WAXING SERVICES

LIP WAX	*$10
EYEBROW WAX	*$20
CHIN WAX	*$15
LEG WAX	*$60
BACK WAX	*$65
LOWER ARM WAX	*$30
FULL ARM WAX	*$50

EXTENSION SERVICES

CINDERELLA HAIR EXTENSIONS   by consultation

All custom hair extensions can be cut and colored
for a perfect blend

*prices starting @

acôte SERVICES

Brochure from Salon Acote, Newbury Street location, Boston.
Copyright © Salon Acote, reprinted with permission. Prices are current as of October, 2008.

Many printers will have an in-house design department who can do the artwork for you, but make sure you have a hand in developing the text. You are the best-qualified person to describe what your business is all about. Also, check for any typos in your phone number, address or other contact information or you will be paying the printer to fix 1,000 brochures or doing it by hand.

If your budget is limited, you can use software such as Microsoft Publisher to design and print your own brochures. For a truly professional look you should enlist a service such as VistaPrint or a printer in your area to do it for you. Look in the Yellow Pages under "Printers."

Distributing Your Menu of Services Brochure

While the challenge of designing an effective menu of services brochure is one thing, how to effectively distribute them is another. Brochures have an advantage over business cards in that they can sit in an office or a waiting room and will be picked up and read by the people waiting. You should of course distribute them through your own salon. Your customers may take them away, share them with friends, and leave them where others can read about your salon.

In addition to your own salon, try to find other places to leave them where people might appreciate knowing about your salon. You might offer to carry the brochures of a complementary business, such as a day spa that doesn't offer hair styling, in exchange for that business making your brochures available to their customers. Brochures can also be distributed by mail, handed out at networking events in conjunction with or instead of a business, and included as part of any packages you prepare.

Flyers

Flyers are essentially a brochure without the fold. They can be colorful and contain graphics, but often do not, making them more cost effective. A run of 250 flyers will cost very little, and the option to create these at home with a decent printer is also there. Many of the tips mentioned for creating an effective menu of services brochure apply to flyers. Again, pay special attention to your contact information and make sure that it is correct.

Attaching a business card to your flyer is also a good strategy. You can post them anywhere there are public bulletin boards, or at places that permit businesses to post flyers. Depending on your community and your salon's niche, you might post them in grocery stores, college campuses, or anywhere else your target market hangs out.

Business Cards

Business cards are a definite must in any business. A business card gives customers the essential contact information for your salon, and every time you hand one out you should think of it as a mini-advertisement.

The cost of business cards can vary depending on how much or how little of the work you do creating them. You can make your own business cards if you own or have access to a computer. Office supply stores sell sheets of cards that come with perforated edges to go through any type of printer.

You can also hire a graphic artist to design a logo, do the layout and even arrange for printing. Most print shops have a design specialist on staff to help with these facets as well. Whichever way you decide to go, make sure the style of your card is in sync with the style you are promoting in your business.

When ordering your cards from a printer, the more you order the less expensive they are. When you order 500 cards, for example, the cost is minimal, generally around $50 to $65 depending on how many colors you have on your card and the card stock you use. Shop around to see where you can get the best deal.

Another alternative when you're just starting out is to use free business cards from VistaPrint.com. You can order 250 cards from them, using a variety of contemporary designs, and you only pay for shipping. The only catch is that they print their company logo on the back. If you don't mind having their logo on the back of your business cards, this is very economical. If you prefer not to have another company's name printed on the back of your business cards you can order 250 cards for about $20 plus shipping from VistaPrint without their logo.

Printers

Your printed promotional tools can be easily designed, paid for and delivered without leaving the house, using one of several online graphics companies. Here are a few you might want to consider:

- *FedEx Office*
  www.fedex.com/us/officeprint/main/

- *Acecomp Plus*
  www.acecomp.com/printing_brochures.asp

- *The Paper Mill Store*
  www.thepapermillstore.com

- *VistaPrint*
  www.vistaprint.com

7.1.5   Your Website

"The only marketing that has worked for us is a website linked to the top five search engines."

> —   Elizabeth Coy, Owner,
> Indigo Salon

A website is an excellent tool for any retail store owner. It lets people know what you do, who you are, how to contact you, and where you are located. Your website can also complement your other marketing efforts. Let people who come into your salon know you have a website, and mention your web address in every piece of advertising or written material you create about your salon.

Ideas for Your Website

The basic structure of your website should include the following:

- Home page to navigate through your site

- Categories pages (types of merchandise you sell), possibly with photos

- "About Us" page: this is where you let your customers know who you are and what expertise you have.

- Contact information with your salon hours, address, phone number, fax number, and perhaps directions or a map

Here are some features and additional information to consider including on your own salon's website:

- A photograph of the front of your salon

- Information about parking around your salon

- Gift certificate information

- Your email contact information

- Articles related to your business, such as product care tips or hot new trends

Developing a Website

If you are already experienced at creating web pages, or learn quickly, you can design your website yourself using a program such as Adobe Dreamweaver or a free program like SeaMonkey (available at **www.seamonkey-project.org**). Otherwise, it's a good idea to hire a web designer through word of mouth or the Yellow Pages. Of course you should visit sample sites they have created before hiring them.

Many salon owners we spoke with cautioned that if you do not have the right expertise or the time to design and maintain your website, you should hire a good tech person to help you with this. Many owners (or salon managers) as part of their regular duties devote time each week to the task of working with their tech person to keep their websites fresh and up-to-date.

You may be able to put up free web pages through your Internet Service Provider (the company that gives you access to the Internet). To present a professional image and make your web address easier for clients to remember, consider getting your own domain name, such as www.yourstorename.com.

There are a number of sites where you can search for and register a domain name; one popular one is **www.godaddy.com**. Microsoft also offers a quick search for domain name availability using their sign-up feature at **http://smallbusiness.officelive.com**. They'll also help you to set up a free website for your business.

Once you register your domain, you will need to find a place to "host" it. You can host it with the same company where you've registered the name. Your Internet Service Provider may also provide this service. You can find a wide variety of other companies that provide hosting services by doing an online search.

> **TIP:** Do not use a free web hosting service unless you don't mind having your customers see pop-up ads for products unrelated to your salon!

Promoting Your Website

A great site is only as good as how many people it attracts. No matter how much you spend on making it beautiful, if people don't know you exist, it won't help you sell your salon or its merchandise.

Make certain you list your site on all your business forms, cards, brochures, signs, and even your car, van or truck. When you list items for sale on any other website, like eBay for example, add your website address. If you spend time on blogs (web logs) or newsgroups, add your site's hyperlink to your signature.

Of course, you'll also want to make sure people find your website when they search for similar retail stores online. Most people regularly use only a handful of search engines, such as Yahoo, Google, MSN, and AOL, so be sure to register your site with them. You can submit your website for free to Google at **www.google.com/submityourcontent**. Once you're on Google, your site is likely to be found by other search engines as well.

Finally, consider creating an email newsletter which your customers and visitors to your website can sign up to receive. Your newsletter could include articles about the types of products you sell and information about holiday specials, salon events, and other news. One popular newsletter distribution service is Constant Contact which you can learn about at **www.constantcontact.com**. You might even be able to get some of your newsletter articles published in magazines, newspapers, and e-zines. A popular site for article distribution is Ezine Articles at **www. ezinearticles.com**.

Photography for Your Website

Digital cameras are now within the budgets of most people, and using them has taken the hassle out of developing film and then scanning them into a digital format in order to show your items to your online visitors. Points to consider for photographs on your website:

Make sure the subject is well lit but not washed out and not under-exposed. Often, taking the shot in the daylight is your best bet. You might find the need to buy a box for photographing small merchandise in order to make your pictures look their best. This is another area where you may wish to hire a professional. Your website is a great opportunity to show off samples of your best work or your stylists' best work as well as how beautiful and inviting your salon is. You may want to try an exchange or barter for services with a professional photographer for services of equal value, since everyone needs to get their hair cut.

You only need images of 72 dpi (dots per inch) for the web as opposed to the higher resolutions needed for printing of 260 to 300 dpi. It's important that, if you intend to use the same pictures for a brochure or any printed item, you shoot the picture at the highest resolution possible. Failing to do so will mean grainy printed pictures and an over-loaded website.

7.1.6 Networking and Referrals

"[Owning a salon] is like any other service business — doctors, attorneys, dentists. You need to network to grow your practice."

> — Billy Lowe, celebrity hairstylist and owner,
> Billy Lowe Salon

"Target complimentary, non-competitive businesses such as a day spa (without hair services) nail salons, boutiques, makeup stores, etc. and personally introduce yourself to the owner. Offer a complimentary service to them. Ask them for their advice on how to get the word out. People love to give advice and have a hand in your success. Offer to come and do free hair consultations on their clientele, and then offer a special "Store ABC" savings coupon. The store owner looks like a hero and you get a new client."

> — Susie Galvez, beauty industry expert and author

One of the best ways to spread the word about your business is through other people. When you open your salon, make sure you get the word out to your family and friends. Consider sending a postcard, and inviting them to your salon's opening. You can also build your clientele by getting to know members of local clubs and by attending as many functions as possible to network with others who might help your business grow.

'The least expensive and most effective marketing strategy is networking. Owners should get out in public as much as possible to meet potential new customers and talk about their business. Join leads groups and business organizations and be active members. Go to community events and participate in what's happening in your city."

— Jill D. Miller, Business Development Consultant,
Creative Solutions

Chamber of Commerce

Often the local Chamber of Commerce and tourism groups are instrumental in getting the word out that you've opened a new business in town. Joining a group like the Chamber usually costs money, but the benefits, which include networking opportunities, educational seminars, and much more, is worth the investment for many business owners.

"It's a great idea to join the local Chamber of Commerce. This sets in good company in the community and positions you as a good corporate neighbor."

— Dalgiza Barros, Owner,
Creative Energy Hair Studio

To find out how to contact your local chamber, visit the national websites. For the U.S. Chamber of Commerce visit **www.uschamber.com/chambers/directory/default.htm**. For the Canadian Chamber of Commerce Directory visit **www.chamber.ca/index.php/en/links/C57**.

Word-of-Mouth

It's time to get your customers working for you. If you can get an emotional connection between you (that is, your business) and your customers they will be your best sales tools. What they say is worth more than hundreds of expensive ads.

One person telling another that your salon is the best place to shop is money in the bank. But how do you get to that point? By being everything your customers expect. Many customers visit small salons for friendly personalized service from knowledgeable staff. So make sure you and your staff keep up-to-date with industry developments and new products. The resources in section 3.6 can help you keep up with what's new, so you can provide the knowledgeable service your customers want, and in section 7.2 you'll get tips on how to provide the customer service that will make your customers more likely to spread the word about your store.

> **TIP:** Ask special customers to write brief reviews of your salon and services. Add these "testimonials" to your newsletter, brochures, and ads.

Get Referrals

One of the best ways to get referrals is to work with other complementary businesses. Put your flyers in their store and theirs in yours. You might also do promotions with them such as offering discounts to customers they refer to you.

> *"All salons should have a referral program to reward customers for sending their family and friends to the salon. My favorites are "win a free year of services" where the winning customer gets a $100 gift certificate every month they can spend on any services with any stylists and "instant gratification" where the salon sends a $5 or $10 gift certificate to customers each time they refer someone new to the salon."*
>
> — Jill D. Miller, Business Development Consultant, Creative Solutions

You can also get referrals from your existing customers. To do this, get to know your customers by chatting with them when they're in your salon. Don't be afraid to ask them if they know of anyone who could use your products and services, and ask them to refer that person to your salon. You might also give a small gift or a discount coupon for bringing in a friend.

Of course, the best way to get your customers referring business to you from others is to offer them the best possible customer service. In section 7.2, we'll offer some customer service tips that will keep your customers happy and get them talking about your salon to others.

7.1.7   Other Marketing Ideas

"Don't just have an opening party, schedule events quarterly if not more often to keep generating excitement. Clients certainly look forward to ours."

— Ronnie Pryor, Owner,
Source Salon

"Another great idea is to have special events that showcase your salon and services offered. I have had success with Client Appreciation Nights held a few times a year. We have wine and hors d'oeuvres and offer complimentary services such as brow wax, hand moisturizing, and color and style consultations. In addition, I ask several clients with complimentary businesses such as jewelry, handbags, fashions, cosmetics, etc...to participate and 'show off their wares.' This adds value to my salon but also offers my loyal clients a chance to mingle and make it a fun night out. My client vendors also enjoy showcasing their businesses. It is a win-win for all."

— Derrick Diggs, Owner,
Layers Hair Salon

There are a lot of unique ways to get the word out about your salon. While you can and should use traditional methods of advertising, keep your mind open to new and exciting ideas as well, because you never know when you might stumble upon one that will be a huge success. Here are some additional ideas you may want to try to market your business:

- Hold a contest. For example, you could have a prize drawing or give an award to the person who comes into your shop dressed in the craziest outfit you have ever seen. (You might even get some media coverage out of it.)

- Print and wear T-shirts or baseball hats with your salon's name and logo. Give them out to your best customers.

- Get your business card printed onto fridge magnets, or put your salon information as pens, coffee mugs, or other items you can sell or give away. (Check online or your Yellow Pages to find companies that print promotional products.)

- Paint your shop logo on your car. If possible, include your web address, location, and a benefit of shopping at your store.

- Contact your local Department of Motor Vehicles to get vanity license plates containing your company's name.

- Post your business card on every bulletin board you see.

- Have a frequent shopper card or offer specials such as 10 percent off one day a month to customers on your mailing list.

- Hold events such as an open house or guest speakers to talk about topics of interest to your customers

Debbi K. Kickham, former Editor of Robb Report Magazine, *is the president of marketing and public relations firm, Maxima Marketing (***www. marketingauthor.com***). Ms. Kickham masterminds marketing plans and publicity for a wealth of businesses, including those in the beauty industry. Her clients include hair salons, skincare salons, plastic surgeons and cosmetic dentists. She has kindly allowed us to reprint the following article.*

8 GREAT NO-COST, LOW-COST WAYS TO MARKET AND PUBLICIZE YOUR SALON ON A SHOESTRING

Many salons simply don't have the budget to hire a marketing and public-relations expert. So - if you're short on funds — what exactly can you do to market your business, to achieve visibility and awareness, by the public and the media?

I'm the co-author of the bestselling business book *Off the Wall Marketing Ideas* (©Adams Media, 2000) and while researching and writing the book, I interviewed hundreds of companies about their make-or-break marketing techniques. To my surprise, many of them simply used their imagination - and not big bucks - to put themselves on the map. That's when I became convinced that smart marketing takes creativity - not cash!

Here are a few of my favorites:

1). Give a scholarship.

A salon can give a scholarship to the local high school or community college, to an art or design student. Better yet, give a small scholarship to a graduate of the local beauty school. Even if it's just for $100, you'll foster goodwill, make a name for yourself and your business in the community, and have a good story to tell the media.

2). Sponsor a day in Chase's Annual Events.

Visit your local library and get a copy of *Chase's Calendar of Events*. You'll find dozens of entries for every day of the year, celebrating special events, worldwide holidays and festivals, and anniversaries. For example, July is National Ice Cream Month. To make the most of this special month, and achieve noteworthy publicity, your business could offer free cones or sundaes to the local homeless shelter, nursing home, or high school, which gets your business name front and center in the community. You also have a great story to tell the media - complete with photos.

3). Create your own day for Chase's Annual Events - just send in your entry.

Here's where you can let your imagination run wild. Why not sponsor a day such as "Good Hair Day" in your town or state? I represented one salon in Massachusetts that did this very campaign, and I masterminded a program to offer discounts, freebies, and Before-And-After pictures of clients with their new haircut - in return the salon received free publicity in several magazines and newspapers. Another one of my clients, a French-owned salon, celebrates Bastille Day every July 14 with similar discounts and freebies, which customers - and the media - love to know about.

4). Visit "dollar stores."

You're bound to find inexpensive giveaways that relate to your business, which you can offer to new and potential customers, and to the media as well. Make sure to put them in designer bags with your logo on them - a company such as Vista Print can handle all of your printed marketing needs (**www.vistaprint.com**).

5). Cross-promote your salon.

Think about your customers and the other types of businesses they are apt to frequent. For example, your salon might prosper and grow by cross-promoting with a local contractor building beautiful new homes, whose target audience is men and women who are concerned with appearances.

6). Write letters.

Make sure to regularly write Letters to the Editor of your local newspaper, discussing issues and problems related to your industry. Include your name, title, and salon name - and you're on your way to free publicity.

7). Donate your energies.

A salon should consider donating its time and expertise to the local high school or college theater group - all of which need hair and makeup done for theatrical performances. As a result, where do you think all of these students will turn when they have a prom or formal night? Also offer to do the hair and skincare/makeup of some of the local news anchor people and TV personalities, on local access TV and your local channels, in exchange for credit on each broadcast.

8). Spend $100 on Lottery Tickets.

Even if yours is a new salon with no marketing budget, chances are you can muster up $100 for this great marketing gimmick. Buy 100 one-dollar lottery scratch tickets, and identify 100 potential customers - either in, say, your hometown, or the city or town where your salon is located. Send them all a mailing introducing your salon, and include the lottery scratch ticket in the envelope, with the words, "Take a chance on my new hair salon." Do not be surprised if you get great results. People love receiving freebies and will remember your pitch - and most important, your business.

> TIP: Remember, it's usually easier and less expensive to keep a good customer than to find a new one.

7.2 Customer Service

As you saw in the previous section, many ideas for marketing your salon involve encouraging your customers to return to your salon.

An even more important factor in getting repeat business is excellent customer service. Exceeding your customers' expectations is a sure way to keep them coming back to your salon for years to come. In this section we will discuss several suggestions for you to follow in order to better serve your clientele.

7.2.1 Booking Appointments

If your business is doing well, most of the telephone calls you receive each day will be from people wanting to make an appointment for one of your service offerings. A receptionist can help you to deal with these efficiently, or, depending on the size of your salon, you may want to deal with such calls yourself or have a designated staff member do it.

In order to book appointments efficiently, you will need a method of keeping track of them. This could be something as simple as recording the name of the client and the service provider along with the date and time in an appointment book that you buy at an office supply store. As business and your clientele increase, though, you might want to consider investing in client-tracking software. See section 6.3.1 for information about software for booking appointments.

7.2.2 Dealing with "No Shows"

It's inevitable that you will book a client for a service and the client will either call in to cancel with little notice or simply not show up. You should have a policy in place to deal with this eventuality.

For example, your client-tracking software might allow you to determine if a certain customer consistently makes appointments and then cancels. In this case, you might choose to inform the client that a credit card number will be required and they will be charged if they don't show up. Alternatively, you might decide it's not worth the bother and politely tell the client you're booked up for the foreseeable future.

In most cases, clients will be considerate enough to call and let you know that something has come up and they will be unable to meet the appointment. They honestly want your services, but need to reschedule. Simply book a new appointment for them at their next convenient time.

When a client calls in with enough notice you then have a "cancellation" to deal with. Obviously, any gaps in service delivery mean less revenues for you. If your business is usually quite busy, you might find someone calling in for an appointment soon after a cancellation. You can inform the customer that you just had a cancellation and ask them if they would like to fill the slot.

One way to prevent last-minute cancellations is to phone clients ahead of time to confirm with them that they are coming for their scheduled appointments. This can be done at the start or at the end of the day a couple of days in advance. Make sure that the person who does the calling is polite and friendly. Reassure the client that "this is just a friendly reminder and we look forward to seeing you."

Confirming appointments can be time-consuming, but can also ensure that you have advance warning if someone needs to cancel so you can quickly fill the slot. Consider that an hour of an employee's time might cost you $10 or $15 making phone calls, but missed appointments can cost you much more than that.

If you find that you're getting two or more cancellations per week on a regular basis, you might want to start confirming appointments ahead of time. You might also want to look into exactly why you are getting such regular cancellations. Perhaps your customers do not feel comfortable in your salon for some reason.

7.2.3   Greeting Walk-In Customers

Most customers behave similarly when they walk into a salon. First, they want a greeting just to know someone is there. Second, they might be cautious for the first few minutes, hoping someone will welcome them. If you have a receptionist, his or her job will be to make the client feel at ease when they first enter. Often new customers don't know what is expected of them during their first visit.

Consider using this three-step approach to greeting customers effectively:

- *Step #1:* When customers enter the salon, greet them. Say, "Hello. How are you?" Smile, smile, smile. Never, ever ignore your customers. Assume the salon is like your home and the customers are your neighbors coming in for a visit.

- *Step #2:* Pause for a minute and then start some chit-chat. "Isn't it a beautiful day outside?" or "I like your necklace." Keep it positive and upbeat. Don't say, "Don't you hate this lousy weather we're having?"

- *Step #3:* Last, but not least, ask if they need help. "Can I help you with something?" "Did you come in for something specific today or would you like to make an appointment?"

Customers do not like feeling pressured. However, they also do not like feeling ignored. We've all been in stores where staff members are busy chatting and joking with each other and ignoring customers, or they're on the phone with a personal call, too busy to be disturbed by a customer. Even if your salon is busy with several customers at once, make sure you at least acknowledge the person when they first come in and let them know that you're around to offer your help if needed.

Greeting Regular Customers by Name

"Know your clients and everyone else's clients by name."

— Marlene Weber,
Marlene Weber Salon

You may not remember every single person who drops into your shop without an appointment, but you should make an effort to get to know the regulars. There are a few visualization techniques you can use to recall someone's name. There are articles you can read online that will help you recall someone's name. One good article is "Remember Names and Work the Room Successfully" at **http://ezinearticles.com/?How-To-Remember-Names&id=470003**. The article introduces devices like mnemonics and "cluster imprinting" for recalling people's names.

> **TIP:** Another way to show customers they are important is to focus on them. If you are working with a customer and the phone rings, allow the voice mail to pick it up. You can return the call as soon as you are finished with the customer who is in the salon.

7.2.4 Refund and Exchange Policies

"Your salon is truly only as strong as your weakest stylist. You must also remember that just because you own the salon doesn't mean that you're always right. In a customer service business your clients are the boss."

— Justin Hickox, owner,
Hickox Studio

For the most part, you are free to choose your own refund and exchange policies. You may decide refunds are not right for you because they create havoc with your bookkeeping. Or you may decide that the customer is always right and since you want them to come back, you will provide refunds or redo the service to their satisfaction.

For products, perhaps you feel hanging the sign "Exchanges Only" is a fair policy, or perhaps you want to keep people happy no matter what and offer a no-questions-asked, money-back guarantee. Many retail stores do not offer returns or exchanges. This will depend upon the items you are selling and whether customers abuse the return policy. This is a personal decision, but try to be flexible. There may be exceptions to any rule you establish.

If you seem hard to deal with (your sign at the cash register screams, "All Sales Final!") you may end up with very unsatisfied customers. Sometimes you will need to give customers their money back even if you think they're wrong or have abused your refund policy. It's always best to have a customer leave your salon satisfied because an unsatisfied customer can be a word-of-mouth disaster for you.

Something else to keep in mind is that certain jurisdictions, usually under specific circumstances, have a "buyer's remorse" rule. This means that a customer has the right to change their mind about a purchase or contract, and back out of the sale within a specified time period (usually 10 days). You have no choice but to comply. Check for rules like this in your locality and retail sector before you implement a "No returns or exchanges" policy.

Think carefully about what kind of policy you want to speak for you. Following is an example of a return and exchange policy for products:

Sample Return/Exchange Policy

[Name of your store] will accept returns/exchanges on unused retail items with receipt only within 10 days of purchase.

Purchasing an item, using it, and then returning it is not an acceptable use of the return policy. Item must be in the same condition in which it was purchased.

If you are not satisfied with any services you purchased at our salon, you may return to the salon within 48 hours and we will work with you to create a style/color/cut that pleases you at no extra charge.

We want to work with you to make sure you are happy with your experience in our salon. Come in during regular business hours to discuss returns/exchanges or refunds with our friendly staff.

7.2.5   Getting Repeat Business

If you set up shop in a busy neighborhood, you may have a steady stream of customers and not need to do anything to attract them. However, if you want to maximize your sales, consider taking a more proactive approach to identify your customers and keep them coming back.

Giving Customers What They Want

To give customers what they want, you need to know something about them. While the amount of customer information you keep in a customer database is entirely up to you, try to keep as much information as your software program allows.

Here are a few of the things you might want to keep track of:

- Customer preferences

- Buying patterns

- Special interests

You will probably at least want regular customers' mailing information and some of their preferences listed. Once you know your customers' interests and preferences, you can make suggestions.

Suggesting services and products that you think will suit the customer can show you're interested in the customer themselves — not just a sale. Take the time to work with your clients and find out what their needs and desires are. Ask your customers what they want, whether it's something you currently carry or not (you could even include a brief survey in your email newsletter). Then create a wish list in a notebook and keep it up-to-date.

Once you have been in business for a while, you will have a few regular customers who do business with you year round. Pay attention to their likes and dislikes and track them. If you have a new service or product that you know they would love, pick up the phone and give them a call. Again, this is excellent customer service. You will more than likely make additional sales as well, because they will likely buy several things while they're in picking up the new item that you have put aside for them.

These extra touches and consultations can keep customers coming back again and again.

Dealing with Difficult Customers

No-shows aren't the only type of difficult customer you will encounter. You may also have customers who are difficult to please. One of the best ways to deal with difficult customers is to gather as much information as you can. Let's use an example.

You have a customer who gets highlights done, then returns the next day to say that she expects the service to be done again at your expense because she's not satisfied. The first time it happened, you didn't mind accommodating her, but it has happened more than once. When you ask what was wrong with the service, do not immediately assume you know the answer. Something in the process may not be working correctly for her. Really listen to what she has to say; practice those listening skills discussed earlier in this guide.

Asking customers for feedback can help you determine what the real issue is and this may help you further develop your salon policies manual as discussed in section 6.1.

Customer Surveys

Feedback can also help you keep your good customers coming back. When customers have a service done or buy items, ask them to take the time to complete a survey, which will include the types of services and products they are most interested in. Keep survey sheets near your cash register and also have a survey on your website. Be careful, though, because privacy laws are very specific, and you need to ensure you customers that you won't be sharing the information you collect and how you will be using it.

> TIP: By offering an incentive, such as a prize (perhaps a gift certificate or discount coupon), you will find people are more inclined to fill out your survey. Let them know that this way, if you get something in they may love, they will be the first to know.

A sample customer survey appears on the next page.

Sorting through the contacts you make this way might seem time-consuming, but setting up a database, either by a simple listing in a spreadsheet, which you can sort and search, or using a database program, is the key to making sure you use the information you have taken the time to collect.

Set up your system to be able to search categories that match your customers' wish lists against new services you offer; for example, a simple category listing that then expands to the various types in that category that they are interested in.

You might want to rate which customers to contact first, perhaps by how well they pay or by how often they have been in the shop. Let them know they are preferred customers.

Sample Customer Survey

Name: _____

Address: _____

_____

Phone: _____

Email: _____

Any new services you would like us to offer? Please describe your wish list.

_____

_____

_____

_____

_____

Can *[Salon Name]* send you newsletters about events and special promotions?   ❑ Yes   ❑ No

Please note: [Salon Name] will only use your information to provide better services to you; your information will not be shared.

7.3 Growing Your Business

You've created a business plan, the roadmap for your new company. Your plan has helped you to put together a start-up budget, find a location and fill that location with inventory, staff and customers. Your customer service is unparalleled and business is booming. It's not only booming, you're outgrowing your old location.

In your business plan, you may have included some ideas about what to do once you've reached this stage in your company's evolution. If so, then you've already realized that it's important for a healthy business to continue to grow and respond to change.

If you haven't given this idea much thought, it's time to think about the possibilities for growth, even at this early stage, while you're still reading about it and setting lofty goals. This section will give you something to think about ahead of time so you'll have some ideas when you get there.

7.3.1   Expanding Your Current Location

You may find that your business might be best served by making your current location bigger. Perhaps you're in a strip mall and the business next door recently vacated, allowing you to expand into their space. Or you might find that you don't need more floor space, you just need to offer more of the same services or a variety of new services. Either way, you're ready to expand.

Signs you are ready for expansion include:

- A consistently full appointment book for several years

- Losing clients because you can't book them in soon enough

- You have more staff members than you have room for

- You have a healthy profit margin

- You have enough resources to be able to shut down for awhile so that you can renovate

Due to the nature of service-oriented businesses, you'll not likely be able to stay open for business during a major renovation project. You don't want your customers' experiences of your business to be ruined because of noise, dirt, dust and mess.

Prepare for renovations by letting your regular clients know that you will be expanding to serve them better. Get them on board by generating excitement about your new facility. If the renovations will be significant, have an architect prepare a sketch that you can show to clients in advance of your temporary closure.

Of course, not every client will be excited about these changes. Keep in mind that you may lose the odd customer, but that your increased capacity will generate even more business. With this increased business as your goal, plan to throw a grand re-opening party. Enjoy this time of rebirth and renewal for your business.

7.3.2   Opening Additional Locations

You may have found that the location next door is not available, but your business is overflowing with clientele and you have no room or time to fit in new clients. It's time to open a second location. This is a big step, but one that many business owners just like you have taken in the past.

A Similar or Sister Business

In many ways, you're right back at the business planning stage as outlined in Chapter 3. You'll need to write a new business plan or add to your existing one, perhaps finding additional financing. You'll need to find a good location to start your second shop, hire staff, find a manager, and so on.

In the start-up phase the new location probably will take up a great deal of your time and energy, just as your first location did. At this stage, it's important that your staff, manager and systems are all functioning efficiently so that they can "fly solo" for a time without you. Of course, you'll still need to be available for any emergency situations, so keep your cell phone turned on.

> **TIP:**   It's most important to ensure at this time that all your operational systems are in place and functioning smoothly. Your service needs to be consistent from one location to the next.

When considering your second location, its distance from your first location is crucial. You want a mix of clients that includes new customers who want to try out your services based on your marketing or reputation, as well as existing clients who appreciate the fact that you're now a little closer and more convenient to them. This will give you a little more room at your old location to bring in new customers to replace the existing ones who will shift to your second location.

Another possibility for a second location is to set up in a nearby town or city. Don't assume that the demographics are exactly the same, since there almost certainly will be different industries and population cross-sections. You may need to "tweak" your existing service offerings a bit to meet the new town's needs. One advantage to opening nearby is that you might be able to move some of your existing staff there who are already familiar with your systems, which will ensure a bit more consistency in service delivery from store to store.

Of course, it's possible that you want to open a new location that is not a clone of your old business. You might want to explore a new concept entirely, though in the context of your existing service offerings. You can generate interest in this "sister" business by celebrating a smaller grand opening in your old location to let existing clients know that they now have a choice in how their services are delivered to them.

Franchising

If you are confident that you have a successful business system and want to share it with other business owner hopefuls, you might want to consider selling your good business name and systems to them. As we described in section 4.2.2, a franchisor is a company that provides a successful business model, including service offerings, products for sale, training, and marketing plan, for a fee to people who want to start a lower-risk business.

Franchising allows you to grow at a faster rate than if you opened several locations on your own. This is because franchisees provide the start-up capital for each new location with very little investment on your part. You still have a tremendous amount of control over how your name, logo, products, and services are presented to the public.

In order to make a smooth transition into franchising, you should seriously consider incorporating as a separate franchising company. You don't want to put your existing business at risk. A corporate structure separate from your other business will ensure that only the corporation is liable for any damages that might result from a franchise deal that goes wrong. See section 4.6.1 for more about this kind of business legal structure.

If this sounds like something you're ready for, hiring a lawyer specializing in setting up franchise corporations is a good way to get started.

Licensing

Like franchising, licensing is another good way to expand your business brand. The lines between trademark licensing and franchising sometimes get a little blurred, making licensing a tricky business sometimes. Generally, a licensing agreement gives you less control over your brand than a franchise does. Also, you can't collect franchise fees because you're not a franchise. You will collect an annual fee from the licensee to allow them to use your trademarks.

Most entrepreneurs who purchase licensing agreements think they already know how to run a business well enough. They just want to get into the market using a recognizable and reputable brand so they don't have to build their own brand. With licensing, you are not legally liable for any mistakes made by your licensees; therefore this has less risk than franchising. Still, mistakes by licensees can damage your brand and hurt your business.

Most franchises start out as licensing agreements because there is less paperwork and expense involved. In addition, you don't have to provide licensees with training. However, you should always use a lawyer who is familiar with trademark licensing to work out the fine details of your agreements with licensees, because of the potential pitfalls in how licensees might end up using your trademarks. Knowing your rights and your obligations to any business partners is an important step when growing your business in this way.

Congratulations! Now that you've gotten this far, you're well on your way to starting a new and exciting career as a hair salon owner. As you forge ahead on this amazing journey, keep in mind the advice of our experts:

"The most important piece of advice I can give any aspiring business owner is to make sure that this is truly what you want to do, and to do a lot of soul searching before starting your business. It is a big commitment and can be truly horrifying at times. I warn people that they will experience "entrepreneurial terror" at some point and that there may be times when money is tight and employees will drive them crazy. I suggest people write out what they want to achieve, their vision, and why they want to own a business. Tuck this information into a safe place and take it out when you're starting to question your judgment about why you ever wanted to take on something as crazy and as wonderful as owning your own business. It takes passion, dedication, tenacity, and perhaps a little insanity to be an entrepreneur, but there is nothing more satisfying than creating your vision and achieving your dreams."

> — Jill D. Miller, business development consultant,
>   Creative Solutions

"Aspiring salon owners should remain open to new ideas, realize that they will make mistakes no matter how well they've prepared, and lastly, remember that their main objective is to make the world more beautiful."

> — Ronnie Pryor, Owner,
>   Source Salon

"Totally love what you do. Keep learning the trends, never stop growing. My personal philosophy about the beauty industry is: beauty is evolutionary, not revolutionary. You must keep up to keep ahead."

> — Susie Galvez, beauty industry expert and author

"Stay focused, but be flexible. It's crucial to remain determined and see your project through until the salon doors open, but don't keep unrealistic expectations. It's always important to stay open-minded to new ideas, unique methods and input from staff and friends."

> — Suki Duggan, Owner,
>   Donsuki Townhouse Salon

More Guides to Build Your Business

Increase your income by offering additional services. Here are some recommended FabJob guides to help you build your business:

Open Your Own Day Spa

As a spa owner you could have a profitable business helping people experience more happiness, health, and well being. In the **FabJob Guide to Become a Spa Owner**, you will learn:

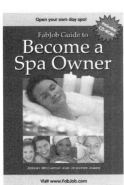

- Your options for opening a new spa, buying an existing spa, or starting a mobile spa business

- Different types of spa and salon services and how much to charge (plus tips on selling retail products)

- How to create a business plan and get financing

- How to choose a location, design your layout, hire staff, and find suppliers

- How to market your spa to attract customers, including tips on booking groups

Get Paid to Help People Look Fabulous

Imagine having an exciting high paying job showing people and companies how to make a fabulous impression. The **FabJob Guide to Become an Image Consultant** shows you how to:

- Do image consultations and advise people about: total image makeovers, communication skills, wardrobe, and corporate image

- Start an image consulting business, price your services, and find clients

- Select strategic partners such as makeup artists, hair stylists, and cosmetic surgeons

- Have the polished look and personal style of a professional image consultant

Get Paid to Apply Makeup

Imagine having a fun high-paying job that lets you use your creativity to make people look good. In the **FabJob Guide to Become a Makeup Artist** you will learn:

- How to apply makeup to best suit someone's coloring, skin type, face shape and features (plus what to have in your makeup kit)

- How to choose a training program

- How to get a job as a makeup artist for a salon, spa, retail store, or cosmetics company

- How to get freelance work as a makeup artist for advertisements, magazines, movies, music videos, runway shows, TV, theater and more

Visit www.FabJob.com to order guides today!